The Challenges of
Educational Leadership

Leading Teachers, Leading Schools
Series Editor: Alma Harris, Professor of Educational Leadership at the
University of Warwick

This series of cutting-edge books on current issues in teaching and school
improvement aims to deal with the practical realities of leading and
improving schools and classrooms, but through the conceptual and
theoretical lenses of teacher development, leadership practice and learning
approaches. Each title therefore shows what its subject means for school and
classroom improvement.

This series is for teachers, headteachers and all those involved in school and
classroom improvement. It is also intended to support Professional
Development Opportunities, NCSL courses and MEd/EdD work.

Titles include:

The Challenges of Educational Leadership

Values in a Globalized Age

Mike Bottery

P·CP
Paul Chapman
Publishing

First published 2004

Paul Chapman Publishing
A SAGE Publications Company
1 Oliver's Yard
55 City Road
London EC1Y 1SP

SAGE Publications Inc
2455 Teller Road
Thousand Oaks, California 91320

SAGE Publications India Pvt Ltd
B-42, Panchsheel Enclave
Post Box 4109
New Delhi 110 017

Library of Congress Control Number: available

A catalogue record for this book is available from the British
Library

ISBN 1 4129 0080 8
ISBN 1 4129 0081 6 (pbk)

Typeset by TW Typesetting, Plymouth, Devon
Printed in Great Britain by Athenaeum Press Ltd, Gateshead

Contents

Tables

Acknowledgements

I have been fortunate to have many friends and colleagues who have helped during the writing of this book. In particular, I would like to single out Chris Sink, Nigel Wright, Derek Webster, Julian Stern and Derek Colquhoun.

I would also like to thank *Cambridge Journal of Education*, *Educational Management and Administration*, *School Leadership and Management*, and *the International Journal of Children's Spirituality*, for permission to use materials previously published in those journals.

Finally, and as always, my love and thanks to Jill, Christopher and Sarah, for all their support, and for being who they are.

And if the blind lead the blind, both shall fall into the ditch.

Matthew, verse 14.

Foreword

Leadership is back in fashion. Across many western countries there has been a renewed emphasis upon improving leadership capacity and capability in the drive towards higher educational performance and standards. Governments around the world are involved in the business of educational reform and are placing a great deal of emphasis on improving the quality of leadership. Even though there are few certainties about the ability of educational policy to secure higher performance from the educational system, the arguments for investment in education, and particularly educational leadership, remain powerful and compelling.

While the education challenges are considerable and the route to reform is complex, the potential of leadership to influence pupil and school performance remains unequivocal. It has been consistently argued that the quality of headship matters in determining the motivation of teachers and the quality of teaching which takes place in the classroom (Hargreaves, 2003; Crowther, 2000; Day et al., 2000; Fullan, 2001). The importance of leadership in securing sustainable, school improvement has been demonstrated in both research and practice (Harris, 2002; Hopkins, 2001). Consequently, from a policy maker's perspective, school leaders are viewed as holding the key to resolving a number of the problems currently facing schools. This has led to a major investment in the preparation and development of school leaders across many countries and has proved a main impetus for the establishment of the [1]National College for School Leadership in England.

Clearly, there is some basis for optimism. The research evidence shows that effective leaders exert a powerful influence on the effectiveness of the school and the achievement of students (Wallace, 2002; Waters et al., 2004). But there is also need for caution. Although the international research base on leadership is vast, the evidential base is very diverse and the nature of studies varies considerably. Yet, there are relatively few studies that have established any direct

---

[1] The National College for School Leadership is located at Nottingham University.

causal links between leadership and improved student performance (Hallinger and Heck, 1996).

This new series focuses predominantly upon the relationship between leadership and learning. It also provides new and alternative perspectives on leadership which offer a direct challenge to the current orthodoxies of school leadership that persist, prevail and still dominate contemporary thinking. This book by Mike Bottery really does trail blaze the message that there are different ways of conceptualizing what leadership is, and should be, within a global society. In an informed but incisive way this book begins to dissect and dismantle some of the prevailing views about leadership, arguing that educational leaders need to engage with the wider, global influences that affect schools and schooling. The 'socio-cultural context', says Bottery, needs to embrace far more than the school, the district or even the educational system.

This book considers the supra-educational pressures on schools and locates them at a global, cultural and national level. It critiques educational leadership arguing that it is simultaneously and paradoxically about control and fragmentation. The dualism of centre versus periphery is explored in some depth along with the important but often sidelined issues of trust, meaning and identity within the current educational context and climate. Bottery rightfully relocates these at the heart of educational change, development and reform. The book argues that the main challenge for educational leaders is to respond in a meaningful and authentic way to these issues and in so doing develop new meanings and understandings about their role. It also argues for an alternative model of educational leader who is not only an ethical dialectician who works from a value base with educational vision but who also has considerable political and pragmatic awareness. Such leaders have an internal moral compass which drives their relationships with others and ensures they rarely stray from an agenda focused on learners and learning.

As the first book in a new series, Mike Bottery has provided a rare balance of challenge, critique and pragmatism. It is unlikely that this book will be read and forgotten. In the contemporary climate of designer leadership, lowest common denominator competences and de-contextualized leadership approaches, Mike Bottery has reminded us of the global horizon and the professional, moral and ethical responsibilities of those who lead within our schools. For this alone, *The Challenges of Educational Leadership: Values in A Globalized Age* should be welcomed.

Alma Harris (Series Editor)

Mike Bottery is Professor of Education and Director of Research Degrees in the Centre for Educational Studies at the University of Hull. He has been Visiting Professor at the Universities of Saskatchewan and Seattle Pacific, and Noted Scholar at the University of British Columbia. Chair of the Standing Conference for Research into Education, Leadership and Management 2004–5, this is his seventh book.

1 The book's intentions

Educational leadership is taken extremely seriously across the globe. There are now a considerable number of initiatives for its development in places as diverse as Canada, the UK, Sweden, the USA, Singapore, Hong Kong and Australasia (see Bush and Jackson, 2002; Brundrett, 2002). While all reflect local culture and needs, and vary in the balance of responsibility for such development between government, local authorities and academics, there remains similarity in the reasons for current interest, and in the content which educational leaders are believed to need to cover. Some of these programmes aim not only at training principals, but also in gaining overviews of the research in the area, and on the back of such understanding, to generate new insights. The reason for all this activity is easy to understand: in a period of massive change, there is perceived to be an urgent need for all professional educators to understand such change in order to better prepare their students for a diversity of potential futures. The UK National College for School Leadership (NCSL) is a good example of this kind of approach. In its *Annual Review of Research 2002–3*, it suggested (NCSL, 2003: 7) that five major issues had emerged during the previous year requiring discussion. These were: definitions of leadership; the importance of context; leaders' professional development; capacity building; and the need for a futures orientation.

Historically, there has been much debate about precise meanings of 'leadership'. It is a highly contested concept. The NCSL (2003: 7) commented that by one estimate there exist 350 definitions of the term: they also remark that they were surprised that there were so few. Indeed, and as Hodgkinson (in Ribbins, 1993: 23) has remarked, there is much 'word magic' surrounding the term which bewitches rather than clarifies. Like the NCSL, then, this book does not want to get into heavy debates about such meanings. However, there are at least two occasions when it cannot and should not be avoided. The first occasion is when meanings have direct implications for challenges being considered. For example, and as developed in the next chapter, particular versions of leadership place such weight of expectation upon individuals, that they exacerbate the situation of many who already feel over-worked and over-stressed. When this happens, when certain duties and responsibilities are attached to particular meanings, then leadership definitions do not simply describe but actually contribute to existing challenges and problems for educational leaders, and scrutiny becomes essential. The second occasion is the need to contrast the officially prescribed leadership qualities and activities to which leaders are currently being steered, with those which research and analyses suggest are needed. Here, it is important to be able to 'name' and delineate contrasting types to help us have a clearer idea of where we are and where we want to go. This book will address both of these occasions.

However, for most of it, educational 'leaders' are taken to be those both in formally appointed role positions and also in informal positions who exercise influence and provide direction to their colleagues. This book, then, is not written to contribute to a literature on 'leadership' meanings. Rather it is written to help individuals, alone and in groups, and at different levels of educational establishments, to help themselves and their colleagues deal better with the forces which surround them, forces which affect the realization of their visions of educational purposes.

So this book also agrees with Leithwood et al. (1999: 4) in Canada, who argue that 'outstanding leadership is exquisitely sensitive to context'. The NCSL in the UK also takes this position when it argues that leadership needs to be seen as a contextualized activity 'because one of the most robust findings is that where you are affects what you do as a leader' (2003: 7), and that such 'context' should encompass more than the type of school, its circumstances or its geographical location. Instead, it needs to encompass personal circumstance, issues of the local community, and looking even further afield, there needs to be the recognition that 'local, national and international events interplay with social, economic and political factors in ways which impact on the equilibrium of the school as a social organisation'. In such an expanded context, then, 'successful school leadership . . . involves being sensitive to these forces and the ways in which they combine, react and influence the school' (2003: 9). The reasons for this are compelling – 'we need to prepare the children in school today for a future where uncertainty and change are a feature of their lives' (2003: 8).

This is indeed a critical time for education, and for societies in general. It is an age of rapid and far-reaching changes, which no longer occur just at the local and national levels, but which have profound effects across the globe. It is a time when we recognize that global warming is no respecter of national borders as it melts polar ice-caps, changes growing seasons and radically affects species' viability. It is a time when we recognize that humanity continues to contribute to global pollution, and yet still seems stuck within postures, both political and economic, which prevent this issue from being properly addressed. It is also a time of great paradox, when massive standardizations of global culture contrast with the easy availability of varied cultures and beliefs. It is a time when some people embrace variety and the freedom while others retreat behind fundamentalist walls as they feel their beliefs are undermined. Perhaps, most importantly, with the demise of fascism and communism as state-sponsored ideologies, it is a time when a version of liberal democracy is the only global political ideology, and walks arm-in-arm across a world stage with an economics of free-market capitalism. The results of this twin domination have been remarkable and striking in their extent and intensity, and while many have welcomed this development, there are others who are much less sanguine. This book, then, suggests that the leader's 'context' needs to be seen as global in nature and, aims to untangle some of these issues and their effects, particularly with respect to the challenges they pose for educational leaders.

These massive changes then pose fundamental questions for society, and in so doing, impose new contexts on the work of educational leaders. They also raise uncomfortable questions for conventional professional assumptions and habits, for this book argues that because of them professionals should be entering domains not previously considered as central to their interests. Yet, for so many, the immediate issue is one of time: as the NCSL (2003: 14) points out 'for school leaders and teachers alike, today always seems more urgent than tomorrow. The daily press of the work of teachers and heads exerts its own influence on them' and in such a press, the larger issues may simply be pushed to one side. So this book may be uncomfortable reading for some, and distanced from more immediate concerns for others. But it argues that these challenges are so fundamental, so important, that educational leaders, and society as well, ignore them at their peril. It also argues that while the challenges described impact upon those within the private sector, they impact even more strongly upon those working within the public sector. Furthermore, and, perhaps unfashionably at the present time, it argues that a public sector with a wide-reaching welfare state is a valuable element of any developed society, that it is worth having and fighting for, and that most of its functions are not improved by being taken over and run by private sector institutions. This argument is not intended as, nor do I believe it depends upon, a feeling of nostalgia for some earlier 'golden period': it argues instead that any future healthy, caring and culturally rich society requires a public sector to provide a set of goods or services which are too important to be left to other sectors – especially if these other sectors have differing values which might result in uneven provision.

Now such public sector 'goods' have varied from country to country, but have usually consisted of educational, health and social welfare provision. Such public sector goods are also linked to the more extensive project of a welfare state, which is based in part upon the belief that providing citizens with more equal access to such goods will generate a more democratic exercise of political power, as greater degrees of health, economic security and educational provision enable individuals to access these rights more easily. Welfare states, rather than emphasizing the kinds of competitive relationships which underpin market functioning, value and nurture trusting, co-operative and caring relationships. Through the stimulation of such relationships, a public sector can then become the repository for the kinds of social values which the private sector itself needs to draw upon if *it* is to function properly. By undermining the public sector, then, the private sector is likely to undermine the societal foundations which it needs if it is to flourish.

The book's argument

While such effects are not normally seen as the kinds of challenges which educational leaders need to consider, this book will argue that they relate directly to the kinds of work that leaders do, and that they tend to steer educational leaders away from particular kinds of education and into other, less desirable areas. Of course, statements about 'more desirable' and 'less desirable' kinds of education need to spelt out a little more, and without going into a treatise of educational philosophy, it is important to make clear the kind of arguments which will be used in this book. The principal argument can be stated in just four sentences:

1 A rich and flourishing society depends, in part, upon the provision for its citizens of a rich and diverse education.

2 A rich and diverse education will only be achieved through the adoption and practice of a number of different educational objectives.

3 All of these objectives are interconnected, in most cases being dependent upon one other.

4 At the present time, one of these objectives dominates and thereby prevents the achievement of the others.

Now while different people will have different ideas of what 'a rich and flourishing society' might consist of, this book argues that, minimally, it needs the following qualities:

- A political underpinning by a version of democracy which encourages its citizens to actively participate in decision making.

- To promote the idea that members should respect and care for one another, and should contribute to efforts to reduce other people's difficulties in participating in and contributing to that society.

- A commitment to helping all members to appreciate the artistic, scientific and cultural discoveries of their society, and those of others.

- A commitment to helping all members realize their full potential, to engage in a process of spiritual growth, and to fulfil themselves as human beings in the widest sense.

- To be sufficiently secure that those within it do not live in fear of either external or internal threat.

- To be sufficiently outward-looking to learn from and help other societies.

- To be sufficiently outward-looking to recognize the interconnectedness of all forms of life on this world, and work towards helping such interconnectedness.

- To be sufficiently economically prosperous to permit the achievement of these other aims.

Clearly, different people will have different views on this subject, and may well want to add or extract from this list. Nevertheless, if the notion of needing a rich and flourishing society is accepted, then precise lists can be left to educational philosophers and healthy democratic debate. What does seem unarguable is that such aims are unlikely to be achieved by chance, and that any society serious about them will have to create systems and institutions to achieve them. Now, given the kinds of aims described above, education is going to have a pivotal role here, and it will need to be as rich and diverse as the society it is attempting to nurture; and like the society itself, such an education system will require a variety of objectives. Without again wishing to write a treatise in this area, such an education would seem to require at least the following eight objectives:

1 *An economic productivity objective*: the need to foster and develop students' skills, knowledge and attitudes so that they are able to earn a living, and contribute to the overall economic wealth of a country.

2 *A democratic objective*: the need to provide students with the skills, knowledge and the self-belief to contribute to the development of a democratic state, and for educational professionals to set an example by their participation in the running of their organizations.

3 *A welfare state objective*: the communication of the belief that a society needs to be more than a sum of individuals but should aspire to be a social and political community which cares for and helps its members, and redresses inequities so that all can participate in this society.

4 *An interpersonal skills objective*: the need to facilitate in students the social skills which allow people to live together in a harmonious and fulfilling manner.

5 *A social values objective*: the need to promote to students social values such as equity, care, harmony, environmental concerns, and democracy within this society.

6 *An epistemological objective*: the need to communicate to students a deep understanding of the nature of knowledge, normally through the study of a particular subject discipline, which not only provides an understanding of this world, and generates a sense of awe and wonder, but also through understanding human epistemological limitations, a constant humility.

7 *A personal development objective*: the need to allow each student to realize their full potential, to engage in a process of spiritual growth, and to fulfil themselves as human beings in the widest sense.

8 *An environmental objective*: the need for students to understand the interdependency of all living things, and of the human impact upon other beings, resources and living conditions on this planet.

It may be tempting to view these as discrete, separate and unconnected. Yet, and as Table 1.1 demonstrates, these can be seen as for example, three complex, connected and interdependent objectives. A first example would be a rich and varied personal development is essential to the growth of a rich and vibrant democracy. At the same time, the development of the democratic norms of participation, respect and inclusion are also essential for the facilitation of rich individual personal development. A second example would be the provision of an education in which interpersonal skills are valued and practised forms a major foundation for the functioning of a sound welfare state; at the same time an education in the values of the welfare state itself – with its emphasis on notions of community, equity and caring for others – provides a vital political and institutional context within which interpersonal skills can be nurtured and practised. A final example is where the provision of an education in social values, in particular an education in respect for truth, respect for other opinions, and personal integrity, facilitates the deeper personal understanding of epistemological issues; at the same time social values themselves are necessarily conditioned by and in part dependent upon a full appreciation of an external reality, and this in itself is conditioned by a full understanding of epistemological issues.

In like manner the provision of an economically productive education – either by making some of its content relevant to the needs of a nation-state embedded within a global economy, or by providing future workers with the skills, knowledge, values and attitudes to enable them to be employable within such an economic scenario – is essential if interpersonal skills, social values and fully rounded personal development are to be practised with a reasonable degree of economic security; yet economic activity can only be properly executed where people have a foundation of social values like trust, respect and care, where they have the interpersonal skills to engage in the kind of teamwork essential in a knowledge economy, and have the kind of well-rounded personality capable of adapting to new changing situations. The development of democracy and a welfare state are dependent on a productive economy, because it provides a secure enough wealth base to support such practices; however, the development of a healthy economy is also dependent on *them*, for both democracies and welfare states are more likely to permit fuller utilization of all talents, the first through its underlying principle of the participation of all, the second by its underlying principle of providing sufficient services for all to engage in such participation.

This book argues that at the present time, *the* dominant objective in many societies, and in many education systems is that of economic

Table 1.1 *Eight essential educational objectives and their dependency on one another*

	Economic Productivity dependent on	Democracy dependent on	Welfare State dependent on	Interpersonal Skills dependent on	Social Values dependent on	Issues of Epistemology dependent on	Personal Development dependent on	Environmental Concerns dependent on
Economic Productivity	X	EP provides secure wealth base	EP provides secure wealth base	EP provides secure wealth base to explore IP	EP provides secure wealth base	EP provides secure wealth base within which E can be considered	EP provides secure wealth base	EP provides base to upgrade environment
Democratic	D provision likely to allow fuller utilization of talents	X	D values of participation and public good underpin WS values	Democratic structures provide context for full exercise of IS	Democratic structures provide context for full exercise of SV	Democratic critical norms provide context for full epistemological discussions	Democratic norms facilitate full PD	Democratic voice mobilizes environmental concerns better than other political forms
Welfare State	WS provision likely to facilitate utilization of all talents	WS provision facilitates democratic ability to participate	X	WS provides strong communal base to explore IS	WS communal commitment provides basis for SV	Considerations of epistemology enhanced by WS norms of participation	Communal norms facilitate PD through enhancing ability to live and work with others	Cooperative underpinnings of WS facilitate environmental voice
Interpersonal Skills	IS particularly important in teamwork of knowledge economy	IS critical to core democratic processes like discussion, negotiation, etc.	Widely based IS form foundation for sound WS aiming	X	Good IS help promote and implement SV	IS skills of discussion and critique facilitate deeper understanding of issues of epistemology	IS facilitate PD through enhancing ability to live and work with others	Environment better protected by joint rather than single voice

Social Values	Economic activity needs strong societal value bases to aim effectively	Care, trust, respect critical to proper democratic aiming	Widely based SV form foundation for sound WS aiming	SV underpin and form rationale for IS	X	SV skills of truth and respect facilitate deeper epistemological understanding	SV facilitate PD	Environment better protected if environmental concern is a dominant social value
Issues of Epistemology	Core to new ideas development	Sound E base essential to democratic criticality	Essential to proper understanding of WS context	IS contextualized by worldview, dependent upon epistemology	Critical component of SV is deep consideration of epistemology	X	Epistemological understandings facilitate PD	Epistemology essential to a deep understanding of environmental issues
Personal Development	Core to having well-rounded individuals capable of adaptation	Mature PD essential qualities for rich vibrant democracy	Mature PD critical in sound WS aiming	IS an aim of maturing PD	Mature PD critical in discussion and practice of SV	Maturing PD allows for deeper appreciation of epistemological issues	X	Mature PD allows for deeper appreciation of environmental concerns
Environmental Concerns	Degraded environment reduces natural resources; pollution is an economic cost	Democratic politics best realized in healthy environmental context	Vibrant WS best realized within healthy environmental context	IS facilitated by healthy environmental context	SV more fully articulated when EC included	Epistemological understanding facilitated by EC	PD more fully developed within healthy environmental context	X

productivity, and that much of this domination is the product of global agendas which transcend the scope of any particular business, or indeed any particular nation-state. The following chapters will discuss the causes and effects of this phenomenon in detail, and two particular effects – those of privatization and standardization – will be singled out as being particularly problematic and challenging for educational leaders. Ultimately, it is argued, the domination of this economic agenda leads to an emphasis on functionality as opposed to a pursuit of other societal 'goods' in their own right. This emphasis ultimately attacks the value of all the other educational aims and endangers their realization by transforming and reducing them to second-order activities.

Developing the context

The NCSL (2003), then, was right in stressing the context of educational leadership, and to expand that context beyond the local to the national and global, for it is at these macro-levels that many forces are acting to prevent education from transcending the aims of efficiency, effectiveness or economic profitability. These forces act in many cases to reduce education to the mastery of a National Curriculum content, and the achievement of pass scores in high stakes testing. Yet, as Fielding (2003) argues, in life we encounter both functional and personal relationships, and while we need the functional (of which economic productivity is clearly one), such relationships and activities are *for* something else – for a sense of personal and spiritual growth, for the growth of caring and vibrant communities, whether these be at local, national or global levels. If educational leaders resonate to such concerns, then they need to include an understanding of the effect of such global actors upon their practice. If, like Bates (2003) we want to conceive of the work of educational leaders as being about more than the delivery and implementation of government legislation, curricula and testing, but ultimately to do with learning to live with one another, learning to support one another, learning to listen to one another, and learning to redress issues of equity, then understanding the dynamics of the global actors which effect such attainment needs to be included in the purview of educational leaders.

And finally, if we care what at bottom causes large numbers of both students and teachers to think negatively of the work they undertake, then this book argues that we need to consider such issues extremely seriously. Pollard and Trigg (2001: 103) conclude on surveying their data on UK primary children's post-1988 curriculum experiences that 'It is difficult to avoid a sense of children in flight from an experience of learning that they found unsatisfying, unmotivating, and uncomfortable'.

Hargreaves (2003: 89), meanwhile, found that many members of teaching forces, trans-nationally, were deeply unhappy about their work and what they were being asked to do, with comments like, 'I used to love being creative; now I'm too busy to try' being the norm, rather than the exception. When pupils find their school experience unsatisfying and unmotivating, and teaching forces exhibit increased 'disengagement' from what they are asked to do, one should take heed of Sennett (1998: 148) when he remarks of regimes that do not place ultimate concerns at the core of their objectives: 'a regime which provides human beings no deep reasons to care about one another cannot long preserve its legitimacy'.

If educational institutions are to preserve their legitimacy, then, such ultimate concerns need to be recognized, articulated and placed at their core. Educational leaders have a critical role to play here. But before this can happen, they need to fully understand the kinds of global challenges which prevent such aspirations from being realized, and come to recognize that a reframing of educational professionalism and educational leadership requires a more critical, extensive and global conception than has been accepted previously. That is the purpose of this book.

2 Shifting frames of reference: the need for ecological leadership

Introduction: a leader's current lot is not necessarily a happy one

There are many empowered, enthusiastic and engaged educational leaders in the western world, who derive deep enjoyment and real fulfilment from their jobs. They hold deep and committed visions of what a good education should look like, they are passionate about empowering their students and in raising their educational achievement, and continue to transmit that enthusiasm to those around them, building a climate of energy, collaboration, trust and self-discipline. In the process they create institutions which are alive, buzzing with the thrill of learning, a joy to be in. Despite increased pressures, there is good research evidence (for example, Day et al., 2000; Gold et al., 2003) that these educational leaders do not sacrifice their ideals, but manage to hold on to their values and lead their schools through their moral visions of what constitutes a 'good education'.

Yet there is worrying evidence that many of these leaders now feel more pressurized than did their peers a couple of generations ago. Their numbers are getting fewer, and there are less and less individuals coming forward to take their place. Such shortages are reported throughout the western world. Fullan (1997), for instance, described a study of principals and vice-principals in Toronto in 1984, in which 90 per cent reported an increase in demands, with only 9 per cent reporting a decrease. Surveying the situation in 1997, he had to conclude (p. 1) that 'we appear to be losing ground [with the principal's leadership role], if we take as our measure of progress the declining presence of increasingly large numbers of highly effective, satisfied principals'. Similarly, Williams (2001) details the same issues in both the USA and Canada. He cites a report by the US National Association of Elementary School Principals, and the National Association of Secondary School Principals (1998: 16), which suggested that 'half the district administrators interviewed felt that there had been a shortage of qualified candidates when they filled at least one principalship in the last year'. His own study in Canada likewise suggested that not only were retirement rates 20 per cent higher than provincial estimates, but the pool of qualified candidates for these positions was also shrinking. In the UK, Troman and Woods (2000) reported the same kind of declining enthusiasm for engaging in senior management positions. Finally, Gronn (2003a), reporting on his own research in Australia, as well as other studies in the USA and the UK, came to the same kind of conclusions: the western world is facing an impending crisis, where insufficient numbers of able people are willing to fill the principal's role.

Why are individuals so reluctant to take on such a role? Evans (1996) argued that despite the fact that there have always been tensions in leadership between such things as managing and leading, between demands and resources, and being a leader yet being dependent on others, what is new is the way the job has expanded and intensified, leaving leaders feeling disempowered, the quality of their lives diminishing. The study by Williams (2001) quoted above provides some of the detail for this argument. His study found that at least 70 per cent of all incumbent principal and vice principal respondents found the following (in rank order) to be issues of job dissatisfaction:

- adequacy of time to plan for provincially mandated changes;
- number of curriculum changes mandated by the province;
- adequacy of time to work with students;
- amount of in-school staff support for principals given workload requirements;
- amount of time the job required;
- resources made available to meet the assessment of the school's educational needs.

Now this phenomenon of increased workloads, lack of time to deal with them, and the stress consequent upon this, is not just a phenomenon of his Canadian principals, or indeed of educationalists generally. Work intensification, and the greater stress and pressure which results, are a reality for many across the world of work throughout the western world, whether in the public, private or voluntary sectors. While Schorr (1992) has argued that US workers have worked longer and harder in order to purchase the goods that would make life in general more satisfying, other commentators have located such intensification elsewhere, particularly in the continued demand by the private sector to cut costs, necessitating reductions in manpower while not necessarily resulting in any reduction in work. Terms like 'delayering', 'outplacement', 'cutting back' and 'casualization' have all become familiar terms as organizations have sought to reduce their overheads. Handy (1989) described the future of work as being that of half the workers receiving twice the salary while doing three times the work. Anecdotal evidence and personal experience both suggest some truth in the first and last parts of Handy's prediction, the middle part seeming much more doubtful. This pattern has moved from the private to the public sector: just as private corporations have cut back on personnel and increased their demands on those remaining, so the public sector has felt a similar bite, as nation-states have retreated from large-scale welfare provision, demanding that their public sectors perform the same kinds of cost-cutting and manpower reductions, while at the same reducing individual room for manoeuvre by increasing the amount of legislative direction. For principals in schools, the result, as Evans (1995) put it, can be the demand for the impossible:

> Wanted: A miracle worker who can do more with less, pacify rival groups, endure chronic second-guessing, tolerate low levels of support, process large volumes of paper, and work double shifts . . . He or she will have carte blanche to innovate, but cannot spend much money, replace any personnel, or upset any constituency.

Yet despite such demands, and increased imperatives for such demands to be seen as legitimate, and to feel guilty if they did not, people continued to go the extra mile, to work the extra evening, to forego the family event. Indeed, and as Gronn (2003a) points out, perhaps even more worryingly, in some cases people have become addicted to this pattern, and in effect are living to work, rather than working to live. The result, he suggests, is that: 'in consuming one's whole being, [work] does more than merely provide the physical and psychological wherewithal for a life. Because it becomes one's life, greedy work consumes one's life, so that work becomes the measure of what one is and not just what one does' (2003a: 153).

Blackmore (1995: 51) has made the same kind of point, arguing that due to the emotional demands of the job and the invasion of personal time and space, 'for many teachers and headteachers, the line between the professional and personal is increasingly blurred', and Fielding (2003: 12) takes this even further, worrying that the personal is not just increasingly utilized for the functional, but rather that '*the functional and the personal collapse soundlessly into each other*' [original emphasis].

These kinds of effects may cause great concern to observers, as they see the person they knew being transformed and not wishing it for themselves. Indeed, there is now increasing evidence that such individuals, to protect themselves, are 'disengaging' from the job, by either seeking early retirement, or by retreating to a level of occupational engagement that they believe is manageable. This is not just a phenomenon in education: Laabs (1996: 1) described individuals doing the same thing in the private sector as 'downshifters', wanting to slow down at work, 'so they can upshift in other areas of their lives'. He also suggested that there were two varieties of downshifters; 'those who want to break out of the corporate mold . . . and those who just want to work less'. At bottom though, was an existential question echoed among educators: 'Who am I and what's my life about?' (1996: p. 3). In education, if individuals have not yet reached a principal's position, such feelings may result in an unwillingness to take on the role, thus reducing the supply of suitable candidates for leadership positions. Gronn (2003a) details examples of this across the USA, the UK and Australia, while Williams (2001) does so in Canada. Those in senior and middle management positions, then, see the stress of the principal's job – the massive responsibility contradicted by the paucity of power, the effects upon families and lives, the emails and texts written in the early hours of the morning – and either realize that they are already well down that path, or decide that this is not going to happen to them. Added to which, and like many in the private sector, they may also come to believe that their loyalty to the organization is not reciprocated: that while greater and greater demands are made upon them, the downsizing, outsourcing, casualization and flexibility of the educational workforce attest to the fact that loyalty is increasingly an outdated commodity. As Misztal (2001: 33) suggested, 'it pays to quit'. When allied to demographic evidence across the western world that a large cohort of the teaching profession is reaching retirement age, this suggests that there is a genuine crisis in the teaching profession, and particularly at the top end. Fullan (2003: 24) seems to be absolutely right then when he concludes: 'The system is in deep trouble. There is a huge need for new leaders, and at the same time there is a set of conditions that makes the job unattractive.'

Labels that kill

So there is good reason to believe that the system is in trouble. Many of those who are capable of leading are increasingly worried about the effects that such a position has or will have upon them. Yet the problem does not just lie in the complexity and volume of the work, and the constraints placed upon the principal: part also lies in what is currently expected, and part of this has come from the labels they have been given, and the responsibilities thereby attributed to them. Officially sponsored definitions of leadership have acquired an impact upon the lives of educational leaders through being prescriptions rather than descriptions, prescriptions that mis-describe the way in which the work should be done. In so doing, they may simply ask too much of educational leaders.

Historically, models have had much less effect. There have been numerous depictions of leadership over the years (see Northouse, 2003). Trait theories, for instance, have suggested that leaders possess certain distinct personal qualities; style theories have suggested that leaders are distinguished by the different importance they place on the management of tasks or the management of relationships; situational theories have argued that different situations actually require different kinds of leaders; and contingency theories have suggested that the best way forward is through the matching of a particular leadership style to a particular situation. However, if truth be told, these different theories seldom actually impacted upon the life and work of educational leaders. They might have helped individuals to reflect upon the type of leader they were, or thought best fitted them and their situation, but they were meant and taken more as descriptions than as prescriptions. If there *was* any message for leaders from such literature (which was largely written for those in the business world), it was that in an age of relative economic stability, the leader's job was a rational job, one of *Transactional leadership*. This, suggested Day et al. (2000), is essentially a form of scientific managerialism, in which leaders exercise power and influence through controlling the rewards in an organization, rewards they can offer or withhold from the workforce. Yet, as the context of leadership has changed, this model of leadership has increasingly come to be seen as inadequate. Designed to deal with stable structures and a predictable economic tomorrow, transactional leadership came to be viewed as insufficient for coping with an age of continual change, when economic certainties and western market-place superiority were constantly challenged. Now, an essential function of leadership would be to generate commitment to change from the workforce by providing a vision of the necessary changes, and of the means of achieving these which others would be persuaded to follow. Transactional approaches did not then touch deeper levels of workers' motivation, which were bound up with beliefs and culture. While transactional forms relied on the use of power and the exchange of favours, the transformational variety attempted to inspire others through vision and through the use of personal consideration. If these traditional theories emphasized rational processes, newer theories needed to emphasize emotions and values. With such unremitting change forced upon organizations and their leaders, *transformational leadership* came to be seen in the business world, and subsequently in the educational world, as an indispensable coping mechanism. Transformational leaders then, were to be social architects, who in creating a vision, developed the trust of their followers, building loyalty, self-confidence and self-regard. As a new age generated new challenges, transformational leadership was seen as a critical part of the response to them.

Yet if inadequately conceived terms are accepted, promoted and then utilized, they transform and corrupt reality, for they reify situations which did not exist before their promotion began. And there is good reason to believe that this happened with the adoption of transformational literature, for there is much to question here. For a start, transactional and transformational leadership may not be entirely separate entities. Certainly, when Burns (1978) first coined the term, he saw transformational leadership as independent, separate and ultimate qualitatively more valuable than its more mundane counter-part. Yet as Bass (1985) subsequently suggested, both may exist along a work continuum, both being needed for effective leadership to take place. If this is the case, then inadequate analysis may, particularly if it is adopted by influential bodies and then used prescriptively, lead to an unnecessary separation, and a relegation of essential duties to a less 'sexy' agenda. Yukl (1999) has also argued that through a preference in this research for exploring the influence of one individual upon another, transformational theories may have too narrow a focus, in the process neglecting such issues as task-oriented behaviour, the interac-tion of a leader with superiors, peers or outsiders, and of the influence and dynamics of leadership upon a group or an organization.

Such concentration on dyadic forms of relationship helps in part to explain the bias of transformational theories towards the depiction of the leader as hero, though one also needs to bear in mind the individualistic predispositions of US culture, literature and folklore from which most leadership theories have originated. It is certainly easier to paint a picture of the leader as heroic individual, and prescribe actions that the individual must perform, than to try and untangle the complex interactive web of group efforts. Certainly, a dominant research methodology in both business and education literature is the recording of successful individuals' stories, and to generalize from these. It should then be no surprise to find that transformational leadership theories are all too easily conflated with charismatic theories of leadership. Yet such conflation is not only unhelpful but can be positively damaging: Yukl (1999), for one, argues that most charismatic leaders don't develop and empower others in their organization in the way one might expect transform-ational leaders to; and this may explain why many of the studies of successful change in effective business organizations were led by individuals who were *not* perceived as charismatic. As he says (1999: 298) 'the vision is usually the product of a collective effort, not the creation of a single, exceptional individual'. Yet such individualist emphasis can convince governments and policy makers that they should be promulgating a picture of the leader as just such an heroic, charismatic 'follow-me-over-the-top' figure, and for incumbent or aspirant leaders to believe that this is what they should be attempting to emulate.

Yet such a model is likely to run counter to the natural predisposi-tions of many excellent leaders, who are not, and never will be charismatic. It is likely to under-utilize the capabilities of others in the organization, as so much stress is placed upon the importance of one individual. It is likely, as Bryman (1992) points out, to suggest an educationally unethical approach to leadership through generating a non-rational commitment by followers. Finally, it is likely to increase the stress on an already stressed leadership group by suggesting that the responsibility at the end of the day is all theirs, leading to the kind of 'disengagement' inclinations mentioned earlier.

This situation – the reification of an activity through analysis and then the official endorsement and prescription of this reification – should be of particular concern to educators, so used as they are by now to the enthusiastic but uncritical advocacy by others beyond education of *their* adoption of business terms and activities. The sceptical might well argue that transformational and charismatic leadership theories are in reality little more than business manage-ment tools devised to mould workers' values and culture into accepting and then enthusiastically embracing managerial/capitalist values as a means of increasing company profitability – what, I (Bottery, 2000) called the 'hot' styles of business management. Such transferences to the educational sector then need to be carefully critiqued for at least three reasons. A first reason is because the emphasis in the business literature has historically been on the techniques of transformational leadership rather than the purposes to which it might be put. A second is because the idea was originally devised to inspire others with a vision which had already been predetermined, and was not intended to include any notion of a shared participative approach in the determining of vision or the solving of problems. A final reason is because the original emphasis was on individuals inspiring others, with a tendency for conflation with non-rational charismatic leadership approaches, which might be used in anti-educational ways to bypass critical faculties in order to gain individuals' commitment.

There already exists critical literature on the impact of poor quality and inappropriate business management 'guru' ideas on *private* sector practice (see, for example, Micklethwait and Wooldridge, 1996); to uncritically transfer such literature into the public sector is double nonsense.

The advent of distributed leadership

Despite its limitations, there are, however, elements of transformational leadership which do lend themselves to educational, and ethical consideration, for it is very important for leaders and educators to have a clear vision of what they want to achieve, and how they want to achieve it. Moreover, when its heroic implications are reduced or eliminated, transformational leadership can also suggest that the processes of both education and leadership should involve the contributions of all parties, rather than being a matter of one person 'doing leadership' to others. Certainly, work in Canada (Leithwood et al., 1999), the US (Spillane et al., 2000), Australia (Lingard et al., 2003) and in the UK (Day et al., 2000; Harris and Lambert, 2003) suggest that, where manifested, it tends to have such characteristics. Indeed, it is partly on the basis of such results that writers like Spillane et al. (2000), Gronn (2003a, 2003b), and Harris (2003), and now the NCSL (2003) have argued that one needs to understand leadership as in reality 'distributed' across a much broader spectrum of individuals within an organization than is normally recognized. Harris (2003: 314) argues that such appreciation has been difficult in coming, most leadership studies in education having been dominated by the studies of individual headteachers and principals, which only further instantiates individualistic views of leadership. Added to this, she suggests that in much educational practice, the 'social exchange theory of leadership' prevails, one which bears an uncommon likeness to transactional forms discussed earlier. Yet she suggests that the work of educational organizations would be better understood if leadership was seen as 'part of an interactive process of sense-making and creation of meaning' in which all members of an organization engaged. Such a view is supported by the work of Spillane et al. (2000), who argue that the degree of leadership distribution is only appreciated when, instead of adopting a methodology of examining individuals' positions and roles within the organization, one instead begins by examining how leadership tasks and functions are actually carried out. From this perspective, leadership is then much more easily appreciated as a shared, group and distributed process than has been generally recognized, either in the literature, or in the way in which roles and positions are created in organizations.

This is exciting stuff for a number of reasons. First, it presents a much more complex – and accurate – description of decision making and leadership activity in organizations than is normally provided. Second, by acknowledging such complex patterns, it may help to prevent the degree of work intensification, and therefore of the kinds of individual pressure and stress described at the beginning of this chapter, for it sponsors a view of leadership which sees many, rather than just the lonely hero, as being involved. Another reason for thinking this is a positive move is that viewing leadership as dispersed helps organizations to more effectively utilize all the talents within them, and in so doing not only facilitates the achievement of goals, but also the empowerment of individuals. Finally, the distribution of leadership could play a critical role in the development of a societal democratic citizenship, because by empowering teachers, it encourages them to develop a more constructive and critical voice, and thus helps to ensure that those who work in such organizations are good role models for the next generation of citizens; for if educators do not show an interest in these matters themselves, how can the next generation be expected to understand the need for such practice?

Nevertheless, even though such a model seems a development over previous ones, a number of caveats must still be made. A first is that one must not get carried away with a *too* distributed vision. Gronn (2003b: 288), for instance, argues that executive level managers appointed as leaders 'surround themselves with an apparatus of secretaries, personal assistants, advisers, deputies, and support groups' because 'to do their job properly, they rely on many other people'. Yet this does not necessarily suggest that leadership is dispersed or distributed: it could just as easily mean that there is so much 'clutter' surrounding the job, that they need these other people to free them up to keep their eyes on the main task. Furthermore, visions of distributed leadership need to take fully into account the asymmetry of power between different actors, which continues to be determined in large part by their formal positions within the organization. It is simply not the case that all actors have equal power or influence in decision-making situations. So while it is very clear that there are organizational leaders who are not institutionally appointed, the formal organizational and professional structure should not be neglected. Fullan (2003: xv), for example, while paying due attention to notions of distributed leadership, by acknowledging that it is only by developing leadership in others that principals can accomplish their tasks, nevertheless recognizes that 'the principal or head of the school [is] the focal point'. If there is other leadership in the school, then it is a leadership normally sponsored by the principal. Even more importantly perhaps, Fullan (2003: 22) recognizes that system-wide change involves going beyond the confines of the school, and that 'the principalship is the only role strategically placed to mediate the tensions of local and state forces ... the solution is to acknowledge the extreme importance of the principalship'. The asymmetries of power could not be clearer, nor could the recognition of the power granted by formal positions.

A second caveat is that while, as Harris (2003) argues, such a view of teacher leadership implies a fundamental redistribution of power, it is important to recognize the full implications of this statement. Leadership, whether by teachers or anyone else, if it means anything, means participation in decision making, and not simply consultation. While such leadership is confined to areas of consensual agreement, or is granted through sponsorship by those appointed to formal leadership positions, then one can envisage reasonably harmonious organizational working. But Harris goes on to say that 'the implications ... imply a fundamental redistribution of power and influence within the school as an organisation' (2003: 322). Indeed they might; but then it must be asked how this is to be achieved if those in formal positions do not wish to have their power redistributed in this way. And what will happen if those beyond the school also do not wish to see this happen? Furthermore, what if those who wish to exercise such distributed leadership see it as something which should not be limited to exercise *within* organizations, but as something which should extend beyond? While distributed leadership is seen as the fairly comfortable functional exercise of cooperative and collaborative relations towards agreed learning agendas, even if this does involve the building of new and complex relationships, then there may be few problems beyond those of actual realization. However, if leadership is about power, which it surely is, and if it is something which by definition has to be wielded, not granted, this potentially involves issues of conflict, both educationally and politically, which are likely to pose very significant questions if those currently exercising power wish to maintain that position. This does not just mean resistance by authoritarian headteachers or principals; it means resistance by those at policy level who, over the last few decades, have been very keen to see the teaching profession as an implementer of externally constructed and driven agendas. As Woods (2003) points out, distributed leadership could be yet one more term used to devolve work and responsibility to those lower in the hierarchy, while not actually engendering *any* real change in the leadership architecture, and he is right to contrast a vision of democratic leadership, which explicitly states what this architecture should look like, with a term which, perhaps all too easily, might be appropriated for less democratic ends. The working out of distributed leadership for both functional learning within the school *and* for participation in wider educational agendas needs to be recognized and carefully thought through.

Such recognition raises a third caveat. As noted earlier, all too often the emphasis in the business literature on transformational leadership has been on the *techniques* rather than the purposes to which it might be put. Distributed leadership faces the same question. For what ends will such leadership be used? Some of the reasons provided for adopting a version of distributed leadership have been given earlier, the central one seeming to be that it will produce more effective learning. Harris (2003: 322) in her discussion of teacher leadership appears to be moving towards a more political vision in her suggestion that this could lead to 'a fundamental redistribution of power and influence within the school'. But questions of power need to be taken further: thus, while distributed leadership may facilitate more effective learning in an organization, this does not address the questions of *what kind* of learning such distributed leadership should facilitate, and for what purpose. And if discussions of distributed leadership produce debate about the redistribution of power and influence in school, they need to ask questions like: should distributed leadership empower a level of participation greater than that required for the realization of the three 'E's of efficiency, effectiveness and economy? Should it recognize participation as a good in itself, a skill which those within a democracy need to practice to become effective citizens? Should it explicitly recognize a commitment to the public sector, that public institutions have a commitment beyond the profit and loss ledger, to concerns of equity, care and justice? In the end the point is simple: debates on the meanings of leadership must not get so wrapped up with definitions that they forget that leadership, however it is construed, has critical effects upon the vision and direction of the school, and needs to constantly come back to this issue.

A final caveat is that while a strong point of some current theories of distributed leadership is an emphasis upon the situated nature of leadership activity, they do not always recognize the extent of such context. Thus Spillane et al. (2000: 27) convincingly argue that understanding leadership in a distributed manner helps us to understand that 'the sociocultural context is a constitutive element of leadership practice, fundamentally shaping its form'. This is extremely helpful in preventing leadership from being seen as some kind of insulated personal quality, pointing instead to the need to understand that there is an interdependence between the individual and the environment (which includes other actors), and which therefore points towards the distributed quality of leadership. But such an understanding should point us not just to the environment of the school but to that beyond it as well. Spillane et al.'s study is prevented from doing this by two factors. One is the methodology: by beginning from the tasks of leadership, they fail to conceptualize such tasks within a macro-perspective. As they say, 'To access leadership practice we must identify and analyse the tasks *that contribute to the execution of macro functions'* (2000: 24) [emphasis added]. This all too easily becomes a fundamentally implementational and functional rather than critical orientation, and in so doing limits itself to a discussion of what leadership is currently concerned with, rather than with what it ought to be concerned. Fullan's (2003) view is wider, explicitly stating the need for school principals to move beyond the functioning of the school to exercise influence and power at the district, even the state level. Yet even this still seems to be unnecessarily restrictive. In his book, Fullan discusses a talk by Michael Barber (2002), adviser and then policymaker to the British government, who described the movement in education in England and Wales over the previous 30 years as a movement from uninformed professional judgement, through to uninformed central government prescription, onto a more informed central prescription, and then finally into an age of informed professional judgement. Fullan's focus in his book is on the development of an informed cadre of professional teachers, developed and led by transformational principals, and he spends little time on the historical background of UK education, apart from some small allusion to the problems which accompanied this 'process'. However, Barber's view is a pro-governmental evolutionary one with which many will disagree, not least because it fails to do justice to the turmoil, anguish, stress and distrust felt by teachers over the last 30 years, and which forms a critical backdrop to the manner in which many educationalists now view New Labour pronouncements. It also fails to address any of the same kinds of issues and feelings which Hargreaves (2003) describes in Canada and the USA. Such functionalist views of leadership which attempt to be ideologically neutral are light years away from the kind of 'bastard leadership' which Wright (2001) suggests is the lot of many English headteachers at the present time, and by implication, far beyond such shores. This is a leadership which feels itself ground down by overwork, by impossible timescales, by enormous amounts of paperwork, whose job is not to lead so much as to implement government policies, which themselves are driven by larger political and economic forces which only occasionally link with the kinds of aspirations and moral agendas which many school leaders still hold dear. Yet this more problematic description of the reality of leadership better fits the picture described at the beginning of this chapter – that of work intensification and leadership disengagement. And to understand such work intensification and leadership disengagement, it seems critical to understand the larger context which has created such conditions, for if this is not recognized and not changed, then those attempts which are made to solve problems will never be more than sticking plasters on wounds that need more extensive attention.

The need for the ecological leader

To understand such issues, it is then simply insufficient to concentrate upon the school, the district or even the educational system. To understand the tasks ahead for educational leaders, the larger context of educational leadership needs to be understood. The 'socio-cultural context' needs to embrace far more than the school, the district, or even the educational system. It needs to describe and understand the quite unique forces existing within societies today, which in many cases emanate beyond them, which condition, constrain and in some cases coerce the work of educational leaders. The rationale of this book, then, is the belief that critical questions need to be asked concerning the purposes of educational leadership, questions which go beyond official recommendations, and to examine the manner in which official sponsorship is often driven by forces which do not always have as a priority the educational, political or social welfare of recipients. This book then aims to be both practical and critical: it aims to help educational leaders and aspiring educational leaders to examine their own values and practice by providing a wider-than-normal framework within which to locate them. It therefore advocates that leaders need, as never before, to be 'ecologically aware' – to be cognizant of those forces which impact upon not only their own practice, but upon the attitudes and values of the other educators within their organizations, the aspirations and endpoints of their students, and upon those in the wider communities they serve. Such leaders, then need to place their practice within both meso- and macro-contexts, and appreciate not only of what these contexts consist, and how they frame educational practice, but what leaders need to do to engage with them to protect their visions.

The book then begins by examining such supra-educational pressures, locating them at global, cultural and national levels. It suggests that the world of educational leadership is a paradoxical combination of control and fragmentation. It examines, in particular, the educational objectives of western industrialized countries, and how some governments have exercised a degree of central direction of educational activity which has resulted in an excess of control, while a paradoxical drive within these societies towards an excess of consumption has exacerbated existing problems of fragmentation. The second part of the book examines the impact of these upon the work of educational leaders, and suggests that these may be best conceptualized as the challenges to trust, meaning and identity. The final part deals with organizing a response, and suggests that educational leaders need to do this by developing an appropriate form of learning organization, and by developing new understandings of the role requirements of professional educators. Such a reframing of professionalism then, finally, suggests the need for educational leaders who are 'ethical dialecticians' – individuals with moral compasses, yet who are sufficiently aware of their own limitations, of the massive changes impacting upon educational institutions, and of their need to listen to others, to adopt a 'provisionalist' attitude to their understanding of the world. At the same time, they also need to possess the political and pragmatic astuteness to help balance a grounded morality, a personal and epistemological provisionalism, and an ecological awareness, leading to the ability to work with others towards the formation of real learning communities.

It will then be clear that a critical area of professional development is going to be a deeper understanding of the etiology of leadership challenges, for only through understanding the sources of these challenges can educational leaders begin to move to realize the kinds of vision that compelled many of them to take up leadership positions in the first place. Furthermore, it is only by understanding and beginning to change the structures and language that discourage potential leaders from continuing their climb that an educational system can be developed which encourages people to work within it, and which contributes to a healthy and vibrant society. This examination begins in the next chapter at the level of global change.

PART 1
SETTING THE CONTEXT

3   *The global challenge*

Why the need for a global perspective?

Many studies of educational leadership are concerned with activities at personal, organizational and local levels. This is hardly surprising when a leader's work is normally centred around individuals and the organization within which they work, and it would be a strange literature indeed which did not reflect this fact. Yet as argued earlier, such leadership focus is not just explained by day-to-day work. The larger literature on leadership, which has had considerable influence on education stems primarily from the US business world, is underpinned by values of individualism and personal achievement, and has therefore long understood leadership as the activities of outstanding individuals. Only recently has this literature begun to look beyond the organization to the effect that particular national cultures have on the practice of management, and that businesses increasingly operate on a global stage (see, for example, Hofstede, 2003).

However, despite the odd exception (e.g. Handy, 1994, 1997), even such enlarged business perspectives are still largely concerned with the commercial success of the organization. Educational leadership, however, both in the challenges it faces, and in the goals it needs to achieve, must be more broadly conceived. If, for example, the education for an entire region is to improve, rather than just that of a few schools within it, then, as Fullan (2003) argues, educational leadership must expand its purview to encompass wider regional issues. If it fails to do this, it is unlikely that the remedies applied to problems will address deeper underlying causes.

Yet even regional approaches may be insufficient. Indeed, if we view the tasks of educators historically, they have also been employed 'to spread the dominant cultures and inculcate popular ideologies of nationhood, to forge the political and cultural unity for the burgeoning nation states, and to cement the ideological hegemony of their dominant classes' (Green, 1997: 35). Their work, then, has largely been contextualized within nation-state aims, and they have been employed for the prosecution of such purposes. Indeed, some writers (for example, Ozga and Lawn (1981)) view the history of education professionals as essentially that of a dialogue between them and the nation-state, with the nation-state largely determining the terms of the debate. Indeed, over the last two decades, educational leaders world-wide have been deluged with torrents of legislation that have massively changed their practice and challenged their values, and most of it has emanated at the national level. It would be a grave mistake, then, to only contextualize educational work at personal, organizational and systemic levels: it needs to be viewed within national contexts as well, and critiqued as such. This is not just so that educational leaders can better understand the implications of such legislation on their practice but also to enable them to engage as both professionals and citizens in the determination of the role of educational institutions in the provision of the knowledge, skills, resources, and values in adjusting to and critiquing the demands of a new information age. This is why Hargreaves (2003) contextualizes the work of schools beyond the local and systemic, arguing that it is the 'soul-less standardisation' of many governments which is destroying the morale of teachers and hampering the ability of schools to provide their students with the skills they will need to work 'within' and 'beyond' a knowledge economy.

Yet there are changes afoot in the world today which challenge even this level of contextualization. With the growth of trans-national organizations like the EC and NAFTA, it is now apparent that the nation-state is no longer the only source of political legitimacy; with the growth of trans-national corporations it is also apparent that the nation-state is increasingly constrained by the activities and aims of the private sector. These issues may seem a long way from the work of educational leaders, but this chapter will argue that such a macro-contextualization of leadership activity helps place in clearer perspective the kind of challenges and values that educational leaders today do indeed face. Such a context, for instance, helps explain that current crises of teacher retention and recruitment originate at least in part from changes which transcend the local and the national. Understanding these crises as global issues is aided by work like that of Ritzer (2004) who argues that a number of global processes are accelerating and exacerbating a trend towards what he calls 'Mac-Donaldization'. A development of Weberian 'rationalization', this is an intensification of the processes of efficiency, calculability and control, not just to industrial operations, but to workers of all descriptions, including those in education, leading to a situation, he argues, where we may be facing the possibility of a world largely stripped of local meaning. As part of this process, many may find themselves steered down roads of training in desired competencies (what Gronn (2003a) described for educational leaders as 'designer leadership'), and in being inspected and rewarded or punished on these competencies. The consequence of such changes may be that many educational professionals will feel less able to employ a critical rationality in their understanding of educational policies, and less able to interrogate their own practice in the light of their personal and professional values – a trend apparently encouraged by some in managerial and policy hierarchies. Indeed, many 'professionals' may feel that a non-standard application of expertize to individual situations through the use of personal intelligence is no longer a requirement – or a desirable quality – for satisfactory role performance. These challenges to educational institutions, then, suggest origins transcending the national, which need to be described and examined as such if they are to be properly understood.

From control to fragmentation

Yet there are other phenomena, trans-national, even global in origin, which generate effects which are the antithesis of such standardization and control. Many daily lives are, paradoxically, as fragmented as they are controlled; a fact reflected in the increasing impermanence of work, and the flexibility required within it, whether this be the numerical flexibility of people in an organization, the temporal flexibility of hours worked, the functional flexibility of tasks undertaken, or the vocational flexibility of movement between worksites. In the business world, practices like hot-desking even reduce presence in the office to the extent that 'work loses its physical embodiment and sense of permanence ... a constant reminder of one's marginal status within the organisation as a whole' (Brown and Lauder, 2001: 152). Such fragmentation challenges and undermines long-cherished value systems and beliefs, leading to what Sennet (1998) calls the 'corrosion of character', as individuals are prevented from building a sense of community and permanence to their life projects. Yet, in this fragmentation of meaning and value, another paradox is produced: the danger that a belief system or organization which can provide structure, control and direction is then welcomed, regardless of where such direction leads. So while Ritzer (1993: 1) points to the dangers of a McDonaldized world, he is also aware that many people welcome it, for those who eat at MacDonalds 'prefer a world that is not cluttered by choices and options. They like the fact that many aspects of their lives are highly predictable.' Ritzer is of course not just talking about the effects of fast-food restaurants on individual's eating habits, but about much bigger issues, for as such predictability is sought for all aspects of life, so that life becomes increasingly controlled. This harks back to Fromm's (1942) analysis of people's fear of freedom, the attempt to locate responsibility for personal choice beyond the self, a direct cause, he suggested, for people's support for authoritarian governments like those of Hitler and Stalin. Such political and existential bargains, however, do not just increase the degree of external control: the practice of voluntary submission also limits the boundaries within which personal and existential freedoms are explored. Giving up one's freedom is an act which gradually ceases to be conscious, and instead becomes a way of life, a self-imposed frame of living, which then becomes an unexamined and unargued psychic constraint on political and existential possibilities. When this happens, the ability to make personal sense of the world becomes that much harder, leading in many cases to the desire for further external direction and further external control, producing a dangerously malign cycle of further fragmentation and control. What this analysis suggests, then, is that control and fragmentation do not then act separately: they interact to synergistically exacerbate existing tendencies; control becomes stronger, more internalized, as fragmentation becomes more real and more effective.

Three reasons for the macro-contextualization

Excessive governmental control and the fragmentation of personal and cultural values are then, this book argues, not issues which educational leaders can ignore; they are ones with which they need to grapple. So one good reason for needing to macro-contextualize the challenges of educational leadership stems from the fact that many challenges may have their origin at such levels. A second reason for such macro-contextualization comes from the fact that many educational problems are increasingly couched in macro-social terms, and conceptions of educational activity and achievement, learning communities, and the role that leaders play within them, in macro-level language. Barber (2000) for instance, talked of the vision of the British government for education as being 'a world class education service; one which matches the best anywhere on the planet', and asserted that 'in this decade we will see educational reform globalising. We will see the globalisation of large elements of the curriculum.' These kinds of comments suggest that the level of comparison should no longer be the national and cultural, but the 'global', and that such globalization will begin to determine the nature of schools everywhere. Whether such claims are true, whether these *are* the proper levels of comparison, can only be judged within a macro-contextualized understanding of leadership activities.

A final reason for needing to include the macro-level in discussions of the challenges to educational leaders lies in the fact that much 'globalization' talk is not descriptive but highly normative. There are usually hidden agendas behind such recommendations of which every educationalist needs to be aware. There is little doubt, for instance, that the globalizing of business markets is a huge prize, and it is therefore unsurprising to find it vigorously campaigned for by large business interests in a neo-liberal/conservative alliance. This places the concept of globalization within heavily contested territory. Some interpretations (e.g. Ohmae, 1995; LeGraine, 2002) suggest that globalization is essentially a force for good, that through opening up new markets, extending competition, and bringing nations into a world order, globalization increases the prosperity of all involved. On this account, any short-term problems – such as greater disparities of wealth, the need for personal flexibility in the search for work, and a greater fragmentation to people's lives – are all prices worth paying. Other interpretations (see, for example, Korten, 1996; Hertz, 2001; Frank, 2002) view globalization in much more negative terms. For these writers, the unfettered free markets of economic globalization have already been seen at the national level, and have produced social dislocation, led to a neglect of the public and civic good, increased inequalities between rich and poor, and produced a poorer quality of life for *all* within communities. Such critics are therefore much less enthusiastic in their embrace of the concept. 'Globalization', then, needs to be deconstructed, and its implications for educational leadership examined.

Meanings of globalization

'Globalization' as a term hides a variety of possible meanings which do not always fit together to produce one neat picture. Yet, in a sense, the term is remarkably straightforward, for seeing the Earth from space can provide a sense of global wholeness and unity, which rather like catching sight of your reflection in a shop window, can be rather surprising. *Is that me?* you ask, realizing perhaps for the first time a new facet to yourself, in the process perhaps glimpsing a little more deeply into who you really are. Seeing the Earth from space is a little similar. It is certainly beautiful, an aesthetic absolute in an age when relativity is the predominant intellectual posture. It is also surprising, as the world of humanity is seen, in comparison with the earth's size and age, as tiny and transitory. What is seen instead is a living planet, on which the human race seems little more than a temporary resident, depending on it as other living things do, for its existence, and yet abusing it rather than treating it with care. As Boulding (1968: 133–48) so presciently said nearly 40 years ago, we live on a spaceship earth, yet treat it like cowboys: 'the measure of well-being [being] not how fast the crew is able to consume its limited stores, but rather how effective the crew members are in maintaining their shared resource stocks, and the life-support system on which they all depend'.

We may also recognize that our treatment could lead to our own extinction. As educators, we may then feel compelled to reflect, and help others to reflect, upon our practices and values, our obligations to others, human and non-human, with whom we currently share the planet, and with those generations still to come. Ultimately, we may reflect upon ourselves, upon the meaning of our existence, and on our mortality, the sense of our smallness and fragility, situated on this small ball whirling through a vast and infinite space. This seems such a core objective of a rich education, and yet how often do educational leaders, deflected by other agendas, find the time to consider such ultimate issues? Thinking at the global level can facilitate such thought, broaden our understanding and experience of others, and allow us to situate our experiences of life in new and remarkable ways.

Three forms of descriptive globalization

'Globalization' as a concept intimately connected with the way we view our place and meaning on this planet, can thus provide unique avenues to self-exploration and self-development. However, 'globalization' also encompasses more than how we look at the world, for it is probably even more concerned with *processes* which would continue whether human beings recognized them or not, and it is these processes which affect nation-states and produce policy mediations, which in turn have a direct impact on the management and leadership of educational institutions. These processes may not be complete, in the sense that not all on this planet may yet have access to, or be affected by them yet they do impact on a sizeable majority, and are likely to impact on many more in the future.

Environmental globalization

Environmental globalization is more than just a description of the growth or impact of oceans, forests and deserts. It is concerned with the ecology and interdependence of these and living things on a global scale. Perhaps the first form of recorded environmental globalization concerned the spread of disease, with the proliferation of smallpox; from its first appearance in Egypt in 1350 BC, to its advent in China in AD 49, in Europe 700 years later, and then 1,000 years later in Australia in 1789. Such globalization of disease has not diminished but actually increased: since 1973, 30 previously unknown diseases have spread from being localized infections to having trans-national incidence, the most obvious and potent being AIDS, largely due to the ease of transport and communication. Humanity's influence is then strongly implicated in such changes to this environment, as it is with deforestation, global warming and pollution. Environmental issues transcend national borders, and are no respecters of national sovereignty.

Cultural globalization

It is worrying that while environmental globalization is a pressing and immediate concern which should help frame the vision of educational leaders, it as yet only marginally impinges upon their work. The reasons for this speak volumes for our present over-riding values – it less visibly affects the financial viability of educational institutions and the political stability of nation-states than other forms of globalization which are more pressing in their immediate effects. Cultural globalization is one such form. It is a curious phenomenon, capable of being conceived in two totally opposed ways. First, there is a *globalization of cultural variety*, where, in a small city such as the one in which this book is being written, I can eat virtually any national dish, attend a ceremony of any of the world's major religions, listen to any kind of music. Such variety can provide education with different windows through which new perspectives are gained on the familiar, where wonder and awe are seen, where it can be realized that others are simply using different roads to pursue the same truths as oneself. Yet others don't necessarily view such experiences as opportunities for spiritual growth. Instead they see them as roads leading only to relativity and fragmentation. Faced with too many choices, they cease to see meaning in any, lose their personal centre, and only *play* with thoughts, ideas, meanings and values. In the process they become one of Rorty's (1989: 73–4) ironic individuals, 'never quite able to take themselves seriously because [they are] always aware that the terms in which they describe themselves are subject to change, always aware of the contingency and fragility of their final vocabularies, and thus of their selves'.

Yet for others – individuals who have used beliefs as protective structures within which to encase their lives, rather than as challenges to reflect upon and deepen themselves – such variety leads to a retreat into rigid, fundamentalist adherences. The globalization of cultural variety is then seen more as incursions by those who lack the truth, but who would infect you and your children with their falsehoods. When such 'incursions' are supplemented by what is perceived as Western imperialist arrogance, such resistance may be translated into physical hostility.

Paradoxically, given the possibility of cultural variety suggested above, another candidate for cultural globalization is precisely the opposite – the *globalization of cultural standardization*, which operates through the imposition of a one-window view of the world. It is Ritzer's (1993) 'McDonaldization' again, with its four classic themes of bureaucracy: efficiency, calculability, predictability and control. It is the world of modern Disney and 'Rainforest Cafes', where the artificial and the commodified come to replace the real; a cultural globalization which is quick, cheap, fast and shallow; where the 'best bits' of a culture are extracted, reformulated and packaged for easy consumption. It is a globalization heavily directed by global markets and free market capitalism, where culture is packaged and sold to be a profit-making activity. When education embarks down such a road, its institutions, rather than being the liberating experience which opens up opportunities to the individual, are in danger of becoming Procrustes' beds in which individuals are made to fit to the standard. In the process, the personal is constricted, the spiritual is shackled.

Where societies embark upon such standardization and commodification there must be considerable disquiet, for cultures and their underpinning values are created by complex relationships between communities, and by individuals reflecting upon, participating in, and debating the values and practices that should undergird their lives. It is through such complex interactions that a rich value base is created, one essential for a vibrant democratic society, and for a commercial sector to exist and prosper. Yet where these primary educational aims are colonized and then pressed into the service of the economic, the base upon which such economic activity relies is destroyed. As Rifkin (2000: 247) says: 'To the extent that the commercial arena tries to sell access to bits and pieces of human culture and lived experience in the form of bricolage and pastiche, it risks poisoning the well from which we draw important values and feelings.'

So while cultural globalization as the proliferation of access to different beliefs and approaches to life can be a force for spiritual growth, it can also drive the less secure and the more dogmatic down very different paths. And in an age of global paradox, we also find an opposing globalization of standardization – again stemming from the West – which may also undermine profoundly held beliefs, leaching out the local and the personal. Such standardization can then have much the same effect upon the threatened, the insecure and the dogmatic. The educational leader, living in a world of both kinds of cultural globalization, needs to be keenly aware of their causes, their synergies, their potential effects. They are both issues to which this book will return.

Demographic globalization

Demographic globalization is a phenomenon with at least two stings in its tail. It may be simply stated as a growing tension between increasingly ageing populations, and those that have a much younger profile. The ageing problem is now widely recognized in the developed West and among the Asian tiger nations, and becoming apparent in developing countries. Its nature and effects are sobering. Simply put, it is the recognition that there is an increasing number of people who are living longer, and that this proportion is increasing. As Dychtwald (1999) points out, in the USA at the beginning of the twentieth century, life expectancy was only 47 years, yet by the end it had risen to 76 years. In Japan, the life expectancy in 1950 for women was 61.4 years, and for men 58 years. By the end of the century, it was 83 years for women and 76 years for men. Significantly, this phenomenon of increased longevity is compounded by the fact that in the same nations, the fertility rate is declining. Assuming that each couple needs to produce two children each to reproduce a population (and probably more, as not all will marry and have children), then many nations are not managing this. The situation of some nation-states is nothing short of dire: Italy has a potentially catastrophic rate of 1.2. Japan, the country with the world's longest living population, has a rate of 1.39.

This combination of increased longevity and reduced fertility has a number of problematic effects. First, it means that a decreasing percentage of the population is paying taxes to sustain core welfare institutions like education, and this percentage will continue to fall.

It also means that, because ageing populations present more chronic medical conditions which necessitate continual and expensive health care, core welfare institutions – and their managers – will be under even greater pressure than formerly. Third, as this ageing population increases in size, so it will wield greater political power. Moreover, as Peterson (2000) points out, because it tends to be more politically involved than younger generations, it is likely that 'gray power' will exercise disproportionate political power, resulting in a skewing of public spending to the needs of the elderly, rather than to investment in education and other services for the young.

This is not an issue for demographers and policy makers alone. Such changes will have a huge impact on the complexion of society, on welfare state institutions, on their leadership, on those who use such institutions, and on individual lives, both young and old, as well as on the changed relationship between young and old. In previous times, and still in some cultures, the elderly were treated with considerable respect, even veneration. More recently, particularly in the west, they have been socially and politically sidelined, apparently irrelevant to the consuming project of greater economic competitiveness. Furthermore, when life expectancy, only a few decades ago, could not be expected to exceed the early fifties, reflections on mortality occasioned by old age was the province of the few. Now it will be the concern of the majority. A longer retirement age for most will present choices which few previously needed to contemplate, and with which policy makers are still coming to grips. Recent legislation attempting to keep people in work longer, and reducing or eliminating state pensions, are symptomatic of this, and are likely to have quite dramatic effects on the elderly and the societies within which they live.

Retirement, then, is likely to lead to an extended period of life, but which could take very different paths. It could be a time of great suffering and bitterness, as concerns about financing elderly care, debates about the responsibilities this places upon middle-aged children, the guilt both sides may feel, and the personal problems of coming to terms with a body which is increasingly frail, all contribute to a potentially dark future. The coming age of the elderly could be traumatic, damaging and spiritually limiting. However, if planned properly, it could be much brighter, in which the elderly aid a generation still in formal education, or, by becoming more politically engaged, develop concerns for generations still to come. It could be a time when lifelong learning means more than just equipping individuals with different working skills for changing employment scenarios, but is related more to the different personal, social and spiritual demands which different ages require. In this brighter future, old age would be a time with great potential for spiritual exploration and development. It is a future which educational leaders need to reflect upon long and hard, not just because it will affect them personally, or because of the impact it will have upon state and institutional finances, but because it will have profound effects upon the way in which a society considers and deals with the core issue of caring for large numbers of its more dependent members. It is hard to exaggerate its social, political, ethical and economic importance.

This then is the ageing problem. However, this is only one side of the issue. The other side is that Muslim countries are not only experiencing a population boom, but an increasingly high proportion of people in their teens and twenties. Huntington (1998) argues that this is a recipe for international tension: an ageing, declining and conservative set of western populations, keen to hold on to what they have, are increasingly going to face expanding populations who have the passions of youth, require greater resources, and are much more likely to want change than their ageing counterparts. When one adds to this scenario the cultural challenges driving holders of non-western beliefs towards fundamentalisms, this does not augur well for the future. As Huntington points out, radicalism is most often seen among the young, and tensions normally occur between those who want change and those who do not. This is why, on his map of international relations (245), he describes relationships between the West and Muslim countries as likely sources of international tension. As he argues, 'to ignore the impact of the Islamic Resurgence on Eastern Hemisphere politics is equivalent to ignoring the impact of the Protestant Reformation on European politics' (1998: 111), only now there are things like nuclear and biological weapons with which such disputes may be prosecuted. Demography, then, is not only intimately connected to the internal economics of different countries, it is critically connected to international politics as well.

Three forms of prescriptive globalization

So far 'globalization' in its various forms has been described as largely a *descriptive* phenomenon. There are, however, other forms which are closely linked to the aspirations of particular political ideologies and particular power groups and these are described as *prescriptive* forms of globalization.

Political globalization

Political globalization is another complex term which is probably best initially conceptualized as the relocation of political power away from the nation-state. One reason for such relocation is the increasing involvement of states in global economic activity, some of which is generated by nation-states themselves as they cede part of their sovereignty in exchange for greater global competitiveness through locating themselves within larger supra-national bodies like the EU or NAFTA. However, by locking themselves into international financial agreements they also limit their room for financial manoevre.

However, not all global involvement and power diffusion is a willing move by nation-states. Some is generated by supra-national economic organizations like the IMF (set up to bail out countries with balance of payment problems), the World Trade Organization (in existence to proselytize the merits of global free markets) and the World Bank (whose prime function is to aid development projects in developing countries through free-market measures). These bodies exert their influence through stipulating that financial assistance to nation-states is conditional upon the dismantling of trade barriers and of their entry into a global system of free markets, which again limits the ability of nation-states to firewall their economies. One further form of global steerage is the activities of trans-national companies (TNCs), who possess considerable capacity to move both finance and plant from one country to another, and thus further limit nation-states' independence. The combination of these forces heavily conditions many other nation-state activities. Education is one such activity, not only in terms of its financing, but also in terms of the uses to which it is actually put. It will be clear, then, that there are intimate connections between political globalization and economic forces.

Nevertheless, while nation-states are perhaps becoming smaller players on a bigger political and economic stage, nation-states are sometimes seen as *too* big, for as individuals come to question whether the nation-state is an acceptable site for their most profound senses of allegiance and identification, political power not only moves upwards but downwards as well. This helps to explain why UN membership in 1945 was 45, by 1960 it was 100, and by 2003 it was 191, and why in all likelihood it will continue to grow. The evidence suggests that many individuals – in reaction against political, economic and culturally standardized globalizations – are re-locating their personal commitments and their very identities to levels below that of current nation-states.

However, the understanding of political globalization as the weakening of nation-state power is too simplistic. One of the most notable features of the modern world is the global interconnectedness of different interests, and the porosity of the nation-states to these interests, which is not easily described in simple power-up or power-down terms. Whether one is talking about the massive influence of the use of IT, international trade, terrorism, or the drugs trade, it is clear that there are forces at work in the world today which limit the ability of even the most powerful nation-state in maintaining the integrity of its borders. Political globalization, then, has probably to be understood as much in terms of the complexity and interconnectedness of present interests and power structures as it does in terms of any ceding of nation-state power.

Finally, political globalization also needs to be seen as the global spread of ideas, and the development of international sets of rules and institutions for political governance. While there are those sceptical of either the idea or the existence of an international community, particularly after recent events in Iraq, a United Nations does exist in which trans-national issues are debated and discussed, and there has also been a global spread of political ideas, particularly those to do with democratic governance, anti-slavery, anti-colonialism, and environmentalism and feminism.

Such global political changes affect educational leaders in at least three ways: first, in terms of the capture of political and citizenship agendas by economic agendas; second, by the call for 'nested' concepts of citizenship rather than a simple allegiance to the national level; and lastly, particularly with the mediation of such global forces at the global or cultural level, by the sheer complexity of situations which make it difficult, if not impossible, to fully comprehend, predict or control the future. Once again, educational leaders will not only experience greater control and direction of their work, but also the increasing complexity and fragmentation of the world around them; and they are going to have to help others to make sense of this as well. Nobody said it was going to be easy!

American globalization

Such debates over political globalization lead naturally into a fifth form of globalization, American globalization. There may be many who will baulk at such an idea. Yet if globalization is to be measured in terms of power and reach, then consider that in military terms, the USA spends more on expenditure in this area than the next eight countries *combined*. In terms of economic power, it has a 27 per cent share of world product, equal to the next three largest economic powers combined. Indeed, the idea of the USA as a form of globalization is not new; it was suggested as long ago as 1902, when an Englishman, W.T. Stead, wrote a book entitled *The Americanization of the World*. The situation today is even more favourable for the USA than it was then. As the French Foreign Minister Hubert Vedrine said in 2001:

> 'The United States . . . swims easily and rules supreme in the waters of globalisation. Americans get great benefits from this for a large number of reasons: because of their economic size, because globalisation takes place in their language; because it is organised along neo-liberal economic principles; because they impose their legal, accounting, and technical practices; and because they're advocates of individualism.'
> (quoted in Nye, 2002: 78)

He might have also have added that a critical skill in global economic power is a facility in IT, and while the USA contains only one-twentieth of the world's population, it has one-half of all internet users.

Indeed, it seems possible to suggest five facets of American globalization:

1 A dominance in the design and use of both the software and hardware of information technology.

2 A massive military supremacy.

3 A massive economic influence through the confluence of American neo-liberal principles, American-dominated supra-national economic organizations, and the functioning of global markets.

4 An enormous cultural influence through the US film industry, the spread of 'MacDonaldized' food, and the casualness of T-shirt and jeans fashions.

5 A widespread politico-cultural influence, emphasizing the supremacy of the individual freedom and autonomy, of democracy, and the dislike of strong and expansionist government.

Nye (2002) divides American power into 'hard' and 'soft' power, and argues that while its hard (military and economic) power is likely to remain unchallenged for decades to come, the disturbing thing for

Americans (and by implication for all other nation-states) is that, because of the more complex distribution of power in the twenty-first century, nation-states are more much porous than they would like to acknowledge. There are, he suggests, more and more things which even the most powerful state cannot control. Recalling the earlier discussion on the limits imposed on nation-states by political globaliz-ation, he argues that particularly after the experiences of September 11, and the invasion of Iraq: 'The US lacks both the international and domestic prerequisites to resolve conflicts that are internal to other societies, and to monitor and control trans-national transactions that threaten Americans at home' (2002: 40). He therefore suggests that the USA 'will have to learn better how to share as well as to lead', fearing that it may be too powerful to be challenged by any other state, but not great enough to deal on its own with issues like terrorism or nuclear proliferation. This suggests that nation-states' power may not be diminishing so much as the complexity of problems is increasing, with nation-states finding it increasingly difficult to resolve them. Nation states could then retain the same level of resources as previously, but would still be less able to deal with issues that arise. And America seems to be in the interesting position of being a form of globalization, yet challenged by other aspects of it.

What are the implications of this for educational leaders? It is probably best to address this through the 'hard' and 'soft' power distinctions made earlier. US soft power – food, fashion, films, political values – will almost certainly continue to exert an enormous effect upon the cultures of other counties, as well as retaining a virtual monopoly in their country of origin. Such soft influences may then be enthusiastically adopted by some, but just as aggressively resisted by others, making it all the harder for the two sides to understand one another. The educational leader will have to reflect upon the implications of this for local identity, culture and education-al community. It is an area global in nature, ripe for both exchange and conflict.

The hard power of US globalization is also unlikely to be far from the headlines. Economic influence and values penetrate the workings of even the most distant nation-state, and affect its functioning (and through this its educational organizations). At the same time military interventions seem a constant possibility, whose outcomes are impossible to predict, but which are likely to raise tensions wherever they occur. Nye (2002) may be right in arguing that the USA would be well advised to restrict its use of hard power in favour of the more attractive elements of its soft power: it remains to be seen whether such advice is followed.

Economic globalization

Claims for the existence of economic globalization have been around a long time. In their 1848 Communist Manifesto, for instance, Marx and Engels argued that 'all old-established national industries have been destroyed or are being destroyed . . . In place of the old local and national seclusion and self-sufficiency, we have intercourse in every direction, universal interdependence of nations' (quoted in Nye, 2002: 77). It is then a long-term trend, currently facilitated, as already seen, by three different forces. One is the rapid, largely unrestricted global movement of finance, a process which prevents nation-states from protecting welfare agendas. A second is the locking of nation-states into free market agreements by supra-national organizations like the IMF, the WTO and the World Bank, which limit the scope of nation-state activity. The third force is that of trans-national companies, who exert force on national government policies through their ability to relocate their capital, factories and workforces around the world, resulting in competition between nation-states to encourage these companies to do business in their country.

Economic globalization not only sets the context for other forms of globalization, but its language is increasingly used to describe their activities – it 'captures their discourses'. It is implicated in *environmental globalization* through multinational companies' activity in extracting non-renewal resources around the world – and thereby raises the question of whether environmental globalization can be a purely descriptive term. It is implicated in aspects of *cultural globalization* through the standardizing activities that much global economic activity has. It is implicated in *American globalization* through the US global sponsorship of free markets, through the close relationship between the US government and multinational financial organizations, massive US economic power, and the lead that the USA has in information technology. Finally, and perhaps most importantly for educational leaders, it is implicated in *political globalization* through the steerage that multinational organizations and transnational companies have on the activities of nation-states. In so doing, such activities, including those of the education sector, are increasingly co-opted: for many in educational institutions, this manifests itself through governmental directives, which thereby tends to be seen as *the* controlling and directing force. Yet, while there are aspects of nation-state activity which are not derivative of larger economic agendas, many – such as the quest by the nation-state to maintain its legitimacy as the primary source of allegiance from 'citizens' – are in large part driven by these larger agendas.

Why does current global economic activity have such profound effects? Part may be due to the fact that, with the departure of capitalism's main competitors – fascism, socialism, and communism – there is no other global system to provide an alternative form of economic organization. But it springs more deeply from the nature of capitalist activity itself, in particular from the fact that the success of a capitalist company is measured by its performance on the stock market, by its continued growth and its ability to generate profits. Such dynamics mean that to be successful, a company, above all, needs to *grow*. This leads to the expansion of businesses not only in the private sector, but into two other critical areas as well.

The first area is the public sector. This can simply mean that private sector companies take over the work of public sector companies, of which there have been many examples around the world. Such physical growth, however, can also lead to symbolic growth, as the values of the private sector – primarily those of efficiency, effectiveness and economy – become the criteria of success, while other values critical to a rich education – like care, trust and equity – are increasingly perceived as second-order values.

The second area of expansion is into the personal and cultural, and, as already seen, if this happens, cultural 'goods' may be turned into articles or activities for consumption – they may be commodified. A number of potential effects of this have already been suggested – the colonization of cultural activities to serve economic activity; the standardization of products to generate greater global profits, and a reduction in local individuality; and finally, the disenchantment of activities, as the individual response to a particular situation is seen as 'uneconomic' and therefore 'irrational'. In its pursuit of profit, the commercial sector tends of its nature to be voracious, turning to commercial advantage whatever facilitates its growth, even things like spirituality (Casey, 2001), emotional intelligence (Fineman, 2000), and informality (Misztal, 2001). Ultimately, then, the dominance of this agenda leads to an emphasis on economic functionality rather than the pursuit of things in their own right, and as it does so, it undermines the value of other aims, transforming and reducing them to second-order activities.

There are two further potential effects. One is the need for continued and expanded growth by encouraging individuals to consume increased quantities of goods. This is most effectively done if people can be persuaded to see themselves, first and foremost as consumers, and to indulge in consumerist activities as activities of first choice. As they do so, however, they will come to value the personal over the shared, the private over the public. A dominant consumerism is then highly likely to lead to the valuing of the self over the valuing of the social.

A second effect is on the nature and role of the organization, and of those within it. It has already been noted how many leaders now feel increasingly stressed by the intensification of work, and the amount of themselves they are asked to commit to the good of the organization. This can in large part be explained by the growth of the 'greedy' organization which attempts to extract the maximum amount of physical and emotional labour and commitment out of the individual, in an effort to reduce the costs of production and increase the amount of its employees' work. All of these should be of interest to the educational leader, not only for the effects they have upon themselves, but also for the way they change the mission of their organization, and the way in which they change the nature of the society within which they live.

Globalization, the changing nature of knowledge, and organizational structures

There are then profound inter-relationships between the different forms of globalization, with economic globalization being the dominant form. This economic domination has one further effect which requires comment, and this concerns the kinds of business organization and functions which are favoured by the changing nature of markets. If markets and physical property have been synonymous for the last 200 to 300 years, as the accrual and control of property has normally meant increased influence and control of the market, this is now much less so. In this new era of capitalism, the critical issue for many has become one of amassing and controlling the points of access to the things that consumers want – whether this is control of access to physical materials (like cars), or, more importantly, the control of access to the ideas and knowledge which generate new products, new ideas, new experiences.

Now such control of access to ideas leads to the perceived need to control and 'manage' knowledge, and from there to the adoption of terms like 'intellectual capital' (Stewart, 1998) and the 'knowledge economy' (Neef, 1998), as once again, the economic attempts to commodify other areas, this time that of knowledge itself. Drucker (1993) suggested that initially in human history knowledge was utilized almost exclusively for personal and social reasons. Only much later, with the Industrial Revolution, did knowledge come to be used in an economic sense, being then applied to the use of tools, methods and products in industrial processes. From there knowledge was applied, through writers like F.W.Taylor, to the process of work itself. Now, Drucker suggests, we are entering an age in which knowledge is applied to knowledge itself. At the personal level, this may principally be in terms of learning how to learn. At the organizational level, the question is increasingly seen as one of how the intellectual capital in a company – the intelligence, innovation and creativity which is increasingly the wellspring of a company's profit base – can be better audited, managed and directed to the purpose and the profits of that organization, to become what Stewart (1998: 67) calls 'packaged useful knowledge'. Now it must be stressed that physical property does not disappear as a business concern, but it does begin in many economic activities to move from the assets side of the ledger to the expense column, to be replaced by intangible properties like human knowledge, imagination and creativity. As this happens, institutions which exercise control through amassing physical capital are challenged, even replaced as market leaders by institutions which control access to ideas, knowledge and expertize. The new economy, then, is a 'knowledge economy', and the new capitalism is 'knowledge capitalism'. There are a number of consequences from this.

One is that businesses – and, by implication, education – needs to understand what is involved in conducting 'knowledge audits', in ascertaining what 'workers' know, what they need to know, and what are the best methods for transferring such knowledge and understanding. Yet this will require a much clearer conception of what 'knowledge management' means than exists at present. Wurzburg (1998: 39) suggests that while there is still much difference of opinion here, there are a number of strategies emerging in the more efficient and effective utilization of 'knowledge workers'. These include:

- increasingly flattened hierarchies where horizontal communication and links are accorded more importance than hierarchical ones;

- information-gathering at more levels;

- better trained and more responsive employees;

- multi- rather than mono-skilled employees;

- an increase in more responsible and self-managing groups.

An important implication of this is that the management of such organizations must differ radically from more 'traditional' hierarchical structures, for as the core of the knowledge-based company rests on the intellectual capital of its employees, this is best exploited, not by top-down direction, but by collaboration at all levels. The central question, asks Leadbeater (1998: 381), then is 'how do you get talented, independent-minded people to collaborate?' And the job of managers and leaders will then move, argues Stewart (1998: 189), from the traditional one of POEM (plan, organize, execute and measure) to that of DNA (define, nurture, allocate), as organizations become 'learning organizations' within which increasingly responsible workers are able to flourish. Such organizations will also need to develop more sensitive and flexible education and training systems for these workers.

This, it is argued, will also help to overcome another major management problem – the development of loyalty and trust in workers who in the light of market conditions, can only be employable as long as there is a demand. Employees then must not only be flexible, but also accept their dispensability. Given this, how can employee commitment be generated? The answer, suggests Stewart, lies in the organization's promise to maintain their employability in the wider job market by constantly upgrading their training and skills. The company then not only gets the best out of workers during their employment, but also provides them with the skills to move to the next company, the next assignment. Furthermore, because of the need for flattened hierarchies, better trained employees and more self-managed task groups, the organization of the future will need to be more empowering, more organic, more democratic, a more collaborative place to work. People with talent – those who have the intellectual capital – will be highly prized and paid, and a critical function of such organizations will then be to ensure that those who lack intellectual capital are given the opportunities to develop it, which will require extensive programmes of training and education.

This is the optimistic side of the theory. On the downside, such a knowledge economy will bring more flexibility in career, more movement between jobs, no jobs for life. Such organizational structures will mean that the middle manager as an occupation may largely cease to exist. If in the past, the 'project manager' was the endangered species, in such knowledge-driven organizations, the order will be reversed. The worker who identifies with hierarchies will be less valued, while the project worker will be favoured, valued for expertize rather than seniority, evaluated on how well the last project was performed. It is, for many, an unnerving scenario, but it is one increasingly described by business writers as the future of business organizations.

Now, while such organizational changes may be ones which outsiders think are ideally suited for transference to education, a paradox easily recognized by many within education is that this does not seem to be a particularly accurate description of what is occurring there. Indeed, and as will be developed further in this book, there seem to be forces at work which actually increase the degree of standardization and inflexibility in education, raising the possibility that education systems are being created, and educators conditioned in ways which make them singularly ill-equipped to help their students in dealing with these challenges. Part of this, it will be argued, is that economic globalization does not produce just greater demands for flexibility. Paradoxically, it also increases demands for standardization and predictability, and many organizations, labeled by Ritzer (1993) as 'McDonaldized', are taking this road rather than any road to flexibility. Educational organizations, and particularly universities, as they are increasingly required to compete in global marketplaces, find themselves being pushed towards standardized rather than flexible destinations. It is therefore important to point out that concepts of the 'knowledge economy' and the 'knowledge society' do not describe a universal phenomenon; they are only one side, the other side leading in very different directions. This problem will be discussed in detail in Chapter 5.

Global realities

This chapter has suggested that different types of globalization interact and influence one another in diverse ways, producing a complex and difficult world, which is likely to produce the following global realities for those living into the twenty-first century:

- There will be increasing awareness of problems arising from *ageing populations* and lowered fertility rates, at first in the developed countries, but increasingly in developing ones as well.

- This will add to the pressures that nation-states encounter with respect to the *raising of tax revenue* for a state spending which can finance not only the support of people in old age, but more importantly perhaps for educationalists, the sums necessary to maintain a rich and diverse education system.

- As states encounter difficulties in this area, they will continue to look for *efficiencies and economies*, as well as seek the help of the private sector in funding these areas, or simply in devolving such responsibilities to them. There will then be continued debates about the respective roles of the market and the state.

● As economic globalization increases, TNCs will expand their power, leading to *a dispersal of state power* and more local financial autonomy. As national governments experience this relative decline in their power, they will feel impelled to find means of strengthening their claims to political legitimacy, in maintaining their economic integrity, and in sustaining social stability within their own borders.

● In the developed countries, there will be a continued shift *from heavier to electronic and service industries*, and an expansion in the use and influence of information technology; all of which will happen as a continued shift of labour to cheaper countries occurs.

● There will be an increased *availability of cultural variety*, which will be counterbalanced by increases in the *commodification of culture* and cultural standardization.

● There will be increased concerns over *population, environment and pollution,* and the spread of disease.

● The USA will have the capacity for and will almost certainly exert its increased influence in terms of both hard and soft power.

● For the individual and the organization this will amount to a continued and increased *rate of change*, which will threaten to produce increased stress and mental disease in the population at large.

National and cultural mediations

While this chapter has described movements and forces which are global in scope, it is important to point out before it concludes that these movements and forces are both culturally and nationally mediated. As mentioned earlier, Huntingdon (1998), provides a political/demographic analysis which locates global mediation at the cultural/national level. Palan et al. (1999) provide evidence that at least seven different national strategies exist in the mediation of economic globalization worldwide. Fukuyama (1999) shows that while in the USA, the UK and Scandinavia, crime rates are rising, and family breakdown is increasing – common results, it is suggested, of the impact of aspects of cultural and economic globalization – this is much less so in Mediterranean countries, while incidence is virtually static in Japan and other eastern countries. Levin (2001) provides the same kind of analysis with respect to educational issues, suggesting that while there are some commonalities of context and strategy, there are also profound differences, due to factors like political culture, geography, and degrees of ethnic diversity.

It may be better to recognize that there exist global drivers which attempt to steer nation-states in particular economic and political directions, but that these are not inevitable. The governments of nation-states, underpinned by different cultural attitudes and values, adopt – or are driven to adopt – different approaches and strategies. Two very different examples will be utilized here to describe this phenomenon, one very western, the other, extremely pervasive but largely not covered in western literature.

The first concerns the mediation of western neo-liberal projects. These are based around labour market notions of 'high levels of mobility, downward flexibility of wages, and low costs for employers' (Gray, 1998: 27) – what Luttwak (1999) describes as 'turbocapitalism'. Such an economy seems to produce less structural unemployment, increased technological progress, better economic growth, more entrepreneurship and less bureaucracy. Yet it also has negative consequences like decreased labour protection, increased worker insecurity, a lower average wage, and a widening of income differentials. The UK, and England in particular, seems located, both geographically and ideologically, between the USA and Continental Europe, as its governments over the last twenty years or so have seemed more ideologically in tune with the USA, intent on continuing policies of privatization and deregulation. Continental European countries like France, Germany and Sweden, however, seem more committed to non-turbocapitalist societies, with the corresponding opposite upsides and downsides. The result of such cultural and governmental viewpoints has been very different mediations of this global ideological project.

A second example is provided by Chua (2003) who points out that many countries around the world have ethnic minority groups controlling disproportionate amounts of a country's wealth and trade. This phenomenon, occurring in Southeast Asia, Africa, Europe, and in South and Central America, produces social divisions, feelings of superiority and inferiority, and on occasions, such strong resentment as to lead to violence and even genocide. However, when global policies of the privatization and marketization of national assets are encouraged, this results in those who already possess large assets and have the strongest social and business networks profiting the most. The result is an even greater concentration of wealth in minority hands, leading to even greater resentment. When one then adds to that another US globalization mantra – the spread of one person one vote forms of democracy, this doesn't create stable democracies, but rather provides demagogues with the fuel to ignite resentful embittered majorities. In such situations, there are likely to be one of three results:

- a backlash against markets, and the targeting of the minority's wealth;

- a backlash against democracy by forces favourable to the dominant minority;

- a violent, sometimes genocidal backlash.

The result is that because US sponsored global free market and democratic initiatives largely fail to take note of national mediating conditions, and indeed exacerbate existing tensions, the USA is likely to be resented because it is seen by impoverished national majorities as the sponsors of such increased inequalities. Chua suggests that this kind of analysis in part helps to explain the actions of September 11, 2001. Simplistic global policies then do not address existing national problems, and are not likely to produce stable and equitable national democracies. It is therefore imperative to understand the national and cultural mediations of globalizing forces.

Conclusion

Such global realities, and such national and cultural mediations are likely to lead to a heightened sense of paradox and tension. For educational leaders, this is likely to manifest itself in the following ways:

1   Attempts to satisfy the greater demands of clients for improved services will likely be hindered by the need to reduce expenditure and increase efficiencies.

2   The need to respond to nation-state attempts to strengthen its legitimacy as the sole provider of citizenship will likely be in conflict with a need to recognize the increased claims by sub-national groups, and supra-national organizations, which result in demands for the recognition of more 'nested' forms of citizenship.

3   The pressure to use private sector concepts and practices, based primarily around questions of efficiency, economy and profit, will likely conflict with contrasting public sector values and practices, based more around care and equity.

4   They are likely to be equivocal about the use of IT, and whether it is primarily a liberating and knowledge increasing force, or more of a means by governments to integrate and control their work.

5   They are likely to be pulled in two separate directions as governments attempt to control and direct them, while, recognizing the need to liberate the intellectual capital of workers, governments simultaneously expect them to be flexible and creative in developing students' abilities for a competitive knowledge economy.

6   They are likely to experience a tension in terms of trust, as governments see the need to allow an enhanced autonomy and creativity, yet feel unwilling or unable to abandon low-trust policies of targets, performativity and compliance.

7   This tension will probably be exacerbated as governments and organizations talk about the need to trust and nurture individual talent, and yet attempt to implement 'designer' and competency approaches in the training of their workforces.

8   There will be a tension between the encouragement to be risk-taking and entrepreneurial and the reality that any failure to meet centrally devised targets is guaranteed to bring an inspectoral body, like OFSTED, down upon their head.

9   A tension will exist, particularly for those in the public sector, between a loyalty to it and its organizations, versus legislation on personal advancement which encourages the individual to take a personal and self-interested approach to career development.

10 There are likely to be tensions for leaders called upon to create organizations which maintain social stability and nation-state integrity through enhancing common values and a common morality, and a potentially contrasting call to also develop organizations which recognize and respect diverse cultural needs and differences.

Overall, for western educational leaders, these tensions are likely to be perceived as being generated by movement towards decentralization, flexibility and empowerment on the one hand, and centralization and control on the other. The feelings are then likely to be paradoxical ones of perceived increases in both the fragmentation and the control of work. The next chapter will examine the manner in which fragmenting forces operate.

4 The impact of commodification and fragmentation

The previous chapter argued that we live in an age of globalizing forces, which take a variety of forms – environmental, cultural, political, demographic, American and economic. It was also suggested that some of these globalizing forces were largely descriptive in nature, while others were more products of the aims of powerful forces, and thus were much more prescriptive. One of these, the economic, was seen as the most dominant and was spreading, not only geographically, but into other domains of activity as well, such as the political and the cultural. In the process, it affected their rhetorics and understandings, turning many of these other-domain activities into primarily economic ones – 'capturing their discourses' and 'commodifying' them. A final claim was that these forces combine to produce a world which seems to be becoming more controlled and standardized, while also more fragmented. This paradoxical combination underpins many of the challenges to educational leadership, and both need to be investigated in greater detail. While the next chaper will examine the issue of control and standardization, this chapter examines that of frag-mentation, by arguing that the uncontrolled and volatile nature of economic activity can result in an unpredictability of national economies, which in turn can have dramatic effects upon the organization and the individual. This chapter will also examine how one major economic concept – consumerism – may not only be undermining rich and diverse concepts of culture, but also re-defining individual self-concepts, and thereby undermining social conceptions of citizenship.

The fragmentation of the economy

It wasn't very long ago that a book written criticizing capitalist economic activity would be in danger of being simplistically categorized as being of 'communist' sympathies. In an age polarized between the political ideologies of American and Russian superpowers, the critic who had reservations about capitalism as an economic system, but did not feel that Russian communism was the answer, might have found serious difficulties in having a third position taken seriously. Times, however, have changed. The fall of communism in Eastern Europe has not left just one functioning global economic system; it has, as Ritzer (2004: 81) has argued, created an era in which for the first time 'capitalism is unchained and free to roam the world in search of both cheap production facilities and labour as well as new markets for its products'.

If communism did manage one thing, it was to keep capitalism on its guard; as Hutton (2001: 11) says 'it kept it aware that it had to have a human face'. The unleashing of uninhibited capitalism has exposed a much less caring face, and there has ensued a more detached and objective appraisal of capitalism, devoid of cold war connotations. Like the taboo on criticizing the UK Royal Family, taboos on critiquing capitalism as an economic system have largely ended.

There is, however, some disagreement over what constitutes current dominant capitalist practice. Joseph Schumpeter (1942) described capitalism's genius as that of 'creative destruction', but there are different views on the degree to which its voracious appetite needs be reined in. Hutton (2001), for instance, is convinced that we are seeing an Anglo-Saxon variety of capitalism, one that believes in the maximization of shareholder value, the flexibility of labour markets, and the ability of capital to invest and disinvest without constraint – what has previously been described by Luttwak (1999) as 'turbocapitalism'. It is also a system which produces widening income differentials, and lower worker security and protection. It also appears to be rather less than global in operation: countries like the USA and those in the EC practice a large degree of protectionism for their home-based industries, yet criticize poorer countries when they try to do the same. It is a fairly cold and uncaring form of capitalism, and is in considerable contrast to a Catholic-European version, which argues for the incorporation into its workings of the notion of a just wage, just price and just profit. If Hutton (2001: 50) believes that 'capitalism does not exist independently of society, and . . . it is proper for the democratic will to be asserted over business and private power', then turbocapitalism is a form of capitalism quite distant from that vision.

It may then be that the current globalizing form of capitalism is a particular cultural variant, but it is still new in a number of respects. Castells (2001), for instance, argues that it is characterized in part by the degree to which corporations utilize new information and communication technologies in enhancing the capacity and speed to do business. Such use of ICT not only facilitates the complexity of what actually happens, as businesses are increasingly organized into networks of production, management and distribution; it also facilitates the deregulation and liberalization of financial trading. The result of such flexibility is for 'this new economy to select its components around the planet, in an endlessly variable geometry of value searching' (2001: 53).

Such information and technological advances have generated real growth and dominance of this form of capitalism, and are in large part responsible for the birth of the knowledge economy. For the individual, as writers like Beck (2001) have pointed out, this has resulted in a world which is considerably more full of risk, uncertainty and complexity. And for other commentators (for example, Elliot and Atkinson (1999)), because this complexity, risk and uncertainty are encountered in an uncaring turbocapitalistist age, it is the age of insecurity, where people feel increasingly lost, fragmented, deserted by the political parties they voted into power. So while there are many positive aspects of the knowledge society, the other side is a high-risk society where people must acquire the ability and resilience to deal with such uncertainty. Educational leaders, then, cannot be concerned solely with servicing this knowledge economy through promoting an education for cognitive learning; they have to help others to cope with its effects, as well as articulating a vision of education and society which transcends it. This means being concerned with people's rights and responsibilities, with issues of trust, identity and citizenship. These are all issues to be dealt with in coming chapters. As Hargreaves (2003) argues, this means that besides requiring an education for the knowledge economy – because students will need the skills and adaptability to survive and prosper – there has to be an education beyond it as well. The economic system then needs to be undergirded and constrained by a wider vision of a good society, where educators are both catalysts and counterparts to the knowledge economy.

Yet Castells (2001) argues that the kinds of technological innovation and liberalization emblematic of 'turbocapitalism' have prevented the understanding, and therefore the ability to control the economic system. For while the technology facilitates investment by individuals, it also decentralizes and thereby fragments decision making; and while liberalization allows many more to join in market transactions, the deregulation and liberalization of the system reduce the flows of information due to the increased secrecy and anonymity consequent upon them. Such uncertainties, added to the manner in which changing national or regional economic fortunes now can have global impacts, lead to greater volatility and fragmentation. The result is that the global economic system increasingly fragments, and is not actually one in which the market alone rules. Rather, as Castells (2001: 57) argues, changes in financial markets are instead caused by a mixture of, 'market rules, business and political strategies, crowd psychology, rational expectations, irrational behaviour, speculative manoevres, and informational turbulence of all sorts'.

This seems a poor way to run a global economic system, for it limits our understanding of what is occurring, and prevents us from controlling its negative effects. Furthermore, it is very selective in its effects. Faux and Mishel (2000) point out that in 1996 the assets of the world's 358 billionaires exceeded the combined income of 45 per cent of the world's entire population. By Castell's estimates, a full two-thirds of the world's population are not benefiting from turbo-capitalism: for them it means lower wages, poorer standards of living, and much greater dislocation and fragmentation; and as Chua (2003) pointed out, when an economically dominant ethnic minority profits by it, it can result in even grosser wealth disparities, the suppression of democracy, or genocidal violence. Even in the USA, the centre and main beneficiary of this system, the figures are stark. Rifkin (2000) points out that Bill Gates has more assets than the poorest 120 million people of the USA combined; while Castells points out that 15 per cent of the population live below the poverty line, while 2 million are in prison. Indeed, in the 1990s, in California, there were more people in prison than in full-time education.

There are good reasons then to doubt that this is economically, politically, or socially sustainable in the long term. The best antidote to problems of instability and, in the long term, to questions of inequity, would seem to be measures at both global and national level. At the global level, financial regulation could be achieved by the use of Tobin taxes to finance such governance. Such regulation is certainly possible – the technology which facilitates the current speed and complexity of financial dealings could also be used to rein them in. Yet the US economy and US firms are the main beneficiaries of the current system, and their agreement would be needed for any action to be taken, making this unlikely in the near future. At the national level, this depends on the particular circumstances encountered. In terms of countries with economically dominant minorities, Chua (2003) suggests that some or all of the following actions need to be taken:

- a greater degree of wealth redistribution;

- the better provision of welfare and health safety nets;

- the better education of economically disadvantaged majorities;

- the greater expansion of social mobility;

- the expansion of equality of opportunity, possibly through positive discrimination;

- the more explicit creation and contribution by ethnic minorities to national projects.

Many of these measures would seem applicable elsewhere. Nevertheless, for the moment, we live in a global economic system which is largely uncontrolled and uncontrollable. It can create a global auction, as nations attempt to attract multinational companies and international finance to their shores. And because of the speed with which such changes can happen, it can produce severe instability for individuals as decisions are made thousands of miles from where they live, and by an intersection of forces which are neither rational nor caring. They are asked to be 'flexible' – temporally, functionally, locationally and numerically – and yet as Sennet (1998: 10 asks): 'How can long-term goals be pursued in an economy devoted to the short-term? How can mutual loyalties and commitments be sustained in institutions which are constantly breaking apart or continually being redesigned?'

This leads to a situation where, as Hargreaves (2003: 38) says, 'children become lifestyle models for their parents, rather than parents being moral exemplars for their youngsters'. This then forms an immensely powerful, unstable and fragmenting backdrop for the lives of nations, communities and individuals. It is a background which poses challenges which educational leaders need to understand, and to which they need to respond. In terms of fragmentation, perhaps the most critical effect is upon the self-concept of the individual, and the manner in which individuals are steered into seeing themselves as consumers rather than citizens. It is to this issue that this chapter turns.

The fragmentation of the citizen

As already suggested, one consequence of free-market influence has been the steerage of many western public sectors into adopting private sector models of management, and private sector language. A particularly influential term is that of the 'consumer'. Now educational entrepreneurs will probably welcome the term as correctly describing the relationship between educators and students; and educational pragmatists might argue that because it belongs to a conceptual universe in which they have to work, they might as well accept it. However, if the public sector and the welfare state are seen as having important parts to play in the development of a participative and caring society, as this book does, then there is reason to be concerned with the use of the term 'consumer' in public sector practice, as it implies a set of values fundamentally at odds with public sector aims, and which over-simplify the educational relationship between professional and client. Furthermore, as public sector education has a role to play within the welfare state project, students and parents need to be viewed as citizens, rather than as customers or clients, for education is one of the principal means of induction into the citizenship role. Further, Marshall (1950) pointed out that such citizenship needs to be concerned with more than just greater personal liberty, freedom of speech, or rights to justice and property, indeed with more than just the right to the involvement in political power. Citizenship, instead, needs to be seen as 'social citizenship' – the right to the health, economic security and education necessary for these other rights to be exercised. Nevertheless, proposing education as in part the promotion of such conceptions of citizenship may be ineffective if proponents fail to recognize that many educational 'clients' may want to see themselves as consumers, may want to define themselves as such. If this is true, then unthinking adherence to such positions simply resembles King Canute's behaviour at the sea's edge of demanding the impossible while ignoring the inevitable. If many want to identify themselves as consumers, then this is where discussion needs to begin.

Consumerism as a term of abuse

It is not just welfare state proponents who have viewed 'consumerism' in pejorative terms. Business discourse itself, as exemplified by the history of its thought for the last 200 to 300 years, has been less than impressed by the activity, seeing it as little more than the rather trivial end point of the much more praiseworthy activity of production. To understand this, one needs to locate business thought within the much broader context of the major western intellectual movement of the seventeenth and eighteenth centuries, the Enlightenment. This movement radically changed views from seeing humanity as subject to natural forces and supernatural whims, to one of believing in its ability to exert control over such forces. One way of doing this was through the increased control over nature in terms of industrial production. This would eventually lead to two unexpected outcomes. One, a perversion of the Enlightenment project, was the turning of a 'control gaze' from nature to the control of humanity itself (see Bottery, 2000). The other was the celebration of industrial production as an outcome of the control of nature, which led to the celebration of materialism as an encompassing value. Such control and materialism would then be major factors in a 'modern' view of the world which suggested that not only could there be ultimate meanings and ultimate aims for humanity's endeavours, but that by a process of reason and scientific effort, these could be achieved.

Both materialism, and industrial production could then be viewed as good things. Yet the end result of industrial production, consumption, was much less favourably viewed: after all, it didn't create, it didn't demonstrate any ability to fashion the world to human purposes. It was simply the destruction of that which was produced. At its best, consumption fuelled the producers, and was therefore a necessary support of man's productive capacities (and the masculine form is used deliberately); but it was nothing to be proud of. Indeed, as the industrial revolution developed, not only were these two processes increasingly separated, but those involved in the separate processes came to have different statuses: men increasingly went out to work (a good thing), while women stayed at home to prepare the consumption (a trivial thing). Such geographical and functional separation of the sexes then meant that men were increasingly assigned the role of heroic producers, while women were relegated to being caretakers of the inferior consumption end of the process. Here was a very important element then in the dominance of patriarchal relationships in the industrialized world – but also, through a kind of cross-fertilization, of the continued inferiority of the consumption end of the production–consumption relationship. Consumerism and the consumer (who was largely identified as female) were then classed as inferior to production and the producer.

Consumerism was therefore an activity which was looked on with disdain, and well into the twentieth century. In commerce, as Zuboff and Maxmin (2003) describe, the literature and the average store manager viewed the (female) customer with almost total disrespect. In industry, the methods developed by Henry Ford for mass-producing cars relegated the consumer to the periphery of organizational interest. His desire to make the car an affordable mass consumer product led to the development and application of earlier ideas of bureaucratization to the car industry, producing through the creation of assembly lines, a standardization of work processes and routines. While such production techniques radically reduced the price of the automobile, and permitted more of the public to purchase luxury goods, the techniques used not only alienated the worker from his work, and focused the worker and manager ever more on the productive process, but also relegated the consumer to the edge of their concern. As James Couzens (1921), one of Ford's early partners said, what the Ford company really did was 'In effect, we standardized the customer.' When Alfred Sloan at General Motors took the management of motor manufacturing to the next 'logical step', instituting the hierarchical divisions of professional managers to oversee the workers so prevalent through much of the twentieth century, the productive sector became even more focused upon the organization and its members, rather than looking outwards to the customer. Leaders were there to lead those within the organization, hierarchies were instituted to more efficiently monitor, control and direct the workers within the organization, and structures were designed to facilitate the functioning of the organization. Consumers, while theoretically the focus of all such endeavour, were in reality consigned to the periphery of this managerial universe. As Lyndall Urwick advised (1943: 29): 'To allow the individual idiosyncrasies of a wide range of customers to drive administration away from the principles on which it can manufacture most economically is suicidal – the kind of good intention with which the road to hell or bankruptcy is proverbially paved.'

Now there can be little doubt that some managerial developments – such as that of TQM – have tried to bring the customer more centre stage. 'Cultural' approaches such as those of Peters and Waterman (1982) have also suggested that the more successful companies are those that stay 'close to the customer'. Yet 'quality' has various meanings, and 'managerial' quality can and does on occasions conflict with 'customer quality' (see Bottery, 2000). And despite some resurgence in the development of consumer-oriented business cultures, there is much skepticism in the public at large about the genuineness of such claims. Some of this skepticism comes from numerous examples of high-level corruption in business, such as the scandals at Enron, World.com and Merrill-Lynch. But part is due to individual encounters: Zuboff and Maxmin (2003), for instance, document how currently 'little murders' are perpetrated by businesses on customers, with those at the receiving end of a commercial exchange being treated with as little interest and attention as possible. It is now commonplace for customers to be able to get through to a business representative on a freephone number if they are going to buy the product, but when having bought the product and now needing assistance, having to ring a premium rate 'help' number and be confronted by canned music for minutes on end, with a recorded voice occasionally telling the listener that their custom is 'valued'. Customers are too often right in feeling that, instead of being valued, they are absolutely the last concern of the business. The *Financial Times* (3 June 1998) suggested, in an article on the growth of call centres, that there is a 'powerful logic' behind their growth: 'Dealing with the vast number of queries and requests for help . . . can tie up central staff . . . to an unacceptable degree. Outsourcing the responsibility to a third party frees people and telephone lines for more productive activities.'

So there we have it: customers prevent valuable staff from engaging in more productive work. The customer remains at the periphery of organizational interest. Nevertheless, while the consumer might be seen as a nuisance and irritation, the consumer is still central to a healthy economy. The logic of the economics of capitalism demands that if production is to continue to expand, consumption will need to be the vehicle that fuels such expansion. The consumer then, as Campbell (1982: 282) describes, has a vital function, nay an obligation, which is 'to want to want under all circumstances and at all times irrespective of what goods and services are actually acquired or consumed'.

The logic of the market has developed this desired model of consumerism throughout the twentieth century. Not only is this model one of obligation, it is also an individual one, for more products are bought if everyone buys one each. Then, as this model is individual rather than social, so consumption increasingly becomes private. And because it stimulates production if industrially produced items replace the labour of the individuals themselves, it increasingly becomes a form of consumption divorced from the individual – it becomes alienated consumption. Finally, because what the consumer is to buy is as much decided by the dictates of the market as by consumer wants, consumption increasingly becomes a passive experience.

The modernist dream of a universal project, then, was in part transmuted into a production–consumption experience, in which the consumption end was operated mainly by women in this obligated-individual-private-alienated-passive manner. And it was largely from such roots that the dominant social arrangements of the mid-twentieth century developed – the nuclear family. View any episode of Bewitched, a favourite US sitcom of the early 1960s, and you will see the wife, Samantha, possessed of unbelievable supernatural powers, who ludicrously continues to be the willing homemaker to her husband, Darren, a mortal advertising executive who possesses neither her powers nor her intelligence. The message is clear: regardless of her abilities, the woman's place is at home, on her own or looking after the children, and she must be loyal, dutiful, serving the needs of the productive husband, who at the office, does the real work. And consumption is a second-rate activity, indulged in by a second-rate sex.

Consumption bites back

This then was a modernist world, its dominant characteristics those of industrial production, capitalist economics, and the use of reason to create bureaucratic structures. This was a world underpinned by the Enlightenment project, the belief in a narrative of universal human progress through the use of a scientific rationality, underpinned by a Newtonian vision of a universe governed by mechanical and predictable physical laws. Samantha and Darren, and millions of other nuclear families like them, thus lived their lives secure in the knowledge that in an ordered physical world, there was only one way of knowing this world. The accepted paradigms of both physics and epistemology underpinned a stable social world which promised the attainment of a universal set of values – a gradually improving standard of living at home, bureaucratically organized hierarchies of management at work, a societal emphasis upon consumption as the motor of productive capacity, and a clear division of gendered roles in producing this. The world was stable, it made sense. All was right with it.

But what happens when such certainties begin to disappear? What happens when it becomes increasingly apparent that there are different ways of viewing this world, when different perspectives, different values, different ways of life seem to work for those who practice them? What if it is no longer clear why women should remain at home? What happens when Samantha and Darren's ordered relationship on television seems increasingly out of touch with the realities of the world, and even women can aspire to be StarTrek captains? What happens when racial segregation is recognized as a gross abuse of power by white majorities? When Miss Daisy is driven to accepting that her negro driver may have rights, even opinions worth listening to? When people question whether their political and military leaders know best, and refuse to be lions led by donkeys? When cynical yet likeable doctors are permitted to comment on the insanity of war in programmes like M*A*S*H?

When this happens, when the old certainties begin to disappear, new doubts begin to surface. Then, Bauman (1996) argues, different personalities begin to inhabit the human stage. There is still the modernist pilgrim, the individual who is convinced that there are eternal truths, and that there should be political and social pro-grammes which try to achieve those ends. But now you also have the stroller, the individual who doesn't want to get involved, but who simply observes what is going on. You also have the vagabond, the one who questioned authority in modernist times and was therefore viewed as a troublemaker and an outsider, but who now is seen as reflecting the spirit of the age. You have the tourist, who moves from experience to experience, culture to culture, experiencing each before returning to the safety of the home – only now the permanency of the home base is disappearing, and he/she is condemned/liberated to be a tourist everywhere. And finally there is the player, who partakes of each experience seriously, but knows that ultimately each is only a game, there being no deeper seriousness or meaning to them, and so, once experienced, he or she leaves the game to partake in the next.

When this happens, the grand social project is likely to be abandoned, and in the process, citizenship as an identity begins to lose its appeal, because citizenship is so closely linked to the modernist project of the realization of the nation-state. In its place, another project – self-creation – increasingly comes centre stage. And this means more than cultural self-creation, where one eats Chinese, or better still, works in Shanghai for a year. This also means physical self-creation: heads are shaved, bodies are pierced, plastic surgery creates a new physical appearance. Individuals engage in personal deconstruction and reconstruction – the consumer in effect becomes the consumed. And in this postmodern world of personal experience, modernist projects are abandoned. Notions of public good are downgraded, even forgotten, the needs of future generations ignored – unless, of course, these serve in the creation of the new altruistic you, a personality which can be tried out, to be abandoned a little way down the road if it ceases to generate the desired personal experience.

In such a world, consumption is then not so much about consump-tion of physical objects as the consumption of experience. In the modernist age, the possession of a car would have been the consumption experience. In the postmodernist age, the driving experience is the object of consumption. Yet such consumption is more than access to sensory experiences; it is the ability to access different conceptual and cultural meanings. This 'Age of Access' (Rifkin, 2000) then means, as we have seen, that power moves from those producing 'hard' manufacturing and industrialized objects, to those controlling access to desired experiences. Moreover, they know that many consumers in the developed world now have the financial ability to access the experiences. In such circumstances, really knowing individual consumer desires, individuals' visions of self-realization, simply makes good business sense. And this can't be done by leaving the individual consumer at the edge of the business universe.

The facilitation and structuring of consumption

On this scenario, then, consumerism becomes the means by which the individual project is accomplished, achieved through acquiring the time and support necessary to pursue a life of personal construction and psychological self-determination. Such a project is also underpinned and structured by two sets of values – one psychological, one socio-political – both of which have quite dramatic influences not only upon the type of consumption attempted, but, perhaps more importantly, upon public sector systems of thought and their management.

One set of values, based upon psychological developmental stage theories, underpins much of the consumption literature. It suggests that motivation and cognitive functioning should be located at the level of the individual, which become increasingly sophisticated as the individual matures, leading to increased individual autonomy and independence. Maslow's (1954) theory of a hierarchy of needs is a standard view of human motivation in business management textbooks, not only locating consumer needs within the individual's physiology, but also suggesting that the lower ones need satisfying before higher ones can be met. And consumers, in a postmodern world with an enhanced standard of living, are now able to reach for such higher stages of self-actualization. Other developmental stage theories, like those of Piaget (1932) and Kohlberg (1981), suggest that as individuals mature, they move to stages of functioning independent of group influence, which again supports notions of individualistic consumerism rather than a consumerism based upon the satisfaction of populations. Such theories, by suggesting that needs stem from biological maturation processes, also deflect attention away from the possibility that consumer needs may be in part the product of marketing and advertising strategies. Such theories also prevent the individual from asking whether it is the needs of an economic system requiring constant and in many cases increasing levels of consumption, rather than individual biology, which create the culture of high consumption seen throughout most of the developed world today.

The other major influence upon current views of the consumer, which has particular potency within the USA, but which is seen increasingly within other western nations, is a set of socio-political beliefs about the relationship of the individual to larger institutions. A first is the strong belief in the primacy of the individual and his/her freedom. This is normally allied with a second, a pejorative view of bureaucratic organizations as stifling individual potentialities. These two beliefs are then linked with a third, that the political state inhibits individual realization. These three beliefs add great strength to the view that the individual should withdraw from grand narratives and from national political projects, suggesting instead that:

- Consumerism, not political involvement, is the best expression of personal freedom; indeed the retreat from citizenship involvement could almost be described as a political act.

- Such consumerism should be, and now can be realized by private sector organizations that respond to the individual's desires and wishes, rather than the individual having to conform to organizational wishes.

- It can therefore be indulged in, to the exclusion of issues of political concern such as citizenship, because the primary vehicle for citizenship – the state – is neither to be trusted, nor, because of postmodern critiques of the validity or possibility of 'grand narratives', is a body to which it is worth giving allegiance.

The combination of these beliefs leads to a view of consumerism which is individualistic, asocial, centred on the realization of the self, and dismissive of larger societal projects. Furthermore, as these beliefs lead to the conclusion that the political state is not a proper vehicle for the realization of this activity, it can then be suggested that the only proper vehicle for human activity is the market. When such socio-political views are combined with individualistic psychological views of need and development, the damage to public services can be crippling.

The new business relationship and the new management thesis

The scene is then set for a culture of consumption focused upon the individual. This entails a radically different conception of business, one requiring a mediating person between the individual consumer and the massive variety of experiences offered by the private sector. It requires a person to provide 'deep support' to the consumer by knowing them as a close friend would, able not only to respond to requests, but to anticipate needs as well. This person then identifies, suggests and provides access to a vast federation of businesses and services which the individual consumer simply wouldn't have the time, energy or expertise to locate. Zuboff and Maxmin (2003: 331) suggest that this creates a new kind of business relationship, as dialogue replaces marketing, 'because only through real dialogue can the other's meaning be known'. And while this kind of relationship is still largely the province of the rich and famous, they expect such expense to decrease dramatically as more customers demand this kind of service, and an increasing number of organizations change existing practice or are created to cater to them.

Benefits and challenges from the new consumerism

Some aspects of such 'deep support' consumerism may be of real benefit to education. It suggests that all educational activity – from policies through to their implementation – should begin from a consideration of the needs, abilities and interests of the individual student, and that only through an intimate knowledge of each could a complete educational experience be realized. This model of consumption would seem to dovetail fairly naturally with an enhanced use of ICT, as classrooms might be much more highly individuated than at present, more sensitive to the changing needs and understandings of each student, and more responsive in supplying materials, experiences, and web sites to match those needs. It would also suggest that the educational professional of the future would be a mediating professional, one able to identify which web sites, which online support, which learning materials, were most suitable to the needs of the individual student. On this model, a national curriculum would only be acceptable if it did no more than spell out general areas of entitlement, which were then translated through deep support mediators into the experience and needs most suited to individual students; and group teaching would only be acceptable where such an activity had a wider social purpose, such as developing individuals' social and cooperative skills.

Even were the reality to fall short of that described above, such a model of deep-support consumerism would nevertheless provide educational leaders with both a blueprint and a stimulus for the development of their institution, for styles of teaching and learning which might be radically different from those currently experienced by many students. Such a model, being derived from extensive practice in the hard-nosed private sector, would probably have a greater chance of adoption than ideas coming from some woolly idealist public sector philosophy. And as costs came down in the business sector, so it would become more possible for a public sector to implement such ideas.

Problems with the thesis

Yet while such a model might engender radical and exciting changes, there are considerable problems with it.

A first problem stems from the very nature of being a consumer, even a deeply supported one. *Webster's Dictionary* defines a consumer as 'a person or organization that purchases or uses a commodity or service'. Yet this fails to fully describe how the current commercial context defines the role of the consumer in the supplier–consumer relationship. A consumer in the private sector, then:

- pays another person for a product or service;
- normally has a number of suppliers to choose from;
- has the legal right to expect a certain quality of product or service;
- is normally not obligated to the seller in any way other than paying the amount of money asked for the product or service.

Such an analysis suggests that the consumer–supplier relationship is an essentially adversarial one, for the market relationship defines them both as self-interested rationalists, trying to get the best bargain for themselves. Such a relationship might also be one where the producer/mediator created the need rather than responded to a genuine one. This – and the fact that the customer can go elsewhere to buy the product or service – suggests that their relationship is a thin and fragile one. Further, in this commercial transaction, the consumer has very few responsibilities: as long as the product or service is paid for, it can be disposed of in any way wished, without any obligation to contribute to its quality.

Finally, this supplier–consumer relationship, built upon the profit motive, is likely to subordinate and transform values like trust, goodwill, sincerity, fairness, as they are primarily used as instrumental values to service a commercial relationship. Yet it is instructive to note that Zuboff and Maxmin suggest that 'deep support' relationships within the new consumer form of capitalism 'cannot exist without the I-You relationship in which individuals cease to be merely means to ends and become ends in themselves . . . Dialogue replaces marketing, because only through real dialogue can the other's meaning be known' (2003: 330).

Such reference to Buber's I-Thou relationships will come as deeply interesting (and probably deeply shocking) to those who fully understand his use of the term, for the quotation above suggests that only when there is unconditional respect between individuals can the business relationship be fully realized. Yet here precisely lies the problem. The relationship is entered into, not out of love, trust or respect for the other, but in order for a profit to be made. The critical question then is: if this is not going to be a financially productive relationship, what should the business person do? In the true I-Thou relationship, this simply isn't a question one needs to ask. In the 'deep support' business relationship, however, this lack of productivity and lack of profit signals the termination of the relationship. The business relationship necessarily reduces all other kinds of relationships to second-order ones for the purpose of commercial gain. Trust, loyalty, respect, all are valued as long as they lead to a more profitable relationship, a greater degree of consumption. If they fail to meet this end, they cease to be of importance. By only walking down the road of commerce and profit, many other destinations, many other areas of human potentiality, are closed off.

The commercial relationship, then, is a necessary one, but it is a peculiar one. It is adversarial, it is fragile, it absolves one party of any real responsibilities to the relationship, it can be manipulated by producers to their advantage, and it transforms and reduces to second-order values many qualities which societies need to see flourishing as first order ones. The commercial relationship is then not one which can on its own underpin a healthy wider relationship. And if this is true of the commercial relationship generally, it must raise severe doubts about a life style or society which bases itself upon it.

Consumerism and the public good

Consumerism is part of this more general problem with the commercial relationship, for not only does it distract us from other kinds of relationships; it also reduces the kinds of relationships into which we can enter, radically depressing our potentialities as human beings. As Barber (1996: 136) argues, it promises a world 'where everything is for sale and someone else is always responsible'. Such seduction works then by promising to place the individual at the centre of a personally specified consumptive universe, with desires being fulfilled by an enormously flexible and adaptable marketplace. In such a world, the only role which the individual needs to fulfill is that of seeking the best experiences for self-realization, and to complain when these are not met.

Such seduction also distracts from other relationships, particularly those concerned with common goods or public interests, suggesting that there is no problem with some individuals and societies having greater access to consumption experiences than others. Should we, for instance, be concerned that the population of the USA consumes over five times more than its percentage of the world's population? On the consumer model, apparently not: we can assume that any failure in the ability to purchase is based upon personal failure, and that if only these individuals worked a little harder, found a job, they could purchase the things that we ourselves enjoy. The consumer model provides no reasons to the affluent westerner to be concerned with starvation in Sub-Saharan Africa, nor with helping the child born of the AIDS-infected mother, nor with those individuals or groups discriminated against because of sex, race or colour. It cannot point the individual beyond the personal to structural reasons for failure, and it seduces the individual into not doing so.

Furthermore, as such seduction distracts us from the structural causes of such injustices, so it also distracts us from working towards common goods which rise above individual short-term need. It suggests that we need assume no responsibility, need raise no voice to change such conditions. In so doing, not only is the individual turned into the consumer: so is the citizen. As Barber argues (1996: 243) 'Consumers speak the elementary rhetoric of "me", citizens invent the common language of "we".' Schools, and other vehicles for the creation of the next democratic polity, and for the nurturance of the public good, are stripped of this function, and instead simply become 'interest groups for people with children' (1996: 283).

In a world dominated by market-based consumerism, the market then becomes the only player in town, translating the world of politics and the citizen into the world of the market and the consumer. When Ronald Reagan said on first meeting his marketing team 'I understand that you are here to sell soap and wanted to see the bar' (Firat and Dholakia (1998: 71), he dramatically illustrated how politics ceases to be concerned with visions of the good society, democratic participation and debate, and becomes more concerned with issues of salesmanship, marketing and image – and ultimately with the furtherance of the market itself. In a world dominated by consumerism, politics, public sector organizations and the welfare state become the major casualties. The state, viewed so negatively, and with its functions hollowed out, is increasingly reduced to an umpire status, existing only to ensure that there are clear legal parameters for markets to work within, that business contracts are kept, and that those who break such contracts are punished. It then increasingly fails to maintain a public sector where essential services are provided for all in a population, regardless of ability or income. It ceases to have a role in the creation of societal projects like the welfare state. It is reduced from being a player in the game of life to being an umpire in the game of the market.

And what of the individual? The market, by seducing us into defining ourselves first and last as consumers, prevents us from asserting our rights as citizens. This may seem perfectly acceptable in the short term if, as postmodern tourist or player, the individual feels neither capable nor motivated to help change the world. Yet such lack of commitment only leaves a gap for powerful others to fill. Abnegating responsibility in the political realm for a life of consumerism in the market realm ultimately circumscribes liberties in the former. For soon there is no body powerful enough to rein in market excesses, to prevent the manipulation of the individual consumer, to redress the abrogation of consumer rights, to build the kind of society and values the market itself needs to survive. As Barber says (1996: 245) the paradox of a marketized world is that 'it cannot survive the world it inevitably tends to create if not countered by civic and democratic forces it inevitably tends to undermine'.

Consumerism and the fragmentation of culture

The individualization of consumption does more than just undermine civic and democratic ideals. It undermines and fragments cultural values as well. It does this, first by reducing first-order cultural values of trust, care, respect, integrity, to second-order commercial values, and thus weakens the cultural base upon which human relationships are founded. Second, by commodifying cultural experiences, and delivering them in safe, packaged and easily consumable portions, it leaches out their true meaning. As with Disneyworld, or the Rainforest Café experience, the oxymoron of a simulated reality is created, in which the most saleable bits are selected, and then stitched together to provide an experience determined by commercial attractiveness. Yet when the commercial sphere replaces the cultural sphere as the centerpiece of people's meanings, two particular dangers present themselves. The first is the fragmentation of a personal narrative, as the immediately experienced becomes the main attraction, and personal meaning is no longer built by deferring the wants of the present for the good of the future. The second danger is the destruction of the societal project between generations. Where commercial concerns accentuate a satisfaction of immediate wants, insufficient attention is likely to be paid to future concerns. This explains why pressure upon nation-states to delay progress in reducing the emissions which cause global warming and damage to the ozone layer has largely come from commercial enterprises whose profits lie in supplying present-day consumption. When 'private want' and 'consumption' come to dominate economic, political, social and educational agendas, present and future 'public goods' are threatened. Commercial interests may be able to determine the price of everything, but they are less concerned with the long-term communal and intergenerational impact.

This replacement of the cultural and the public sphere by the commercial sphere has been dramatically seen in Common Interest Developments (CIDs) in the USA. These are private developments, commercially owned, access to which is heavily restricted, in which people obey the rules set by the companies who own and run them. According to Rifkin (2000), 150,000 of these are now in existence. They seem to be the outcome of what Reich (1991: 268) prophesied when he commented that 'the symbolic analysts and their families have seceded from public life into ghettos of affluence, within which their earnings need not be redistributed to people less fortunate than themselves'. Such CIDs appeal because not only is a greater degree of safety guaranteed, but so is an interaction with those of similar lifestyles and values. Yet their expansion restricts participation in the public space, damaging both democratic and cultural values. While CIDs may guarantee an initial security, they reduce the sharing of different experiences, and the learning of tolerance and respect for different lifestyles and different values, and in so doing, they weaken and fragment wider communal values.

The same kinds of problems are also increasingly seen in the educational sector, not only through the increase of overt and covert advertising and sponsorship in public education, but through agreements in which equipment is loaned to schools upon agreement by them of student exposure to corporate advertising during school time (see Bottery, 2000: 212). When this happens, educational organizations become less promoters of a critical induction into a civic culture, and more an arm of commercial sponsorship. The overall result of such commercial invasion into the public and cultural spheres is that individuals are less engaged, less critical, contribute less to the process, and become more interested in the consumption of the next experience provided by the commercial arena. When that happens, a sense of individual and cultural direction is fragmented and lost, and the immediate and the now become the predominant concerns.

Consumerism and financial scarcity

One further scenario vis-a-vis the public sector needs to be explored. As already seen, one of the reasons for public sector and welfare state decline has been that of problematic finances. Given such constraints, how could such deep-support consumerism be afforded? Writers like Gilliat et al. (2000), for instance, argue that the reality of much public sector work is one where 'consumers' are increasingly being induced to take on former 'producer' responsibilities, or perform many activities for themselves. This, the authors argue (p. 333), has served to 'co-opt service users into the management of scarcity, rationing and/or technological change', the result being (p. 347) that 'the organisation rather than the consumer is empowered.' This possibility – that deep-support consumerism may not be realised in the public sector – needs to be recognised. Yet the result is more likely to be that as we travel down a privatised road, the unequal access so characteristic of the private sector will be replicated in the public, so that the best services will go, as one would expect, to the consumer who can pay the most. For those within a residual public sector, then, deep support will go only to the wealthy. In such a way does the public sector come even more to resemble the private, and support for citizenship is even further undermined.

Consumerism and political advocacy

However, there *is* one view of consumerism which does not undermine citizenship so much as replace it as the context for political advocacy, and there are both inclusive and exclusive variants of it.

The exclusive variant is seen in Davidson and Rees-Mogg's (1999) vision of a form of citizenship driven by consumer wants: where the individual has the responsibility to search out the best 'deal' they can find on citizenship and 'buy into' that country's provision. Different countries will have different 'brands' of citizenship, some with high taxes, some with low, some more inclusive, some more exclusive. Individuals then 'shop around' to find the deal that most suits them. This thesis, clearly economic/consumerist rather than political in origin, is premised upon the (dubious) belief that in an age of increased global movement, not only can money move easily around the world, but so can many of its inhabitants. Citizenship then becomes a matter of consumerism and choice. It is pretty obviously a citizenship biased to the rich and powerful, for it is they who can move the most easily. The nation-state then finds itself in competition with other nation-states for the citizen-consumer's business, and rather than being a body concerned with a 'public good' – a concern for all – it becomes increasingly concerned with selling its 'services' to the highest bidder, and in the process its activity, its very language, is captured by the market.

A more inclusive vision is provided by Hertz (2001), who suggested that we live in a world where the politics of the nation-state is ceasing to provoke interest and electorate participation. This is in part, she argues, because populations are beginning to realize where the real power and influence lies, and this is increasingly with global corporations. In such a situation, where the economic producers are the real power in the land, if people are going to change anything, they need to pressurize not their national politicians but the leaders of business. Hertz (2001: 116) approvingly quotes the Church of England-approved prayer book, New Start Worship, which advises its readers that: 'Where we shop, how we shop, and what we buy is a living statement of what we believe ... shopping which involves the shopper in making ethical and religious judgements may be nearer to the worship God requires than any number of pious prayers in church.'

The message is clear – business is the group to address, for it has the real power. Indeed, there are recent examples of consumer pressure groups having real effects upon the policies of multinationals – with Shell (on the dispensing of one of its oil rigs) and Monsanto (on its policies on GM crops) being only two of the latest examples. Hertz (2001) even suggests that if pressure groups want to influence political regimes abroad, then the people to whom these people will listen are not their nation's politicians (who may have very little persuasive power) but the heads of multinationals, who may be able to dangle the inducement of relocating a factory – or withdrawing it – from the country of the regime.

In some ways, this is a more appealing thesis, as it is far more inclusive, far more concerned with achieving public goods rather than, as with Davidson and Rees-Mogg (1999), achieving individual wants. But in doing so it acknowledges the de facto authority of the economic and private sector over the political and public, and leads to the dangerous game of playing within private sector rules, rather than asserting the primacy of the political and societal, within which the private should operate. Furthermore, it is still tied to the voice of consumerism, and therefore is still largely dictated by market rather than democratic forces. While it is a more inclusive and social view of consumerism, it would still be dangerous to see it as a substitute for a proper balance between the various sectors.

Conclusion

This chapter then has suggested that the current version of global capitalism provides a backdrop to cultural life, the work of educational institutions, and individual understanding, which is complex, fast-moving, risk-intensive, knowledge-driven and insecure. It has also suggested that it has the effect of harnessing, controlling and directing educational efforts to the delivery of private sector values, locating them within a vision of consumption as it deflects attention away from issues of the public good. In so doing it ultimately fragments the purposes of culture and citizenship, posing serious threats to pluralist democratic societies.

Professional educators – and their leaders – therefore need to develop a role beyond the provision of the skills and qualities required by workers for the marketplace, but also beyond a simple nurturance of students' personal and social skills, and even beyond the appreciation of education for its own sake. They need, as Hargreaves (2003) argues, to be both counterpoints and catalysts to the knowledge economy and its products. They need to be able to understand, track and articulate concerns about the nature of current globalizations, the effects of the knowledge economy, and the impact upon national circumstances. They need to develop a critical research-based societal ecology, in which economic activities are seen as vital but second-order functional activities in the pursuit of first-order individual and social goods. They need then to keep in view the question of the ultimate purpose of their activities, which calls for an extended and probably more politicized role for the educational leader than is normally conceived. The next chapter – which examines the standardizing and controlling effects upon education – reinforces and develops this view.

5 *The impact of standardization and control*

The previous chapter traced the particular nature of current global economic activities and argued that by understanding the nature and dynamics of the dominant model – the Anglo-Saxon 'turbocapitalist' one – it is possible to begin to understand the fragmented backdrop to much national, local and personal activity – both within education and beyond it. It was also suggested that such fragmentation was exacerbated by the increased influence of current versions of 'consumerism', which undermine cultural concepts, redefine self-images, reduce personal citizenship visions and increase the neglect of notions of public good, the need for a public sector and a healthy welfare state.

One set of fragmenting consequences, particularly from economic globalization, stems from the nature of capitalism itself. However, another set of consequences, stemming in large part from the model of business production which such an economic system tends to prefer, are, paradoxically, much more centralizing, standardizing and controlling. Together they provide a backdrop which is *both* fragmented and controlling, and which, it is argued, reflects much educational reality today.

Now the previous chapter argued that one of the major driving forces behind globalization (or 'grobalization', as Ritzer (2004) describes it, in an attempt to describe the drive to expansion) is the nature of capitalism itself. In particular this was seen as the need by a business to 'grow' – to expand its production, sales and profits, and to demonstrate that it has potential for future growth. This necessitates expansion, not just geographically, but into the cultural and political arenas, and into the public and non-profit sectors. Such expansion is a principal measure by which the company is rated on the stock exchange, by which its success is judged. These kinds of dynamics, it was argued, have led to a situation of considerable complexity, turbulence and instability, leading to concerns of fragmentation from the personal through to the global. But herein lies the paradox. Because while this kind of explanation reflects one of the dominant theses of nineteenth-century sociology – that of Karl Marx – the actual *manner of production* is much better explained by one of the other great theses – that of Max Weber's apparently contradictory emphasis on the increased ubiquity of rationalized and bureaucratic processes and structures, with their stress on efficiency, calculability, predictability and control; and from there to its twentieth-century realization through the work of F.W. Taylor's 'scientific management', with his stress on the breaking down of work into its constituent actions.

Now why would globalizing firms want to employ this kind of Weberian/Taylorian rationality in their quest for growth and profit, particularly when we are told that this is an age of increased diversification? Weber suggested that these kinds of processes were ideally suited to a capitalist system of organization, possessing many qualities which capitalists value. When the ultimate aim is that of making a profit, then the more efficient the structures, the more likely profits will be generated. And such efficiency in many cases is greatly facilitated by other characteristics of bureaucracy – particularly high degrees of specialization, hierarchical authority structures with restricted command and responsibility, an impersonality of relationships, the recruitment of individuals on the basis of ability and technical knowledge, and the application of impersonal rules to all, so that those new to an organization can be immediately aware of how that organization functions. Then if one adds to this Taylorian methods of breaking down and analyzing the most efficient way of performing a task, there is real financial incentive for managers to heavily control and direct their workforces. So even if we live in an age apparently calling for greater flexibility and creativity, there are still, as Ritzer (2004) argues, sound commercial reasons for standardization, as such mass-produced products tend to be less expensive to produce than more complex and distinctive ones. Furthermore, because of their simplicity, they are easier to market and advertise, and are therefore likely to have greater demand. In terms of consumption, because they are cheaper to produce, and can be cheaply priced, more people are likely to buy them. But not only will they be bought because they are cheap; for some people at least, their comparative simplicity and lack of distinctiveness will be appealing because they will be easier to appreciate, to consume. They are then

likely to have a wider general appeal, as well as being less likely to
offend particular cultural tastes.

Moreover, such 'rationalized' forms do have other uses beyond
those of mere profitability. In today's world, many things work well
– and we appreciate them – precisely because they have all the
hallmarks of this phenomenon. The credit card is a good example.
Here is a piece of plastic which is simple, quick and convenient to
use, precisely because it is standardized, calculable and controllable.
It is certainly a lot easier to use than carrying large wads of money
around – and a lot less dangerous as well. It is a lot more convenient
and efficient to use than having to change currency when traveling
abroad. Internet banking has many of the same qualities: it is easily
accessible 24 hours a day, and it dovetails better with the pressures
of a busy lifestyle than dealing with a physical bank. So, given the
inevitability of living in a fast-moving world, such adaptations may
actually help us not only to be more effective, but perhaps more
relaxed through having less to do. So such 'McDonaldization' may not
only be to the advantage of large corporations: it may in part be to
the consumer's benefit as well.

Indeed the reverse side of such rationalism, the local, is not always
an unalloyed good. So often in the past it has been an example of the
bigoted, the insular, and the parochial, rather than of the nurturing,
communal and caring. The local has constrained freedoms and
abilities just as much as it has nurtured them. And the extreme of the
local – what Barber (1996) rather unfortunately and inappropriately
calls 'Jihad' – an uncritical communal adherence to fundamentalist
values and doctrines from which individuals attempt to depart at
their peril – suggests that a force like McDonaldization may have
much to recommend it. Our concern then must be to understand and
counter its excesses, rather than to reject it out of hand.

Problems and excesses

Nevertheless, the problems caused by its excesses *are* real and felt by
many. First, its predominant mode of reason has, historically, had the
effect of corroding attachments to a warm and communal world. This
'reason' was the product of the Enlightenment project, which some
have seen, and continue to see, as an illuminating tool, helping to cast
light into the attic rooms of superstition and unthinking compliance.
Yet such reason is a double edged sword. For many, as it divides,
analyses, classifies, and dissects, it also removes the security of order
and hierarchy, it undermines a belief in the mystery of life, and

destroys belief in a world ordered and managed by a concerned Deity. It then *disenchants* the world, and makes it a much harder, less caring place. As Weber said (1948: 155)

> The fate of our age, with its characteristic rationalization and intellectualization, and above all the disenchantment of the world, is that the ultimate, most sublime values have withdrawn from public life, either into the transcendental realm of mystical life, or into the brotherhood of immediate personal relationships between individuals.

Second, its predominant mode of organization – the bureaucracy – has undoubtedly increased the degree of equality in society through allocating positions on the basis of ability rather than on birth and social position. It has also made such organizations more efficient and effective by the careful and rational analysis of what needs to be done, and created the means to accomplish those ends. So it is very important to recognize the necessity for a fair degree of bureaucracy in virtually all organizations. Nevertheless, it has had a number of adverse consequences for both organization and individual. Adherence to such rationality can lead to a 'ritualism' (Merton, 1952) towards rules where little or no effort is made to use personal initiative, or to improve the service. When such ritualism occurs, motivation and morale normally decline, and people not only become inflexible to external change, but may fail to provide appropriate service to individual clients or customers. Perhaps most critically, a rigid adherence to bureaucratic rules may leave 'street-level bureaucrats' (Lipsky, 1980) feeling that they are being driven to treat clients or customers in a routinized and dehumanized manner, which may not only fail to address the particular problems such clients have, but may reduce street-level bureaucrats' morale and effectiveness as they are unable to treat clients in the individualistic way they feel is necessary.

Such rationality then, almost inevitably produces a series of *ir*rationalities, the most tragic perhaps being that while rationality should be pursued in order to meet the needs of our humanity, yet so often it seems to be used, irrationally, to destroy it. By the standardization of procedures, the activities and relationships with which we are engaged tend to be dehumanized and disenchanted. Furthermore, this restricted rationality so often, in pursuing one goal, irrationally prevents us from pursuing more important ones. Finally, and when used in a competitive situation, it can destroy that which is socially valued in the pursuit of that which is personally desired.

A major result of such processes, this standardization, argues Ritzer (2004: 3) is what he calls an increase in 'nothing' – 'a social form that is generally centrally conceived, controlled, and comparatively devoid of distinctive substantive content'.

Economically, if the ultimate aim for many firms is 'to create a formal model based on a limited number of principles that can be replicated virtually anywhere in the world' (2004: 85), the result will be a twentieth-century version of Weber's rationalization – what Ritzer calls 'McDonaldization', the drive towards an efficient standardized product, where everything, being predictable, can be calculated and controlled, and out of which all or most substantive, meaningful and human content is extracted. And because of the dominance of global economic agendas, this model spreads beyond the economic sector to affect all other aspects of society. For Ritzer, the ultimate irrationality of this is that we live in a world which produces an over-abundance of such forms of consumption, largely empty of any form of local or social content, thereby reducing or destroying forms which are more valuable and precious because they cater to our deeper personal and communal needs.

Does 'McDonaldization' add anything?

So there are major problems with such standardization. Yet, given the previous discussion, two further questions spring to mind. One is: does Ritzer add anything (apart from large amounts to his bank balance) by using the term 'McDonaldization' rather than Weber's concept of rationalization allied to Taylorian Scientific Management? This is important because the answer leads to some significant conclusions about US globalization. The other question is: given that both the Marxian and Weberian perspectives seem implicated in economic globalization, which is the more important? This is important because the answer provides a richer understanding of the paradoxes of globalization, and of the ways in which it impacts on individual lives.

So, Ritzer's coining of 'McDonaldization', and the fame resulting from this has been viewed with no little envy by some academics (see, for example, some of the critiques in Smart (1999)). Indeed, there are times when Ritzer *is* doing little more than interrogating Weber's ideas in the light of developments in the late twentieth century. Yet, Ritzer is saying something important, particularly when he argues that 'highly McDonaldized systems, and more importantly the principles that lie at the base of these systems, have been

exported from the United States to much of the rest of the world'
(2004: 84).

Ritzer does say that McDonaldization can be seen springing up
around the world, but his point is that the kind of large-scale,
rationalized and standardized organizations dedicated to consumerism, have almost without exception in the last 50 years originated in
the USA. This focus on consumerism, and on the USA as the place of
origin, does make this a new, if slightly derivative phenomenon. The
emphasis on consumerism reinforces the belief expressed in the
previous chapter that consumerism is no longer the handmaiden of
business activity, but now needs to be seen as a central player when
we try to understand the ecology of forces that surround educational
organizations. The second, the USA as locus of origin, is equally
important, because it points to the fact that McDonaldization has two
faces – the face of Weberian rationalization, *and* the face of US
globalization. Critically, were an American to be asked how they
thought of McDonalds, Coca-Cola, or any of the other massive firms
emanating from the USA, their reaction is likely to be a triumphalist
'made in the USA' one, and not one which simply describes them as
large corporations producing burgers, soft drinks, and so forth.
McDonaldization, then, is as much about Americanization as it is
about economic globalization. Indeed, attacks on McDonalds restaurants around the world need to be seen as attacks on what is perceived
as a representative of US cultural imperialism as anything to do with
global capitalism. And linked to this, in like manner, current forms of
global capitalism need to be seen as both 'turbo-capitalist' *and*
'Anglo-American' in origin. So once more, it is highly likely that the
average American will see 'capitalism' as as much American as
economic in fundamental nature. It is a 'brand' which rules the world
and which is perceived alongside the McDonaldized fast-food restaur-
ant, as intrinsic to the American identity, and indicative of America's
health, success and standing in the world.

If this is the case, then while Americans may celebrate McDonaldization and turbocapitalism as twin representatives of the success of
the American way of life, it might be expected that others might react
against them for twin opposed reasons. A first would be because of
the negative effects that such forces have upon them and their ways
of life; a second would be the result of the association of these
forces with America, and would therefore be a reaction against
America and things American. As Ritzer himself says: 'Empty forms
can come to be seen as the product of the United States, an inherent
characteristic of American culture that is being aggressively exported
throughout the world. Thus empty forms may be resented not in

themselves (for their emptiness) but also because they seem so American' (2004: 168).

Thus, when Ritzer says (2004: 149) 'the reality and sense of loss is far greater in much of the rest of the world than they are in the United States', the reason is almost certainly that such 'loss' is not felt in the US because such corporations are 'filled' with the 'something' of Americanization. For those outside the USA, however, this may not be a filling they want, when what is taken away is their own cultural distinctiveness. If this is the case, then many in the USA may fail to understand the antipathy that some of their most loved institutions provoke elsewhere, and those elsewhere may fail to understand why many in the USA regard these 'institutions' with so much affection – unless they conclude that American intentions are either malevolent, or they are so far lost that they cannot be saved from themselves.

Marx or Weber?

The second issue is whether the Marxian perspective, emphasizing the economic aspects of globalization, or the Weberian perspective, emphasizing the rational/cultural, is the more important influence. Is, then, the fragmentation caused by the instabilities and fluctuations of a largely uncontrolled and uncontrollable world economic system more important? Or are the prescriptive, centralized, standardizing and directive forces caused by the rationalized and McDonaldized processes? The answer is probably that such is the inseparable interpenetration between the two, that we need to recognize the importance and influence of both if the complexity and paradoxical nature of the forces surrounding educational organizations are to be understood. This interpenetration is part explained, as argued elsewhere (Bottery, 2000) by the fact that Weberian rationalism and bureaucratic organization are products of the Enlightenment project – the western attempt to fashion a concept of progress sustainable for all humanity through the application of reason. Such processes then predate current capitalist structures in the economic organization of society, yet there can also be little doubt that those engaged in capitalist activity saw early on that such rationality, and such bureaucratic organization, were both ideally suited to their objectives as they provided clear divisions of labour, transparent hierarchies, an absence of ambiguity, and the placing of the most qualified person in the right position. As Weberian rationalism predated and in some respects laid the cultural ground for capitalism to grow, while capitalism took on and further developed and incorporated this rationalism into its own activities, we may simply have to accept that such is the interdependence of the relationship between the two, that it would be foolish to try to separate or locate one in dominance over the other. The conclusion must be that the expansion of global activity in the economic and cultural spheres is to be explained by the growth of *both* turbocapitalism and McDonaldization. This helps to explain the widespread paradox of feelings of both fragmentation and control in everyday life, the former emanating from the instability and turbulence of capitalist activity, the latter from the standardizing and controlling effects of McDonaldized rationality. It is also a paradoxical situation which is unlikely to disappear in the foreseeable future.

The rationalization of educational systems

Globalization is then a complex and paradoxical group of forces, generating both a fragmentation and standardization/control of cultures and individual lives. Moreover, one country at least – the USA – is as much the generator of some of these forces as it is a recipient of others. One would expect – and in fact one sees – a considerable mediation of such global forces depending on culture, political orientation, and status in the world. Nevertheless, in education systems across the western world, there has been a quite dramatic movement towards the standardization of frameworks characterized by detailed legislative frameworks of pupil testing, precise definitions of curriculum standards, and high stakes processes for inspecting, monitoring and intervening in school performance. Now, once again, it is important to point out that there is not a simple causal link between McDonaldization tendencies and such rationalization. Given that globalization *is* such a complex term, and that there *are* national mediations of what happens at the global level, it would be surprising if there were such simplicity in causation. Instead, it is probable that such rationalization/standardization is due to the interplay of the following six elements:

Global rationalizing processes: the centralizing and bureaucratic logic of many McDonaldizing businesses might be very attractive to policy makers, as it may seem to enable simple translations of practice from private sector successes to organizations where there are concerns over poor performance, and over which they have responsibility and control. When this occurs, standardization may then be seen as one means of raising a base level of achievement.

Neo-liberal thinking and markets: as noted previously, much of the drive to economic globalization is underpinned by neo-liberal thinking, one aspect of which involves a dislike in granting power or status to producer groups because of the belief that these producers – of which professionals in general and educators in particular are seen as very representative – will use such power for their own purposes. In such circumstances, policy makers influenced by such thinking can be expected to require indicators of success independent of professional judgement.

The drive of global capital for continued growth and expansion: this drive leads to the viewing of all sectors as ripe for 'commodification', as being objects for commercial gain. The public sector is clearly not exempt from such gaze, and public education may then be seen as an area ripe for plucking. This might be accomplished by making education unappealing as a public sector activity. Standardizing public sector schooling might then make education sufficiently unattractive for parents to consider moving their children to private schools.

The logic of economics: when an economic model is utilized to evaluate the activities of other sectors, its methods tend to be used within these foreign sectors. Broadbent and Laughlin (1997) argue that the transference of 'acccounting logic' into education and other public sector areas is a logic built on two assumptions:

- that any activity can and should be evaluated in terms of measurable outputs, and in terms of the value added in the course of the activity; and

- that such evaluation can be undertaken in and through the finances used in the activity.

This means that that any evaluation will be framed in terms of what can be measured in quantitative terms; and a standardized education system would facilitate such accounting logic. Further, such economic logic would be predisposed to the much greater use of international statistical comparators of student achievement in judging public sector success. Indeed one of the strongest reasons given by western policy makers for school reform has been the perceived 'economic miracle' of the Asian tigers, which seems in part to have led to the adoption of similar standardized and controlled systems. Economic logic may then have favoured the adoption of global statistical comparators, which may have further encouraged policy makers to adopt frameworks which deliver to these kinds of numerical standards.

Reactions to fragmentation: in terms of the previous analysis of the instability, complexity, change and fragmentation caused by the economic turbulence, it might well be the case that politicians and public alike would welcome a type of policy which was relatively straightforward, simple, and understandable by specialists and non-specialists alike. In an age of great confusion, the clarity of greater standardization might be welcomed by many.

National drivers: the reduction in state funding, for reasons of both demographics and market ideology, has meant that states have found it increasingly difficult to maintain levels of funding: greater standardiz-ation might be appealing to policy makers as a way of achieving cheaper versions of education. Furthermore, many policy makers are pragmatic politicians who have, within democratic systems at least, fixed terms of office. To be voted back into power, they are driven by timetables which differ considerably from those of educationalists. They need to formulate educational policies which can be swiftly implemented and which yield relatively quick (and simple) results, so that electorates will be sufficiently impressed by their performance to re-elect them.

While some of these reasons can be traced to national issues, many of them can be traced to the effects of global forces. The irony is that while standardization, micromanagement and tightened inspection systems may therefore have been adopted in large part as a consequence of global pressures, it is likely that they are exactly the opposite of what is required to meet the challenges of this global future. It is to this issue that we now turn.

Organization, standardization and control

One of the principal governmental means of achieving standardiz-ation and control has been through the re-engineering of organiz-ations, and a critical strategy here has been the creation of a cadre of managers and leaders to oversee such reculturation. In the public sector in developed western countries, in contrast to former more facilitative strategies, such 'New Public Management' has come to be seen as 'the guardian of the overall purposes of the organization, and therefore it is wrong that another group of staff should be able to work to a different set of priorities' (Pollitt, 1993: 113).

Now once again, there has been a paradoxical combination of 'empowerment' for managers to be more entrepreneurial, yet at the same time being asked to implement and come into line with more and more central directives. And perhaps just as paradoxically, such management practices have experienced considerable swings over the last twenty years, as attempts at 'hot management' strategies have been utilized in the attempt to capture the minds, motivation and commitment of employees, only to be replaced by more 'cold management' strategies, which have aimed more at compliance, and the capture and utilization of the time, motion and bodies of individuals. Hoggett (1996) suggested that governments in the early 1990s were committed to what he called 'high output/low commitment' management – in essence neo-Taylorian strategies – which Pollitt (1993: 56) described as being principally concerned 'to set clear targets, to develop performance indicators, to measure the achievements of those targets, and to single out, by means of merit awards, promotion or other rewards, those individuals who get "results"'.

Since Pollitt and Hoggett, this process has, if anything, intensified in the public sector, combined with an even firmer commitment to the development of a more marketized, privatized and deregulated educational sector. Gleeson and Gunter (2000), for instance, in their analysis of the introduction of Performance Related Pay in Public Sector education the UK, argue that this has completed a circle of 'cold' managerial control and direction. It is but one instance of a situation across the western world where the managers and leaders of public sector organizations have been smothered in a stream of directives, targets and steers in the attempt to create predictable, error-free and risk-less organizations in which professionals don't need to be trusted in any but the most minimal sense because everything is so controlled, so micro-managed, so *known*. Yet the creation of such an environment has a number of damaging consequences.

First, while such management practice may attempt to leave trust out of the equation, it actually results in people feeling distrusted and demoralized, for they know that they are constantly the objects of surveillance. Second, through its incessant stipulation of more targets and performativity, such managerialism forces individuals into the playing of a game rather than concentrating upon the true purposes of the educational endeavour. Finally, it limits the development of any meaningful concept of a learning community by steering educators into becoming what Hargreaves (2003) calls 'performance training sects'. These consequences need to be examined in greater detail.

The consequences of distrust and demoralization

There is now strong evidence that throughout the western world, there are many public sector professionals, and educational professionals in particular, who are deeply unhappy with their current work. This is seen in the number who wish to leave, those who want to take early retirement, and those who are having to leave through ill health brought on by stress. Some critics may say that this is simply professional shroud waving, yet the situation is serious for reasons other than a concern for teachers' states of mind. One reason is that unhappy teachers don't make good teachers. A second reason is that sufficient numbers are leaving and depopulating a profession to the extent that replacement crises are now firmly on governmental agendas, resulting in the adoption of policies of 'workforce remodelling' in which less qualified individuals are allowed to take on activities previously reserved for professonals. The result for the organization, the students and the society in general is then extremely worrying.

Now, as already seen, in study after study (e.g. Hargreaves (2003); Gronn (2003a); Fullan (2003); Bottery (1998)), at both senior management and classroom teacher level, the same issues of overwork, demoralization and alienation are repeated. Hargreaves (2003: 91), for instance, in his studies in New York State and in Ontario, Canada, reports many teachers feeling ' "demeaned" and "degraded" . . . "unfairly criticised" and "sick and tired of being asked to justify their existence"; . . . of "constant government put downs" that teachers were "poisoning young minds"; of government mandates to "slander and deprofessionalise" teachers as whole'.

Part of this came from worries over creativity. As one teacher said:

> the primary motivation of the government has been to increase productivity at the expense of creativity. I do not have the time for professional development . . . I also don't have the time to fit the curriculum to the needs of my pupils . . . what a waste of my intelligence, creativity, and leadership potential! (2003: 83)

Yet this does not just apply to teachers. As Fink (2001: 232) said: 'There is . . . not a great deal of room in most of the test-driven reform agendas internationally for pupils to construct knowledge, and to demonstrate their creativity, imagination and innovativeness.'

A major consequence of teachers' treatment was their lack of trust in the integrity of governments and policy makers in introducing educational changes. As another of Hargreaves' interviewees said: 'I think the government has done what it set out to do. Many parents are choosing private education. The state system will become second rate without money and vocal or involved parents' (2003: 97).

When teachers distrust governments so much, it is worrying that a governmental pamphlet like *Professionals and Trust* (2001) by a former Secretary of State for Education in England is exclusively devoted to governmental difficulties in trusting teachers, but which says nothing of the difficulties teachers have in trusting government, and therefore says nothing about what might be done to remediate this.

Now it has to be said that while teachers may complain that governments don't recognize their problems, it also seems fair to say that on many occasions teachers don't recognize governmental concerns. This points to the fact that trust is a two-way process, in which the dynamics of relationships are absolutely critical. The next chapter will look at this in much greater detail, but it is important to point out here that the kind of trust discussed in *Professionals and Trust* is very much as one might expect from foregoing discussions about economic agendas reducing first order values to second order ones – trust is here viewed as a management tool, rather than as something which is deeply personal in its effects. Such a second order use of trust can have immediate and negative effects upon the morale of workforces, for if leader/managers/policy makers see trust simply as a tool, they may fail to see that those on the receiving end – those being trusted or distrusted – take this in a very personal sense. *Being distrusted* is not perceived as the absence of a managerial tool but as a normative judgement about one's character. In that situation, workforce reactions are predictable – anger, deep distrust and dislike of those not trusting them. Tragically, those who began the mistrust may perceive such reaction as confirmation of the validity of their initial adoption of 'cold management' approaches – and both sides may then be locked into vicious circles of mutual distrust. And when perceptions of educators as self-interested workers who cannot be trusted to define their work, or be trusted to reach high standards on their own are confirmed, it may then seem sensible to subject them to intense micro-management and detailed levels of accountability. Two strategies in this process need describing here.

The use and abuse of targets

While the general notion of targets as a way of specifying what is intended, and how it might be achieved, is a sensible means of getting people to plan ahead, there are a number of issues with their use which contribute to the problems begun by the creation of low-trust environments. A first is that targets are never neutral. As Fitzgibbon (2000: 260–1) argues 'one of the aims of indicator systems is to attach value to that which is measured'; and where targets are attached to inspections, and rewards and punishments, it would be a strange – not too say foolish – management, that did not put a great deal of effort into achieving them, an amount which might be disproportionate to the contribution they make to a richer education for students. Similarly, if individuals know that in annual reviews of their work they will be judged – and pay awards will be made – on their ability to show student progress in those target areas, it would also be strange if they did not adopt strategies which targeted the enhancement of these specified areas. They will also realize that they would be better off being assigned teaching groups with whom they can demonstrate most progress, and this may make them more selective with the groups they take. They may also be more inclined to take over groups from weaker colleagues, and more reluctant to take over those from strong ones, for they will be able to show more progress by taking over from the former than the latter. They may also be less willing to teach outside of their specialist area, or share classes with less competent colleagues. And they may become increasingly reluctant to move schools to teach in difficult areas.

The result of the creation of such excessively directed and punishment-oriented regimes may then be a *distortion of* aims. Individuals, faced with perverse incentives, may be tempted to work for personal benefit rather than for collegial good. The combination of an organization distracted from its real aims by inappropriate targets, and of individuals pursuing 'rational' courses of self-advancement at the expense of collegial benefit, could then do great damage to the achievement of a 'learning community'.

Now, it must be acknowledged that successful change requires a degree of pressure and support from above; bottom-up creativity and invention will not suffice. Yet as this is a question of balance, oppressive central standardization does not achieve this. Furthermore, there is evidence that, under current target-driven regimes, some individuals do manage to work the system successfully, as they knowingly 'play the game' while at the same time keeping their eye on 'the real' issues, needs and desired developments of their organizations (see Day et al., 2000). Indeed, where there is some flexibility in external directions, astute leaders and managers may well subvert the spirit of individualistic target regimes by incorporating more collegial targets, which strengthen rather than diminish an organization's learning environment. Yet this cannot be an argument for keeping such a system in place. Managing to survive in an unsympathetic environment is hardly as conducive as flourishing in a supportive one.

Furthermore, excessive external imposition is a problem in a number of other ways. Not only does it indicate a lack of trust in those close to the process, thereby generating low morale; it also cannot see the needs of the institution in the richness that those internal to the process see it; and it can deflect effort away from responding to such context.

Critically, externality tends to generate largely extrinsic rewards, such as financial incentives. Yet going back as far as Herzberg et al. (1959), the evidence suggests that while such extrinsic rewards may remove dissatisfaction, they do not generate motivation or satisfaction. Too great a degree of external imposition of work content and reward may then be self-defeating, resulting in the reduced morale of a workforce unable to realize the things they believe are central to their work. And this, as Jeffrey and Woods (1998) report in their research on UK teachers, may lead to intense feelings of guilt and loss of self-respect. One teacher talked of 'resenting what I've done. I've never compromised before and I feel ashamed. It's like licking their boots' (1998: 160).

Another said: 'My first reaction was "I'm not going to play the game"; but I am and they know I am . . . my own self-respect goes down . . . Why aren't I saying "I know I can teach; say what you want to say" and so I lose my self-respect' (1998: 160).

This echoes other research, which talks not only of demoralization, but of teachers seeing themselves as prostituting their professionalism 'in the service of ends they regarded as morally indefensible' (Hargreaves, 2003: 92).

So excessive standardization through externally-imposed targets can negatively affect the aims and objectives of a school, reduce trust in policy makers, and depress educators' self-concepts. Sadly, however, this is not the end. Not only can targets deflect attention from the prime concern of an educational organization, but, because of their ever-changing nature, they can prevent people from ever being satisfied with their efforts. Now it is important to be clear that 'satisfaction' does not necessarily imply 'complacency'. It is perfectly possible to do the best that one can, to realize that change and improvement are never-ceasing, but still feel able to celebrate attainment and be proud of past and current achievements. Yet when the achievement of constantly changing external targets is made the overriding objective, morale can be dramatically lowered, for such targets create constant feelings of *self-doubt* (at having to replace carefully acquired professional judgements with externally imposed targets), of *anxiety* (at having to constantly attain targets), of *guilt* (at being unable to achieve increasingly difficult targets), and of *complaint* and *blame* (as consumers are led to believe that the focus of their educational aspirations should be on dissatisfaction with producers' attempts to reach such targets).

Indeed, and only half-jokingly, one might argue that somewhere there exists a manual entitled 'The Rules of Good Management, Leadership, and Teaching in an Age of Target Setting and Low Trust'. It probably amounts to the following five rules:

1 If you're happy at work, then there's something wrong.

2 If you're satisfied with what you've done, then you're complacent, for satisfaction is the same as complacency.

3 Your best is never good enough.

4 If you're not dissatisfied with your current performance, then you're not doing it properly.

5 The good teacher/manager/leader is the one who is unhappy and anxious.

Such rules may help to explain the fact that in the UK the number of working days lost to stress in the general population between 1995 and 2002 rose from 18 million to 33 million, and that this was *60* times the number of days lost to industrial action (*Guardian*, 6 January 2003).

An excess of performativity

The cynical might want to add one further rule to this list: 'The good teacher/manager/leader is the one who is able to convince external observers that he/she is doing what is externally demanded, while managing to get on with the real job.'

This, in a word, is 'performativity', and it is highly interesting that as influential a commentator as Sergiovanni (2001: 5–14) has as the fifth of seven basic principles of leadership that of 'building with canvas', for as he argues, like the decoy tanks built in canvas during the war, such strategic deceptions can help leaders respond to external demands which require that school look as they are supposed to. However, performativity is even more ubiquitous, for whenever a leader or manager makes demands which are not totally consonant with a subordinate's view of the job, then it is likely that some degree of performativity will be attempted. Furthermore, one cannot assume that such subordinates are always right, for they may reject reasonable demands out of self-interest, or may misunderstand the true nature of the situation occasioning the demands. So exercises in 'performativity' do not necessarily indicate where the fault lies, nor how issues should be resolved. However, there *is* likely to be a damaging degree of performativity when external direction is excessive, for when this happens, it obstructs strategies aimed at coping with the unique and changeable nature of a particular situation.

Moreover, one of the principal functions of performativity in a culture of low trust is to make individuals' activities constantly public. Yet, as Elliot (2001) points out, such transparency is not always possible, partly because of the tacit nature of some of the activity, partly because of the time involved, and partly because of the transaction costs incurred. Where it is attempted, the result is likely to be no more than a 'highly selective objectifications of performance' (2001: 194). Moreover, because such transparency assumes that there are 'fixed and immutable standards against which to judge performance' (2001: 195), it may actually hinder the flexibility necessary to meet the ever-changing learning needs of students.

What is especially worrying is that even those leaders and managers opposed to steerage by such means, may find themselves engaging in it – and in the process hating themselves for it. This seems particularly the case when there is a squeeze on budgets, for where extra income generation is not possible, either people have to be 'let go', or the best use needs to be made of the resources available. In this situation, a manager/leader may feel impelled, not only for financial, managerial and strategic reasons, but for those of *equity* as well, to consider adopting performance measures. Thus, as finance is reduced, they may try to ensure that all contribute fully to helping the institution meet its obligations, and thus may attempt a greater transparency of effort through the introduction of performative strategies like workload models. These may be considered for what may seem the very best of reasons, yet they may still generate the kind of damaging effects described above. Even Stephen Ball (2001), an arch-critic of performative systems, is forced to admit the temptation to urge people to submit ill-prepared articles in order to meet the next UK Research Assessment Exercise, which allocates research monies to university departments. As he says: 'Some of the oppressions I describe are perpetrated by me. I am agent and subject within the regime of performativity in the academy' (2001: 214).

The results of such performativity can then be profound. At the institutional and strategic level, it can lead to a perversion of the true objectives of the organization, as attention is focussed on external demands and not on internal needs. It can also prevent a necessary flexibility of response, as well as limiting the degree of creativity and risk-taking, with which any learning organization needs to be concerned. At the personal level, it can generate a variety of negative and damaging emotions, involving individuals in inauthenticity and fabrication, as they find themselves compelled to deny their true instincts with respect to the betterment of the institution. Not only then may individuals feel depressed at what is happening externally: they may feel depressed at their own actions. This lack of self-respect, of self-betrayal, of guilt and of dissatisfaction permeating a working life is seen in all of the studies mentioned so far. As Stephen Ball (2001) said, individuals find themselves being both 'agent' and subject' in the creation of their unhappiness.

Crippling the learning organization

What is the likely effect upon people within a learning organization, in terms of their attitude towards students and teaching? Some of this has already been covered, in the suggestion that demoralization may well lead to greater exhaustion, lower morale and lower commitment. However, there are two other aspects of excessively standardized approaches which further cripple the learning organization.

The first is, somewhat paradoxically, the fragmentation of the student experience. This can be understood by re-examining the main thrusts of excessive standardization. By placing priorities on performance standards, targets and competence checklists, the emotional dimensions of education are neglected and undermined. By portraying schooling as a predominantly clinical exercise devoted to the achievement of targets, creativity and imagination may be neglected, as may the magic of relationships which needs to underpin teaching. In the process, teachers are disengaged from the act of teaching, and students from the act of learning. This is particularly true at the secondary level, where students' experiences may be initially fragmented by the lack of absorption and excitement which such standardization causes, and which may then be further fragmented by a system which is built around the delivery of separate subjects, delivered by different teachers, who may have neither the time nor the opportunity (nor, indeed, if driven by subject delivery, the interest) to get to know the students in the way that is possible at the primary level. A further problem with this system of organizing education is that it demands of pupils a mastery of a variety of subjects areas, when the experts teaching them do not demonstrate this themselves. The final fragmentation is encountered by those least able to deal with it – those who come from fragmented and disrupted homes. If this book has already dealt with a number of instances of the irrationality of a restricted rationality, here is a final one – an education system which by doing the 'rational thing' of increasing the tests, targets and amount of teaching, disengages the student by preventing or neglecting precisely those things which give meaning and coherence to the educative experience, and which undergird the true learning organization – the sense of identity, care, respect, trust, community and belonging.

The second effect of such standardization and control derives from the more recent decision to launch large-scale reform strategies, such as *Success for All* and *Open Court* programmes in the USA, and the National Literacy and Numeracy Strategies in the UK which Hargreaves (2003) argues have a number of key similarities. These are:

- heavily prescribed teaching strategies in key areas (normally numeracy and literacy);

- rigorous monitoring of ambitious targets for improvement;

- expectations that all pupils will achieve these standards;

- relatively generously funded intensive training in these programmes.

Now there is evidence (see, for example, DfES, 2003) that these strategies have shown some significant early success, and have challenged the assumptions of teachers with low expectations of their pupils. Furthermore, such heavily scripted materials may benefit both novice teachers and those teachers working at unsatisfactory levels. Nevertheless, in terms of developing genuine learning organizations, these programmes raise a number of serious medium-to long-term problems. First, while reasonably successful in terms of achieving limited aims, these programmes may be less successful in more complex and critical areas. Second, because these programmes stress particular areas of the curriculum, and external interrogation of schools is largely based on these areas, other areas of greater creativity and criticality may be neglected. Finally, and despite the fact that the originators of such programmes never intended this to happen, it is possible, as Hargreaves (2003: 144) argues, that: 'Professional development becomes like being inducted into an evangelical sect where the message of pedagogical salvation is presented as a divine and universal truth.'

The danger, then, is that teachers may be steered into the adoption of a set of values light-years away from those of genuine learning communities. These values are:

Pedagogical exclusivity – the belief that there is only one externally-defined way of teaching; and that the examination and critiquing of different approaches, or the intellectual movement from thesis, antithesis, to higher synthesis of different approaches, are neither values nor options open to the professional.

Epistemological monopoly – the belief that research results of the particular orientation are objectively 'true' and not to be disputed; educational truth is a monopoly exercised by bodies in authority, and by researchers who have official approval.

Implementational obeisance – the belief that the job of the teacher is not to critique claims to better education, but to implement what they are told; critique, if it has a place, has to remain at the level of implementation, and if aspects of implementation are designated as 'true', then these are not to be considered within the orbit of teachers' professionalism.

What is *really* disturbing is that while Benjamin Barber's (1996) contrast between the McDonaldization of standardization and the *Jihad* of fundamentalist resistance has already been mentioned, it might be tempting to see this *Jihad* as a response by some religious group in an underdeveloped country, somewhere suitably distant from our more 'civilized' western world. Indeed, as mentioned, Barber's use of *Jihad* is an unfortunate choice, for not only does it mis-describe the proper meaning of the term, but it distracts us from the realization that one-sided, fundamentalist demands for unthinking adherence to a set of (contestable) beliefs are just as likely in the West as they are anywhere else – and the reform strategies being discussed have many of the qualities, having both a fundamentalist orientation and demanding an unthinking allegiance. The arguments of the followers of *Jihad* are the same the world over, being founded on authority and simple assertion rather than on debate and reason. We do not have to travel too far from home to encounter their values, arguments and effects.

Such values then militate against research and criticism, except for the 'normal' scientist working within a research paradigm, concerned only with making its operation more understood, more efficient. The paradigm breaker, who questions whether the standard or traditional way is the correct way of doing things, is then positively discouraged. Such values also militate against a reasoned epistemology, and send profound anti-democratic signals to student populations, for they see themselves being taught by adults who are not allowed to question what governments say they should do, and who are told that the best form of education is a paradoxical and contradictory form of the McDonaldization of standards and targets, and an unthinking allegiance to government-sponsored teaching approaches. This is problematic in the extreme.

Conclusion

There are two principal issues to be drawn from this chapter. The first concerns the nature of a learning society. As the UNESCO Delors report (1996) argued, there are four essential functions of learning. Two of these – *learning to know* and *learning to do* are core functional means for a healthy economy; but the final two – *learning to be* and *learning to live together* – are ends in themselves, and are fundamental to any life worth living. The message is clear: learning for a healthy economy is a means to an end of a healthy society. More than this, a healthy knowledge economy *depends upon* a learning society, and this in its turn needs to be constituted of individuals and groups who keep learning in new and innovative ways, which is not aided by excessive standardization. Yet while western governments may have based their standardized approaches on perceptions of economic successes which occurred in the Far East, these same Asian governments have now largely realized that their future prosperity depends instead on a different flexible, creative and adaptable response. A skilled, predictable but inflexible workforce may have been of use in more traditionally hierarchical times, but such prescriptive direction will not create the flexibilities either a knowledge economy or a learning society requires. Indeed, such directive approaches will almost certainly produce the kinds of people who are *not* able to compete in global markets in the next few decades. If, as Leadbeater argues (1998: 375), in the new economy all companies will need 'knowledge-able motivated employees who can take responsibility for solving problems, delivering services to the highest standards of quality and coming up with new ideas', then standardized and controlled structural, organizational and leadership forms within present educational systems are likely to be extremely counterproductive. And as Lauder at al. add: 'If we are not careful, policy settings which emphasise results at the expense of methods will lead to a *trained incapacity* to think openly and critically about problems that will confront us in ten or twenty years' time' (1998: 51) [emphasis added].

Second, and even more critically, not only does standardization standardize, and thereby inhibit flexibility and creativity, and drive out humanity; it also fragments. And as it fragments, it steers people into the opposite of standardization, into unquestioning fundamentalisms. Indeed, as Castells argues 'Fundamentalisms of different kinds and from different sources will represent the most daring, uncompromising challenge to one-sided domination of informational global capitalism. Their potential access to weapons of mass extermination casts a giant shadow on the optimistic prospects of the information age' (1998: 355).

This chapter has largely agreed with this assessment, but has also suggested that fundamentalisms lie much closer to home than might at first be recognized, and that a primary place to guard against them is within a society's educational system. Like Castells, Giddens argues that: 'The battleground of the twenty-first century will pit fundamentalism against cosmopolitan tolerance ... Cosmopolitans welcome and embrace this cultural complexity. Fundamentalists find it disturbing and dangerous ... they take refuge in a renewed and purified tradition' (1990: 4–5).

But yet again, he fails to locate the fact that such fundamentalism is already in some respects with us. Giddens' world of cosmopolitan tolerance needs to be developed not just by looking outwards, but by looking inwards as well, and particularly to the nurturing of educational institutions as a primary base. This book now moves to consider the qualities that are needed for this. One critical area is the creation of a greater degree of trust. It is to this that the next chapter turns.

PART 2
EXAMINING THE IMPACT

6   *The impact on trust*

Previous chapters have already alluded to issues of trust when describing global and societal changes. In terms of global economic changes, as markets become more unstable and volatile, and change becomes more rapid, trust becomes increasingly more critical. Misztal puts the case for the need for trust very well:

> In a global economy where risk-taking, innovation and information sharing are seen as paramount, companies will only be able to prosper if they create a high-trust culture. In an electronic world, where businesses are geographically far from their customers, a reputation for trust assumes even greater importance. (2001: 24)

Yet if trust is leached out by such instability and fragmentation, the other side of globalization, the control/standardization agenda, has also led to the use of low-trust cultures. So while excessive fragmentation can lead to misunderstandings and to difficulties in assessing risk, producing strong feelings of confusion and distrust, excessive standardization can also produce a distrust in the exercise of professional autonomy.

Trust as a topic is extremely current in other ways as well. Trust in political leaders, in business tycoons and their dealings, in professionals like doctors and teachers, is never far from the headlines. Yet the concern with trust is more than contemporary: it is also vital. At the societal level, it is essential in building the kind of relationships necessary for a flourishing society, as well as in building better relationships between governments and public sector workers. At the institutional level, it is essential in building better relationships within teams in a knowledge economy, in building relationships within a learning community in which knowledge is socially created and shared, and in building the kinds of group relationships that boost student achievement. At the interpersonal level, it is central to perceptions of individual integrity, and therefore critical to good leadership; it is also essential in building the kinds of student–teacher relationships fundamental to good teaching. Finally, at the personal level, trust is essential to individual morale, in maintaining self-esteem and feelings of self-worth, and is central in any attempt to deal with uncertainty, unpredictability and risk. At bottom, it is a critical existential need. It is hard, then, to over-estimate its importance, yet this chapter argues that failure to recognize its importance and complexity currently impedes the raising of morale and student achievement, prevents the development of not only effective but acceptable management strategies, and hinders a leader's ability to cope with the longer-term demands of a knowledge-based society.

Government, trust and teacher morale

It was mentioned earlier that in 2001, the then Secretary of State for Education in England and Wales, gave a speech on 'Professionalism and Trust' (Morris, 2001) as part of a strategy to heal damaged relationships with the teaching profession, as well as an attempt to address an ongoing teacher recruitment and retention crisis, a problem common in many other countries. In England, teaching resignations had risen in 2001 by 4 per cent, 30 per cent of students qualifying as teachers did not enter the profession, and 18 per cent of NQTs quit the profession within three years – and when 61 per cent of the current teaching force was over 40 (*The Teacher*, December 2001: 5). Furthermore, while the current government was committed to increasing teacher numbers by 10,000, by their own admission (Morris, 2001: 11) that still left a shortfall of nearly 25,000 teachers. However, this pamphlet was largely utilitarian in nature, its concern being with trust by government of teachers; it did not consider whether there was an issue with the lack of trust *of* government *by* teachers. It therefore failed to recognize the two-way nature of trust, and discussed it as little more than a pragmatic calculation on the government's part, failing to see that *being trusted* evokes very different emotions, being perceived by those upon whom the judgement is made as a moral judgement about them and their character. Such failure to recognize that utilitarian trust judgements produce deep emotional reactions, because they are taken instead as ethical judgements on individual integrity, suggests a lack of awareness of the nature and dynamics of trust, which this chapter addresses.

Such apparent lack of trust stems from a number of sources. Table 6.1 suggests that there are three principal foundations for trust underpinning this loss of trust by government of teachers, and that

Table 6.1 *What happens when governments don't trust professionals?*

Trust foundation	Lack of trust leads to following 'low-trust' policies
Values: Agreement over the necessary values and value priorities to make the activity successful	Legislative requirements; training priorities; promotion geared to value and value priority compliance
Integrity: A perception that professionals say and do the same thing	Increased frequency and detail of inspection; more accountability; more testing
Competence: A perception of competence of those doing the job	Emphasis in training on assessed behavioural competencies, increased inspection, speedier dismissal procedures

where such foundations are undermined, specific 'low-trust' policies tend to follow.

The first foundation area for trust is an agreement over values and value priorities. Some of the foundational undermining of professional practice, then, can be traced back to Hayekian (1944) arguments that welfare state bureaucracies, and self-serving professionals who work within them, are likely to replicate the authoritarianism of Nazism and Communism. Some can also be traced to the work of Friedman (1962) and his belief in the supremacy of markets and the voice of the purchaser.

The second foundation area is based upon people doing what they say they will do. Professionals have increasingly been characterized as not being trustworthy in this respect. Some of this can be traced to the work of critical sociologists like Collins (1990), who painted professionals, not as groups centrally concerned with clients' welfare, but as producer-workers attempting 'occupational closure' – the creation of work monopolies which maintained their salary levels and permitted considerable discretion at work.

The third foundation area of trust is perceptions of job competence: and governments worldwide have acted upon (and in some cases engineered) critical reports of performance standards, after which blame has then largely been attached to the incompetence of professionals.

Such undermining of the bases of trust in professionals has then provided legitimation for government action worldwide. Such action has also been spurred on by increasing concern with declining tax bases, and the need to extract the best value from the money available, which has involved ensuring that public servants, educators included, deliver what governments feel they need to achieve. In the process, governments have developed an increased intolerance of public servant professional autonomy, and have moved from what Pollitt (1993) described as a desire to see professionals from being 'on top' to being 'on tap'. Such assaults on professional autonomy have resulted, depending on your point of view, in either radically improved educational provision and greater access to a good education, or with the promulgation of questionable official statistics, and a disempowered profession afflicted by stress, apathy, and a desire for early retirement. As already noted, even on an optimistic scenario, there is now widespread official concern over teacher supply across the western world. Teacher morale and trust, then, are topics high on governmental agendas.

A growing interest in trust

An educator's interest in trust, however, should not be confined to just these concerns. Trust is also heavily implicated in agendas involving the transformation of organizations from hierarchical structures with long-term employment, to flatter ones with greater worker flexibility and impermanence of employment – what Grey and Garsten (2001) describes as movement from bureaucratic to post-bureaucratic structures. The problem, as seen by management theorists, is that of generating individual worker predictability and organizational control, for, so the argument goes, trust was not much of a problem in bureaucratic structures, precisely because the bureaucratic form extracted the need for trust – individuals were made predictable and controllable through the careful delineation of their functions and roles. Now such structures have increasingly been criticized, not because of the way in which they leach out values like trust, but because of their inability to adapt to changing market conditions. Writers like Peters and Waterman (1982) have argued instead for the creation of organizational cultures which can generate worker predictability and control by inculcating them into the values and norms of organizational cultures. An individual thus wedded to, or indoctrinated with, particular organizational values could then be made quite as predictable and controllable as within a bureaucratic regime. However, this approach to the creation of worker control now also looks increasingly outdated, for as we have seen, many organizations now need to be so flexible that their workers must not only be flexible, but dispensable as well. Such workers will then probably not be around long enough to be socialized into a set of norms. And if the individual cannot trust the company for long-term career employment and advancement, why, one may ask, should the company expect the individual to trust them? And here lies the paradox: even though trust is now seen as a critical factor in organizational – and economic – functioning, the kind of organization which needs this quality also feels pressured to develop structures and forms which run counter to its generation.

So trust is a topic of increasing interest in a number of arenas. Perhaps, given the apparent lack of need for it in bureaucratic and 'culture' organizations, it should not be too surprising that much of the work on it has been partial and fragmented. Influential books like that of Fukuyama's (1996) are conceptually quite limited, an inadequacy of analysis which is noted more generally by Dasgupta (1988), Luhmann (1988), and McLagan (1998). Yet there are pockets of solid research. Gambetta et al. (1988) explore and develop the conceptual complexity of the term; empirical research by Kramer and Tyler (1996) developed the understanding, dynamics and development of trust within organizations generally, while Uslaner (2002) reviewed and developed both empirical and ethical arguments for its necessity. Finally, Bryk and Schneider (2002) and Louis (2003) have produced important work in education. It is time to examine trust in more detail.

Understanding trust: the developmental stages

There are at least four different stages in the development of a trust relationship. These will be called the *calculative, role, practice* and *identificatory* stages. They are both developmental and normative in nature, becoming more complex and valuable as they move from an essentially cognitive platform, to incorporate motivational, affective and principled elements.

Calculative trust

Trust is involved in dealing with risk and uncertainty, both inescapable facts of the human condition. We cannot, and never will be able to know all of the contingencies in a situation, nor their likely interaction. This ubiquity of risk is important, because it suggests that trust is an inevitability of human existence, no matter how hard individuals and organizations strive for certainty. For such appreciation of risk does not entail simply abandoning ourselves to fate: human beings constantly attempt to understand, control and predict future situations, and use an array of sophisticated mental processes to do so. It should be no surprise then that Gambetta's definition of trust is necessarily complex, suggesting that it is:

> a particular level of the subjective probability with which an agent assesses that another agent or group of agents will perform a particular action, both before he can monitor such action (or independently of his capacity ever to be able to monitor it) and in a context in which it affects his own action. (1988: 217)

This definition of trust suggests the need to take a variety of factors into account, and to make judgements concerning the probability that someone will do something that is beneficial to us, or at least not harm us. From these calculations, a decision is then normally made as to whether someone can be trusted. This is calculative trust which, Gambetta (1988: 218), argues should be seen as a 'threshold point' on a continuum from complete trust to complete distrust, the actual decision to trust being a variable point, determined by such variables as personal predisposition, the amount of information known about a situation, knowledge of a person's past performance, the risk and harm attached to trusting, the ability to bring sanctions to bear on someone likely to break that trust, and the knowledge that that person knows that you can and will bring those sanctions to bear, and for these sanctions to matter. All of these conditions will then feed into an individual act of rational calculation of whether to trust or not.

Role trust

Now a useful element in the calculation of an individual's trustworthiness is supplied by the manner human beings are inducted into particular organizations and occupations. They learn through such induction to accept and practice certain values. Western doctors, for instance, are inducted into a medical profession underpinned by a set of values, principal among which is that of not harming others. Now, because the general public believes in such values, and tends to trust doctors to practice these values, we think we know how a doctor will react when a situation arises in which a person is injured. This helps explain, as Meyerson et al. (1996) argue, why 'swift trust' is possible, for individuals within a group can come together for a short space of time and yet trust others within it to carry out their role, even though they have neither the time nor opportunity to form strong personal bonds, or develop detailed knowledge of each other. This is because these workers all accept the same cultural role and share the same value code; when these conditions are put in place, they help to short-circuit the normally lengthy period needed for people to build a satisfactory degree of trust. Such occupational values, then, act as 'flags' by which uncertainty is reduced, for they help people believe that individuals belonging to that occupation will act on those values. The case of Harold Shipman, a doctor in the north-west of England who murdered over 200 elderly people while claiming to be treating them, is disturbing precisely because his actions undermine this deeply held societal belief. This form of trust, then, introduces an ethical component to trust to an extent not seen in calculative trust. If the metaphor for calculative trust was *the logician*, the metaphor for role trust is *the professional*.

Now if one accepts that many professionals' practice is underpinned by such ethical commitments, it is easy to see why relationships between professionals and managers and/or governments might be strained, and why professional morale might be low. For the use by governments and managements of increasingly calculative forms of trust in their relationships with professionals will in most cases be taken very personally, as they will be seen as attacks on an individual's integrity. Moreover, the situation will be exacerbated if professionals come to believe that their occupational values are being downgraded or replaced by a set concerned more with cost-cutting and economic competitiveness. A potent mixture is then created for producing lowered morale. A profession will not only believe that it is distrusted by government (or, even worse, believe that government is not concerned with what it thinks), but it will now distrust the government, the body determining its practice and conditions. Finally, and as this distrust is conveyed to government, a vicious cycle of declining trust is generated between the two parties.

Practice trust

So far, then, trust has been portrayed largely as a matter of personal calculation, aided by the 'flags' of occupational values. But trust needs to be underpinned by more than this. A further method is to engage individuals in continued interaction, to engage in practice trust. Now such practice trust can be performed simply as an extension of calculative trust, for repeated encounters increase the amount of knowledge about a person, and therefore facilitate more accurate calculations concerning an individual's trustworthiness. However, such practice trust is also different in that, as Axelrod (1986) argued, repeated encounters 'enlarge the reach of the future'. Knowing that further meetings will take place ensures the greater likelihood of future sanctions. Such possibilities probably ensure that promises are given more weight, just as the person to whom the promise is being made is also aware of this, and will calculate this into their decision of whether to trust or not.

Such reasoning expands the calculative context, but does not change the basic cognitive nature of trust. However, repeated encounters also create a new form of trust, because they facilitate the development of interpersonal bonds. These do more than merely create a larger calculative context, for they require that each acknowledges and respects the other's integrity, introducing to the relationship additional ethical and affective components. The partners now begin to construct the discipline of an ethical system upon which the relationship will be based, rather than merely basing it upon rational calculation, or role attribution, and are highly likely to be offended if such a system is broken unilaterally. A relationship then begins to develop which is now nurtured for its own sake. It is this combination of elements – the calculative, the ethical and the affective – which provide educational managers and leaders with dilemmas when they are asked to make utilitarian calculative decisions which run counter to the ethical and affective dimensions of a relationship, and lead them to question where their ultimate loyalties lie.

The inclusion of personal and ethical elements into a trust relationship helps to explain that trust may become depleted through lack of use, and may be strengthened by continued use. Importantly, it also suggests that practice trust is the level at which we begin to think 'trust' becomes a reality. Thus, as Kipnis (1996) found, being trusted generates very positive feelings, for individuals who feel that they are being trusted believe that not only does the other party like them, but also that they are regarded as persons of ethical integrity. More than that, because trust involves risk, it sends an even more powerful message:

> Even though this situation is potentially threatening to me, I still believe in you enough to place my trust in you.

The reverse of this – of not placing trust where it could be placed – provides precisely the opposite message:

I don't have confidence in you and your abilities; you are not dependable, and when there is a threat or a risk to me, I do not believe that you are someone to be relied upon.

This then is the kind of trust which contains both affective and ethical judgements of another person. The results, unsurprisingly, are benign and vicious circles: the more I trust you, the more complimented you feel, and the more likely you are to react favourably and repay that trust by carrying out what is expected – and the more likely I am to extend that trust on a future occasion, when the situation is perhaps even more threatening. Alternatively, the less I trust you, the more demeaned and insulted you feel (particularly if you feel you should be trusted) and the more likely you are to dislike me, to react negatively to future offers, and therefore for me to reduce the times I extend trust to you in the future – even when there may be relatively little risk to me.

So, if the appropriate metaphor for calculative trust was the logician, and for role trust the professional, the appropriate metaphor for practice trust, Lewicki and Bunker (1996: 12) argue, would be *the gardener* 'tilling the soil year after year to understand it . . . gathering data, seeing each other in different contexts, and noticing reactions to different situations'. To become a significant feature in the social landscape, trust then needs to be practised. And this can be done in all sorts of ways – by living and working closely with someone, by sharing in joint products or goals, by committing to jointly shared values, in larger groups, by attempting to develop a collective identity. Furthermore, for a kind of trust whose metaphor is the gardener, lack of practice also sows seeds of distrust, for not only do insufficient interaction and communication prevent the generation of a deeper understanding, but not practising trust may be interpreted as not being trusted, liked or being dependable. And finally, missing or insufficiently emphasizing the crucial involvement of affective and ethical components at this level, or of demoting trust to a purely calculative level, can have very damaging effects upon the relationship.

Identificatory trust

Identificatory trust is very special, limited in number, and involves an intensity of relationship not seen at other levels. It contains a calculative component, but this is relatively little used; it is nourished by a practice component, but this is not needed as much as at lower levels; and it draws from an ethical base, but moves beyond any mechanical application to a complex intertwining of personal thoughts, feelings and values. If the lowest level is one of pure cognition, and others build in affective and ethical components, this level builds in an interpersonal commitment not seen nearly so markedly elsewhere. Here, for Lewicki and Bunker (1996), the metaphor is that of *musicians* playing together: individuals who have grown to know each other so well that they intuitively *know* the other will extemporize in a manner which complements their own creative insights, without needing to calculate, without needing to gather information, without needing to refer to role expectations. And critically, its metaphor is of more than one person. The logician calculates the consequences of a relationship; the professional declares a set of ethics which will guide others as to his/her behaviour; the gardener cultivates the relationship; but these musicians have moved to a level where the whole is greater than the sum of the parts, and where two people begin to act as one. Trust, here, is very special.

A normative hierarchy of stages

This analysis then provides a developmental view of trust based on the following stages:

- calculative trust (the logician);
- role trust (the professional);
- practice trust (the gardener);
- identificatory trust (the musicians).

Now I want to argue that this is a normative hierarchy, that relationships containing more developed trust are better than those with less developed trust, because trust leads to deeper more meaningful relationships, in which people come to respect each other's integrity and care for one another. These are spiritual goods virtually all would value. This does not, however, mean that all relationships require the highest levels of trust, for even though they may be intrinsically desirable, there is seldom the time to develop such a degree of understanding. Nor indeed may there be the need, given that many organizational interactions are low-level functional ones. Nor, finally, may such identificatory trust be possible, for there needs to be a high degree of compatibility between individuals for such a relationship to develop. Many relationships may be conducted at calculative, professional or practice levels, such levels of trust being quite sufficient to ensure the success of that kind of relationship.

However, two other things do follow from this analysis. First, while the further a trust relationship evolves, the more valuable and significant it becomes, it also means that violations of such levels of trust are more hurtful and damaging. The breakdown of such trust will then be much harder to repair. As Lewicki and Bunker (1996: 127) argue, trust violations here 'tap into values that underlie the relationship and create a sense of moral violation. They rend the fabric of the relationship and, like 'reweaving', they are expensive and time-consuming to repair, such that the fabric may never look quite the same.'

Second, and as noted above, because most people assign different value to different levels of trust relationships, loss of trust, or unilateral movement by one person from a higher to a lower level, is likely to be taken personally. Loss of trust hurts: people may never get over the breakage, may seek revenge, may even attempt to physically harm the trust breaker. Such perceived breakage can simply be through one party failing to keep a promise to another. But there are other, more subtle, breakages which cause just as much harm and animosity. Thus, as Sitkin and Stickel (1996) point out, loss of trust may result from the leadership and management of an organization – or the government of a country – imposing unduly detailed, restrictive or inappropriate procedures upon a professional workforce. This workforce – which sees its work as being defined at role or practice trust levels – now feels that it is being treated at a lower level of trust. Such trust 'demotion' then feels as if one were regarded as untrustworthy, and this is normally deeply hurtful, producing a vicious cycle of increasing distrust, leading to an increasing polarization of attitudes between the two parties. Any further sensible ideas by the other side are then rejected because of their place of origin. When this happens, 'party lines' become tightly drawn, and individuals may find that their 'group' demands of them an increasing 'groupthink' (Janis, 1972) – which is an ironic position for a group of professionals who initially defined themselves by their right and ability to make personal autonomous decisions. The likely consequence of this is a downward spiral: professional/worker distrust of government/management is interpreted as hostility to good intentions, or simple obduracy in the face of progress, and even more detailed prescription and low-level calculative trust is employed.

Understanding trust: the different levels

Micro-level trust

So trust has different foundations, and developmental levels, and in its various forms clearly operates at the individual, person-to-person micro-level. It has already been noted that it is a central component in any view of a person's integrity, and is therefore fundamental to people's perceptions of good leadership. It is also central to the kind of student–teacher relationships essential for good teaching. Being trusted is also critical to a person's morale, to self-esteem and to feelings of self-worth. Yet individuals need to believe that they exist within an organization, community or society which provides them with feelings of self-worth, which can guarantee them sanctions against those who would use the threat of force or violence, or who would break the trust embedded in a commercial transaction. Other levels then need to be invoked to provide individuals with psychological, spiritual and physical security, and we need to be able to trust these levels just as much as the individual we have just met. Such reflection suggests that there therefore exist at least two other levels of trust besides *micro-trust*: what will be called the *meso-* and *macro-* levels.

Meso-level trust

The meso-level of trust is that trust we have for the institutions within which we work. Meso-trust is widely dispersed, concerned essentially with belief in the culture and ethos of an organization. It is particularly important when any process of change occurs, for the management of change, suggests Louis (2003), is concerned with a number of issues: understanding the nature and purpose of the change, the behaviours required for it to happen, the outcomes which will result, and how and when the success of the change will be assessed. Louis (2003: 31) argues that trust is 'the bridge that reform must be carried over', but that this bridge 'is not solid, but built on changing emotions.' Her research suggests that loss of trust can happen with any area of change, and that when distrust is created, events are *interpreted* through this distrust. Trust is therefore critical to the success of any change. In her study, with respect to both the implementation of TQM policies, and the appointment of a new superintendent, she found that existing levels of trust or distrust shaped, and in some cases even determined, the perceptions of changes and therefore of their likelihood of success.

It is also significant, given previous discussion, that trust and distrust were talked about within a language of ethics, with terms like integrity, honesty and respect being used. And yet – and this is also deeply significant – despite the fact that Louis reports that neither she nor her co-researchers had any reason to believe that the administrators in low-trust districts were less honest, or less concerned about school improvement than those in high-trust districts, and this study took place over several years, she believes that existing low levels of trust almost certainly doomed their efforts to failure. Trust, then, seems to act like a lens through which people and proposals for change are interpreted, and which therefore affects the success of those aiming for transformational change. Unsurprisingly then, where there is a legacy of mistrust, 'reclaiming it during a change process appears very difficult'. And as worrying is 'the ease with which trust appears to be broken during periods of significant change' (2003: 31), no doubt because of the perceived threat and risk to the practice of those facing change. A final comment by Louis is just as sobering: 'we know very little about how leaders repair trust once it is perceived as violated.' Extrapolating from personal experience and literature, it is highly likely that such repair is a difficult long-term process, requiring the restoration of perceptions of integrity, honesty and respect. After all, as Iago said to Othello:

> Who steals my purse steals trash; 'tis something, nothing;
> 'Twas mine, 'tis his, and has been slave to thousands:
> But he that filches from me my good name
> Robs me of that which not enriches him
> And makes me poor indeed. (3.3.161)

Bryk and Schneider (2002) provide further insights into meso-level trust, for through their work in Chicago in elementary schools, they argue that trust at the meso-level should be understood not as trust between individuals, but rather as a 'relational trust' – a trust between the different groups (parents, teachers, principal and local government) who each play a vital role in attaining institutional objectives. They found that the development of such 'relational' trust was strongly correlated with school academic attainment when each group carried out their role obligations, and each group saw that the other groups were doing likewise. Where one or more groups failed to do this, school improvement was much less significant. Specifically, Bryk and Schneider argue that relational trust facilitated school improvement through:

- reducing the feelings of vulnerability that participants involved in major changes normally feel, and thus encouraging the use of innovative and creative ways of dealing with issues;

- reducing the transaction costs involved in such major changes, and thus allowing people to get on with their jobs;

- facilitating the sharing of problems between the different groups within these learning communities;

- the clear understandings by all the parties of their specific role obligations, and other parties' expectations;

- sustaining a focus by all parties upon advancing the best interests of the children, rather than individuals or groups concentrating upon their own personal interests.

This piece of research is extremely important, then, in supporting the view that trust is a vital ingredient in improving student achievement. It once more backs up the argument that low-trust, standardized educational institutions and systems, which depress the growth of trust, work against school and student improvement rather than for it.

Macro-level trust

The weakening of the third level of trust in western societies, the macro-level, is currently unmistakable, and points once more for the need to see the generation of trust as a two-way process, in which the representatives and creators of macro-trust need to consider not just whether they can trust the individual citizen, but whether they are providing the environment within which such citizens feel that *they* are able to trust others. Three groups in particular create this societal context.

A first group are politicians. Because they set a country's legislative framework, they frame the context within which people explore their existential possibilities. Yet it is a sad commonplace that politicians are among the least trusted of all occupations. From Nixon and the Watergate tapes in the USA, to the 'cash for questions' scandal in the UK, and onto invasions of other countries, politicians are increasingly viewed with suspicion. One result of this is probably public apathy in the political process, and a decline in the percentage of electorates bothering to vote.

A second group, that of the senior representatives of business, is a cause for as much concern. Businesses which recognize the responsibility they owe to their society increase the overall sum of macro-trust. Yet examples of company directors paying themselves huge pay rises while providing poor quality service to their customers, and cutting the pay or sacking thousands of workers, do little to promote trust in their practices. In the USA, three scandals in 2001–2002 – Enron, Merrill Lynch and World.com – severely undermined the trust of the general public in the business community, as massive lies were told about company health and profitability, and loyal employees lost their life savings and pensions, confirming for many the belief that in business the only rule seems to be ensuring you get away with wrongdoing.

The final group is that of the media. Here, macro-trust is lost when newspapers are irresponsibly used for political or financial gain. The power of newspaper proprietors allows them to distort the truth, to publish inventions as fact, and to vilify individuals who have neither the financial nor legal clout to fight back. Such a situation is serious; worse occurs when pusillanimous governments are as much concerned with keeping such journalistic pirates from criticizing them and their policies as in policing and enforcing ethical standards of journalism. The result is an increased perception that major representatives of macro-trust are colluding together, further reducing ordinary citizens' belief in the probity of society's representatives.

Yet the integration of macro-, meso- and micro-trust into an individual's view of life is not performed in some rational utilitarian calculative way. It is instead a long-term, deeply existential process, more felt than reasoned, one which underpins much of the individual's confidence in the rightness of the world. Healthy levels of macro-, meso-, and micro-trust provide a personal assurance, 'that in living, things "hang together" and without this there is no meaningful social/cultural activity' (Webster, 2002). In most instances, such confidence is pre-rational and unacknowledged, yet provides the support which allows us to explore ourselves, our relationships with others, our encounters with the unknown, and with the 'border situations' of our spirituality. Such existential trust then, is produced not only by stable relationships, but by the support of one's community for 'the community is not only porous to the invisible (to mystery, to our quests, to our exploration for meanings), it also offers the conditions that make its perception possible'.

And yet critically, 'the confidence in the worth of things is eradicable. Coherence, the context of meaning on which human activities depend, can crumble ... the communal basis for our identity is also a threat to its realisation'.

Such descriptions of the connectedness of micro-, meso- and macro-levels of trust, then suggest that not only are relationships at

Table 6.2 *The possible trust relationships between different levels*

	Macro-trust	Meso-trust	Micro-trust
Macro-trust	Macro–Macro (e.g. one government's feelings about another government)	Meso–Macro (e.g. institutional perceptions of government)	Micro–Macro (an individual's trust in governmental pronouncements)
Meso-trust	Macro–Meso (e.g. government attitudes to educational institutions)	Meso–Meso (e.g. one school's view of another)	Micro–Meso (an individual's trust of the institution in which they work)
Micro-trust	Macro–Micro (e.g. governmental views on the depth of specification on individual work)	Meso–Micro (e.g. institutional views on trustworthiness of individuals)	Micro–Micro (one person's view of another)

these different levels important, but that perhaps those *between these levels* are even more important, and particularly if such inter-level relationships then affect existing intra-level ones. Meier (2002) provides a good example of this when she argues that when teachers are not trusted by governments, teacher–student relationships may also be damaged, for if governments do not trust teachers, why, students may ask, should we trust them? Table 6.2 suggests the possible relationships and the synergy created between these levels.

It is also worth repeating the issue of benign and vicious circles – that attitudes on one side of a relationship will almost certainly affect the attitudes on the other side to *them*. Thus, governmental lack of trust in individuals is likely to generate dislike and lack of trust by individuals in the government. There is, then, an inevitable interactivity in all trust relationships which educational leaders need to bear in mind.

Understanding trust: the different functions of 'thick' and 'thin' trust

A final aspect of trust which needs noting is that provided by Uslaner (2002) who describes a difference between 'thick' and 'thin' trust.

Such a description is not a recommendation for one or the other, but rather the observation that they have different but equally valuable properties. Thick trust is seen between those individuals who have strong shared values, such as members of strongly inclusive communities like religiously-based schools. They tend to exhibit an understanding of one another which generates excellent community spirit, and which can provide a real sense of support to staff, pupils, and the general community. It is likely that human beings were biologically constructed as 'thick' trusters – prehistoric evidence suggests that human beings lived in small closely-knit communities, and it therefore would make excellent adaptive sense for extensive thick trust to be cultivated.

So far, then, so good. 'Thick trust' can be immensely helpful in generating good relationships, and in providing the citizen of tomorrow with a strong affective base. It promotes a strong inclusivity, which in a world of rapid change and constantly threatened fragmentation, can act as a much-needed bulwark. Yet strong 'inclusivity' implies 'exclusivity': for individuals to be identified as having such similar tastes and values that they can constitute a 'community', others who do not share these must necessarily be excluded. And by strongly identifying with people of similar values, beliefs, habits and practices, there is, suggests Uslaner, a real danger that walls will be built to others different from ourselves. The kind of trust that builds bridges with strangers, with people of different religion, colour or culture, is a different, 'thin' trust. It is a kind of trust which seems to be generated more by genetic inheritance, early experience and the example shown by one's elders, than by group norms. It is also built by long-term experience – for instance, by how an individual of a minority group member is treated by a majority culture.

These, then, are very different forms of trust. Yet, suggests Uslaner, the evidence is that 'thin' trust can lead to 'thick' – if we extend our hand more often than not to the stranger, we are much likely to develop healthy 'thick' relationships with those who are different from ourselves than if we don't. 'Thick' trust, however, if over-emphasized, may actually depress the likelihood of building thin trust – one is so wrapped up in one's community, that one either doesn't feel inclined or simply doesn't want to find out about others. Yet such a development might, in a globalized world, lead to many other kinds of problems besides those of fragmentation – we may become too keen to stereotype, to pigeonhole, to fear those who do not look like us, talk like us or dress like us. The implications of this for educational leaders should be clear: they may wish to create communal support for their learners, but they must not do this in a manner or to an extent which leaves these learners unable to reach out to those who are different. And this issue becomes all the more serious when allied to questions about fundamentalist and absolutist views of epistemology, for all too easily such views reinforce 'thick' trust orientations and prevent the kinds of thin trust increasingly necessary in a globalized age. This issue will be returned to in the next chapter.

Educational leaders and the generation of trust

Given the importance of trust demonstrated in this chapter, what can educational leaders do about it? The analysis of trust here suggests a number of different strategies which might be considered.

A first strategy, *acting upon the dynamics of trust*, stems from an understanding of the developmental stages of trust. An appreciation of these stages, and of the effect that promotion or demotion within these can have upon an individual, could provide a greater awareness of the reasons for low morale within institutions, as well as enabling leaders to articulate to others that the perhaps unwitting message of a particular piece of policy is precisely to send a message of demotion. An understanding of the dynamics of interaction upon these stages could also help educational leaders to understand and explain how easy it is to get into vicious or benign cycles of trust, and therefore be able to devise ways of reversing vicious cycles, or of initiating benign ones.

A second strategy, *understanding and dealing with the foundation areas of trust*, recognizes that trust is generated in three different ways: by agreement over values and value priorities; by individuals doing what they say they will do; and by demonstrating competence. Table 6.3 uses the relationship between professionals and government to show how trust might be enhanced. Here, educational leaders need to work towards strategies which harmonize the different value priorities, which help demonstrate the integrity of the two parties to each other, and finally, for both parties to demonstrate their competence in their own areas. Such measures, it must be stressed, need to come from both parties: in this case then, not just from policy makers, but from professionals as well.

A third strategy, *appreciating the mechanisms by which meso-level relational trust works*, implies a need to understand how everyday issues can help build trust between the different parties in an institution, and perhaps, by extrapolation, to build better trust beyond. Actions like reducing peoples' feelings of vulnerability in times of major change, of reducing transaction costs in change

Table 6.3   *Re-establishing governmental–professional trust*

	By government	By professionals
Harmonizing value priorities	Greater commitment to explaining reasons for policy, to provide the ecological context; policy creation recognized as both top-down and bottom-up; showing appreciation of professionals' work	Better explaining of educators' commitments; recognition of government rights and professional responsibilities
Proving integrity	Moves from calculative to practice and role trust; providing appropriate time for consultation and implementation of initiatives; incorporating feedback into policy reformulations	Providing research evidence on consequences of overwork; creation of, commitment to, and practice of, explicit set of professional values; viewing clients and stakeholders as partners
Proving competence	Recognition and reduction of aspects of teachers' workloads; commitment to meeting and discussing with varied stakeholders	Provision of evidence on student progression and improvement; commitment to evidential base for practice

processes to allow individuals to get on with the real job, of ensuring that problems are shared between the different groups within the institution, of facilitating a clear understanding by all parties of the obligations attached to their specific roles, and of focusing all parties upon the core objective of advancing student interests, all help to develop not only trust but higher student achievement.

A fourth strategy, then, is to *recognize that trust is a multi-level concept,* stemming from and across micro-, meso-and macro-levels. An awareness and understanding of this could help a greater appreciation of the location of a particular trust impact, as well as enabling articulation of the level at which a response needs to be made. Most educational leaders normally operate at interpersonal, organizational and interorganizational levels; however, the kinds of 'ecological' contexts described in this book, and the kinds of trust articulated in this chapter, suggest once more that educational leaders need to become increasingly aware of and proactive at the macro-social level as well.

A final strategy, *appreciating the natures of 'thick' and 'thin' trust*, can sensitise the educational leader to the need to develop both qualities in their organizations, and of the danger of a too-vigorous prosecution of either. A too-thin approach may lead to a lack of security and grounding for pupils; a too-thick grounding may lead to a lack of appreciation of other viewpoints, and a tendency to categorize and pigeonhole others on limited information, instead of reaching out to others, and through the exploration of differences, developing the existential growth and well-being of all. For the evidence seems increasingly clear that when people are trusted, their self-esteem is raised; when they feel good about themselves, they are able to feel good about others and to reach out to them; altruism is then more likely to be seen. And heightened trust, self-esteem and interpersonal altruism are strong foundations for better societies, and from there to the creation of a better and safer world.

Conclusion

Official recognition of morale problems in the teaching profession across the western world has placed trust back on governmental educational policy agendas. There are at least three pragmatic reasons for governments to take it seriously. First, lack of trust seems clearly linked to poor morale, and poor morale is heavily implicated in crises in teacher retention and recruitment. Such crises are good ammunition for opposition parties, and reflect badly upon governments at election time. Second, inability to develop and retain a highly skilled teaching force severely jeopardizes the achievement of official human resource strategies, and again has long-term political implications. Finally, research reviewed in this chapter suggests that enhancing trust is linked to the major governmental objective of increasing student achievement.

There are, however, other reasons for believing that trust will continue on governmental – and educational leadership – agendas for some time to come. One, as noted earlier, is that trust is increasingly recognized as a core element in the management of organizations working within a knowledge-based economy. These organizations are seen as needing to generate both greater intellectual capital, and a more flexible workforce. These are currently unarguable mantras in economically developed nations, and depend much more strongly than past arrangements on healthy trust relationships. Where flexibility is a desirable characteristic, discussion of trust becomes almost inevitable.

Other reasons are much less utilitarian. First, a happy, tolerant and healthy society depends upon the blossoming of trust relationships, both within communities and between them. Second, happy, tolerant and healthy individuals require a large degree of existential trust – the belief that others can be depended upon, as can the meso- and macro-levels of their society. If the first-order values of a society are not economic, but personal, social and moral, then trust has to be seen as a first-order value that should be promoted for its own sake. In such a society, educational institutions, and the relationships between teacher and student would necessarily be allowed, indeed encouraged, to promote the growth of trust.

However, once trust is lost, it is hard to recreate, and is normally replaced by mechanical and quantitative forms of external accountability, and such low-trust cultures have been endemic to the management of educational organization for so long that it is unlikely that this situation will be quickly turned around. But there is now a reasonable understanding of how trust works, and of the strategies to increase it, to believe that some of this lost trust can be regained.

Nevertheless, even when greater trust is sought from government, it cannot be seen as a license for professional autonomy. There can be no return to the teachers' secret garden, where only they knew what was happening. As Middlehurst and Kennie (1997: 59)) argue, the trust that must be built can no longer be built on mystique, it must be built on transparency, and this means a radical re-think of not only trust but accountability, and the forms with which professionals need to engage. This is a subject taken up more fully in the concluding chapters, where it is argued that professionals need to take a much more proactive approach. Trust is a two-way process, and if it is to be gained, the reasons for granting it must be clear and transparent. If those external to the educational process are to trust those conducting it, then professionals need to provide evidence of their practice, and justification for their conclusions. Educational professionals need to consider very carefully what committing themselves to becoming an accountable research-based profession would mean, and what giving evidenced-based robust reasons for their practice would entail. While fuller consideration will be developed later, the question here needs to be asked: if educators are to provide such robust evidence, what will be their basis for this? In an increasingly fragmented, postmodern world, some claim that all understandings are equally valid, just as others retreat into fundamentalisms which claim that only they have 'true' knowledge. It is also a world where some governments, in similarly fundamentalist mode, seem keen on creating teaching bodies that resemble training sects. In such a world, what should be the status of a teacher's knowledge base? This is the question of next chapter.

7 The impact on truth and meaning

The last chapter ended by asking what is the educators' basis for robust evidence. The epistemological basis for evidential claims is perhaps *the* critical nexus of questions for educational leaders. Yet, for reasons deriving from pressures of both commodification and control, they are increasingly difficult questions for leaders to ask. Commodification pressures ask for a primacy of the question '*is it useful?*' over that of '*is it true?*', deflecting educational leaders away from questions of truth and towards concerns of utilitarian worth. Pressures of control also steer leaders from educational concerns, for as Gunter (2001: 96) argues: 'the mandated model of headship . . . presented within current government documents does not see the headteacher as a head *teacher*, but as a leader and manager in an educational setting' [original emphasis].

When this occurs, leaders are diverted from questions of truth towards concerns of management, and from problem-posing to problem-solving. Yet if they are to be *educational* leaders, the question of robust evidence bases, and of the interrogation of the integrity of epistemological bases, have to remain central professional challenges. There are at least four reasons for this: professional, ethical, political and cultural.

First, then, if claims for the necessity of a flexibility of practice, the exercise of personal judgement, and of a degree of professional autonomy are to be taken seriously by outsiders, then professionals need to convince others that questions of truth are a critical element of professional ethics. However, for the last quarter of a century and more, that claim has been doubted as a rash of literature has argued that professional activity and an attendant autonomy have been no more than attempts by an occupational group to maintain what Collins (1990) called 'occupational closure' – the maintenance of power by preventing others from engaging in similar practices. The belief of such accusations was part of the reason for the curtailment of professional freedoms, and the introduction of systems of external surveillance and accountability. If professionals are to move beyond such frameworks, they need to be able to show that their practice transcends such self-interest. Part of this, as just argued, lies in a commitment to truth-searching, which is in part exhibited by the construction of a clearly articulated and argued evidence and research base for their practice. This then needs to be linked to moves towards a proactive accountability, which encompasses not only external quantitative measures as summations of the 'truth' of professional practice, but other more qualitative measures which pay due attention to the richness and flexibility of actual practice.

However, such action should not only be directed towards a search for the truth in some abstract sense, but as a recognition of the fact that professional practice is likely to be better realized by incorporating the different perspectives of those others who contribute to and are affected by such practice. This takes professionals' knowledge from a position of apparent unassailability, to one which makes it a contribution towards a larger picture. And this larger picture is one where professionals and others work towards a greater public good, and a more tolerant and caring society. And to realize such collaboration will involve professionals in a project of constituency building, in which all participants ultimately benefit the larger society.

So the development of such a core of expertise needs to be much more than a self-interested move – it needs to be part of an ethical and a political commitment as well. But finally, it needs to be part of a cultural commitment. Previous chapters have explored the greater fragmentation and standardization/control arising from globalized forces. These contradictory tendencies tend to steer individuals, cultural groups and societies into a too-rigid adoption of views, either in an attempt to maintain a simple picture of the world, or as a reaction against the economic and political excesses of other groups. However, individuals can also be steered into epistemological supermarkets, where one viewpoint is seen as acceptable as any other. Both positions pose significant problems for society and educators. One steers them towards an unthinking allegiance to the practice of performance sects, and from there to acts of intolerance and aggression, as decisions are made on the basis of authority, dogma or revenge, rather than from reason and critique. The other may lead to an individualism of taste and consumption as an offshoot of a larger 'postmodern' movement, which increasingly disbelieves in the possibility *or* validity of any large societal projects. The final result is a relativist view of the world, where there can be no universal truths, no one right way of doing anything, nor indeed any way of differentiating and judging one approach from another.

At professional, organization, cultural and societal levels, then, issues of epistemological absolutism and relativism need to be taken very seriously. This chapter examines four different perspectives on this, arguing that a 'provisionalist' epistemology not only best explains our understanding of the world, but provides a way for dealing with the challenges of relativism and absolutism, and provides a means of balancing cultural needs with those of individual identity.

Moving beyond absolute perspectives

It might be best to begin by stating the obvious: human beings *never* attain an absolute perspective on the world. As Scruton (1997: 120) remarked: 'We do not even have a concept of the world as it is in itself.' We are creatures of this world, with specific sensory capacities, who perceive the world through these. But our sensory abilities are limited instruments: we do not have the sensory capabilities to detect ultraviolet light like a bee, sense damp like a woodlouse, locate heat like a rattlesnake. However, not only our sensory apparatus limits us: because we are each born with different physical and mental capabilities, into particular times and cultures, which fill us up with expectations and assumptions before we can be critical with *their* take on what this external reality consists, we also know that we will have a particular (perhaps distorted) view of this reality. This will not only differ from member to member of the same culture, but be even more pronounced between individuals from cultures distant in geography and time. Wittgenstein once said that if a lion could speak, we wouldn't be able to communicate, so different would we be: some would say that the same may be nearly as true with other human beings at a cultural and historical distance. And of course we don't just perceive the world: we select certain things from that external world, both consciously and unconsciously, and ignore others. In so doing, we actively *construct* our reality. And when one adds a limited perceptual ability to a necessary construction of reality, there can then be little likelihood of any full apprehension of this reality. Only some supreme being could do that. Most of the time, we muddle through, living within our personal and social preconceptions.

Yet a critical function of education is to help improve on such muddling by critiquing the truth status of our knowledge and beliefs, and there therefore needs to be viable epistemological educational positions located between the absolute objectivity of a supreme being, and a postmodern social and personal relativity. How is this to be done? We can, for a start, ask whether there are any absolutes to which educators *can* turn. A first, I would suggest, is in the utilization of the basic canons of rationality. The laws of identity, non-contradiction and deduction are so integral to the fabric of the universe that it does not seem possible to imagine a world where other forms of thinking would be more appropriate: a thing, after all, either is or it isn't, and if *a* entails *b*, and *b* entails *c*, *a* absolutely *must* entail *c*. If we cannot function without such fundamentals of logic, then educators cannot choose to be rational or non-rational, nor should they suppose that this is an arbitrary choice for others. Here, perhaps, is one absolutism they can and should adopt.

At a less absolute level, it might still be argued that while human beings differ in their cultures, their histories and geography, all share the same categories in structuring and sustaining their experiences. Thus we all use the same mental categories of motives, thoughts and intentions; we all use the same perceptual categories of sight, hearing, touch, smell and taste; we all use the same moral categories of care, truth-telling, equality, freedom, justice and fairness; and we tend to divide our understanding of the world into the same knowledge categories of history, geography, music, mathematics, language, etc. Now such claims necessarily are much more guarded, in part because of doubts as to their universality: some cultures, like the Ituri pygmies, do not divide their understanding of the world into the same knowledge categories as we do. Furthermore, even if there is agreement on the categories, there is likely to be large differences on the importance of the contents within – societies like ancient Sparta placed much higher value than we do on bravery, as opposed to care. Nevertheless, if we can get people at least to talk the same language, to discuss these assumptions, then some progress is made towards understanding and agreement. Discussion on such categories is a good start.

Moreover, despite the debates upon objectivity within the philosophy of science, norms which attempt to transcend cultural preference are available: Lysenko's views on genetics became a laughing stock, not because the critiques were western or bourgeois, but because his theories were scientific nonsense, and were demonstrated as such. The nigh universal acceptance that the Earth orbits the Sun is not western propaganda, but the result of a rigorous examination of a theory by the scientific canons of empirical investigation, rationality and logic. The same kinds of approach needs to be taken with creationist views, with the myths of the Oglala Sioux, or with any other beliefs (and that of course especially applies to beliefs held by dominant cultures). Minimally, they can be celebrated as expressive of a group's approach and adaptation to changing conditions, and so should be treated with interest and respect, but if claimed as 'truth', need to be treated with the same epistemological scrupulousness as Lysenko's theories or the manner of the Earth's orbit.

Four epistemological positions

But even with such logical imperatives, and categorical parameters, educational leaders will still be faced by substantial variation and disagreement, and they are likely to meet and adopt one of four possible approaches in resolving knowledge claims (Table 7.1). These must be examined in further detail.

The fundamentalist

The first – *the fundamentalist* – may accept that they personally cannot know any universal reality, any absolute truth, yet still believe that this 'reality' or 'truth' is revealed by either a supreme being through particular holy books, or by the writings and speeches of a political guru. Most practices and values may be included in this description of reality and truth, and following the text of the book or speech in a literal and uncritical manner will therefore be seen as both essential and mandatory. From this position, educational leaders can derive great spiritual and practical comfort, for their role now is to find the best methods of inculcating such truths into their students. Where they are in the majority, policies of assimilation will not only be sensible and acceptable, but an act of great generosity on their part (even if the individual or group being assimilated does not at first see it that way). In situations where they are in a minority, there may well be a strong tendency for them to develop a 'thick' trust within their community of belief, and to build both physical and psychological barriers to others. Multiculturalism – the sharing and celebration of different views – will be anathema, and tolerance will in many cases be an undesirable leadership quality, for tolerance may suggest a weakness in following the revealed path. Organizing and running an educational institution in which a variety of beliefs were present would also be intolerable and nonsensical. Why would you expose students to false beliefs when the truth is known and can be taught?

Of course, the reality of the fundamentalist educational leader's life is not that simple, not that black and white. While there may be something of a gratifying clarity to the direction of their decision making, all educational leaders are normally faced by a plethora of

Table 7.1 *The Meeting of Minds? Four approaches to epistemology and their likely opinions of each other*

	Fundamentalist	Objectivist	Provisionalist	Relativist
Fundamentalist attitudes to:	*Fundamentalist:* Profound agreement or profound disagreement, depending on whether beliefs coincide	*Objectivist:* Strong resonance, but suspicions of backsliding from full commitment	*Provisionalist:* Some insight, but antipathy to such ideological weakness	*Relativist:* Profound disagreement, even antipathy to such a false position
Objectivist attitudes to:	*Fundamentalist:* Strong agreement, but a wariness over the too-passionate nature of the commitment	*Objectivist:* Profound agreement or profound disagreement, depending on whether beliefs coincide	*Provisionalist:* Some understanding, but concerned by such weak commitment	*Relativist:* Profound disagreement, even antipathy to such a false position
Provisionalist attitudes to:	*Fundamentalist:* A wariness: much too certain about what is necessarily uncertain	*Objectivist:* Understanding but wariness: too certain of what is necessarily uncertain	*Provisionalist:* Intellectual comfort; strong resonance	*Relativist:* An understanding of the position, but concern over implications of the position
Relativist attitudes to:	*Fundamentalist:* One take on reality, but not supported by the facts; worried by the social implications of the position	*Objectivist:* A possible take on reality, but not supported by the facts; worried by the social implications of the position	*Provisionalist:* Understands the need, but suspects P is too weak to follow through the full implications of the P position	*Relativist:* Paradoxically, must recognize that this (their own) is only one position, no better than any other

tasks during the day of quite short duration, which may be as simple as deciding how many toilet rolls to order, or deciding which brand of computers the school should use. Answers to these questions are not normally the domain of holy books or political beliefs, and in such situations a tolerance of views, the welcoming even, of other and different insights from within a 'faith' community, will be a normal and welcomed part of life. It is in the larger challenges – the school's direction, its curricula selection, its attitude to government policies – that the epistemological orientation will be seen.

The objectivist

The objectivist leader, like all others, will be faced by minutiae – the decisions made for pragmatic rather than educational, ethical or religious reasons. However, on the larger questions, objectivists, like fundamentalists, believe that they possess *the truth* on a subject. This may stem from a document which they believe is the revealed truth of a supreme being or a political thinker. It could, however, stem from an indoctrination in a particular culture – the English major in Africa in the nineteenth century who had no doubt that he was bringing civilization to savages. Yet both kinds would normally want to make a distinction between eternal truths, and other practices which, it is believed, are reflective only of the times and are not seen as a core element of their beliefs. The objectivist educational leader may then have a more difficult job than the fundamentalist, for there may sometimes be disagreements over what constitutes eternal truths and peripheral practices (for instance, the food one eats, the clothes the sexes wear, the education the different sexes receive). Nevertheless, the objectivist educator will, like the fundamentalist, see the inculcation of their truth as their primary responsibility, and assimilation of others as a proper goal. They will also normally be concerned at the idea of an educational organization which welcomes different beliefs, and which admits students from different cultural and value positions. The objectivist educational leader will, like the fundamentalist, see a primary responsibility in building a 'thick' trust between the members of the community.

The provisionalist

The provisionalist educational leader breaks radically with both of these positions. Like the fundamentalist and the objectivist, the provisionalist believes that there is a 'reality' out there, and that it is possible to come closer to an understanding of this reality. However, their optimism is now limited by many caveats. In terms of religion, he or she may believe in a supreme being who has an absolute perception of reality, but will not be convinced that this has been revealed sufficiently for human beings to have a 'road map' of what to do, and is deeply worried about those who would act out of such beliefs. In terms of politics, they will not wish to assign omniscience to another human being, no matter how cogent and learned their arguments appear to be. Professionally, they will exhibit a similar kind of humility: they may have expertise derived from professional training, but are convinced that better solutions to practice are provided when all parties contribute to the understanding of the problem. For the provisionalist, then, without a belief in the revealed truths of a supreme being or a political thinker, or in their own professional superiority, there can be no absolutist epistemology, but instead a need to accept that there must be a less than perfect appreciation of reality, and that different systems of belief are no more than different paths – and imprecise ones at that – to the appreciation of any 'truth'. Assimilation *of* others to a provisionalist point of view is then almost a contradiction in terms, while assimilation *by* others will be seen as an unjustified authoritarian imposition. Professionalism is an occupation of empowering others and listening to their viewpoints; multiculturalism a justifiable expression by others of their 'take' on some external reality.

Furthermore, their basis for reaching decisions is likely to be quite different from the fundamentalist's and the objectivist's. While they will use logic in their arguments, and use approximations of the 'objective' categories described above, yet at the last, both fundamentalist and objectivist will refer back to the revealed truth as ultimate justification for practices and judgement. These, being positions of revelation, where judgements and actions are dictated by a faith orientation, require a leap of faith in the validity and acceptance of the message transmitted, and cannot be fully open to an empirical examination or validation by the facts. Provisionalists are unlikely to refer to revelation. For them, justification must be based upon the processes of empirical enquiry, reason and logic. More than that, however, they will probably argue that use of these tools as ultimate justifications is a moral necessity, for once it is felt permissible to accept a position on authority, rather than interrogate and question it, they will feel that the road to tyranny and authoritarianism is open. Education – the opening out of possibilities – is for them then transformed into indoctrination – the convergence into specified solutions.

Nevertheless, provisionalist leaders may well feel pulled in absolutist directions. The need to make decisions may tempt some into working with the comfort and certainty of objective beliefs; and as Lindblom (1959) has shown, the reality of leadership is not one of examining and choosing between all alternatives, but rather, necessarily, of choosing from a limited selection. However, for the epistemological provisionalist, reflection is likely to suggest that the process of decision making needs to recognize a degree of uncertainty in the personal – or group – perception of the situation, and of a tolerance, a welcoming even, of others' views. A provisionalist leader's requirement to decide and act may then pull them towards the judgemental black and white, while their more philosophical side, as well as the pragmatic recognition that getting colleagues on board is better done by consultation, will suggest that many judgements and decisions must contain elements of tentativeness and sensitivity, a continual process of dialectic, of thought, testing and reflection.

The relativist

Yet the bases for a provisionalist position may seem very unsteady. By accepting that there can be no full appreciation of reality, and no certainty of how near one is to it, provisionalists may well feel pulled towards a more radical position which argues that because there can be no guarantee of certainty, no 'take' on external reality can be more valid than any another. This is *the relativist* position. The logic is inexorable: if we can only bring to an external reality the perceptions, understandings and values of, for instance (say) an early twenty-first-century white English-speaking male individual, then, consciously and unconsciously, so much is missed, so many assumptions added, that a reality is 'constructed' rather than seen. Who, then, is to say that one version is better than another? The 'truth', for the relativist, may then be no more than personal or cultural group truth. So when Banks and Banks (1996: 5), in an authoritative US text on multicultural education, stated that knowledge was no more than 'the way a person explains or interprets reality', by explicitly stating that knowledge *is* synonymous with a person's reality, one may be tempted to conclude that one person's reality is as valid as any other's, and that there can be no external standard by which to judge the validity – or acceptability – of a person's viewpoint. If such a position is reached, then the logic suggests that an educational institution should do no more than welcome or accept all and every point of view. The logic of the position will turn the organization into

an epistemological and values supermarket, where each epistemological 'consumer' may 'shop' for what suits them, and for which no
criterion other than personal taste is possible or necessary. Now
Banks and Banks do argue that knowledge contains both 'subjective
and objective elements', and that we must not abandon the quest 'for
the construction of knowledge that is as objective as possible' (1996:
65). But where 'knowledge' is seen as no more than an individual
expression – or choice – of a viewpoint on reality, it becomes difficult
to see how a relativist viewpoint can be avoided. And worryingly for
others, relativism doesn't necessarily entail a tolerance of other
opinions; it must accept that intolerance is as acceptable as any other
viewpoint. Paradoxically, then, cultural relativism can lead to the
establishment and practice of absolutist perspectives just as pronounced as those at the fundamentalist end of the spectrum.

The challenges of multiculturalism

So there are problems with all epistemological positions for educators, but particularly with respect to the treatment of different
cultures. Historically, absolutist, assimilationist views have been
most evident in many western countries, though with some variation.
Initial official US attitudes to different cultures, for instance, were a
schizophrenic mixture of the welcoming, the assimilationist and the
discriminatory. While pursuing what virtually amounted to the
genocide of indigenous native populations, and the enslavement or
apartheid of its coloured numbers, it nevertheless enthusiastically
accepted many persecuted minorities, mostly from Europe, in the
creation of a nation founded on individual freedom, personal responsibility, distrust of big central government and a passionate patriot-
ism, though even more paradoxically through the adoption of an
absolutist, assimilationist 'melting pot' mentality. As one state board
of education put it in 1884 (quoted in Hersh et al., 1980: 18):

> The danger to civilization is not from without, but from
> within, the heterogeneous masses must be made homogene-
> ous. Those who inherit the traditions of other and hostile
> nations; those who bred under diverse influences and hold
> foreign ideas; those who are supported by national inspira-
> tions not American must be assimilated and Americanized.
> The chief agency to this end has been the public school and
> popular education.

The Canadian experience was very different. Instead of the absolutist melting pot, the model was more that of a provisionalist/relativist mosaic. For while the USA was in large part defined by what it did (have a revolution and create its own identity), Canada was more defined by what it didn't do, which was to reject the American invitation to join them in revolution, and instead to remain within the British empire. With such comparative lack of revolutionary self-belief, with less ideological zeal, and with an already existent and vocal French minority (as well as an indigenous native population), there was within the Canadian psyche a much greater toleration of different views. The joke that the Canadian national character is one in search of a natural character, may well be a reflection of the much more tolerant view and less assimilationist treatment of minorities than was seen in the USA.

England, by contrast, has had many waves of immigration, yet, because of a very settled Anglo-Saxon culture, has tended to adopt an absolutist, monocultural approach, and assimilationist views such as the following were the official approach to immigrants as late as the 1960s:

> a national system of education must aim at producing citizens who can take their place in a society properly equipped to exercise rights and perform duties which are the same as another citizen's. If their parents were brought up in another culture or another tradition, children should be encouraged to respect it, but a national system cannot be expected to perpetuate the different values of immigrant groups. (Commonwealth Immigrants Advisory Council, 1964 quoted in Troya and Williams, 1986: 12)

Given these different cultural backgrounds, perhaps it is not surprising that multiculturalism originated as a term and a policy in Canada, when, in October 1971, Premier Trudeau introduced it in a visit to Winnipeg, in a move to placate groups who felt excluded by previous emphases on Anglo-French biculturalism. Some of these groups, however, were not cultural or ethnic in nature, but feminist or gay who felt that they had undergone similar kinds of oppression. Multiculturalism as a policy, then, not only spread beyond Canadian borders to challenge and then largely replace assimilationist policies in most other western countries, but also developed into a movement within which many different kinds of groups demanded greater recognition and rights. This also began a process of what Hollinger (2000: 102) calls the 'diversification of diversity' – where initial attempts to recognize particular groups led to members of these groups coming to see such descriptions as too constrictive for their proper individual or group expression. Why, after all, should a member of the Iroquois nation have to accept the label of 'Native American' when such a label hides a much greater variety of affiliation?

Provisionalists and relativists might both welcome such moves as more in keeping with a relaxed tolerance of views. Surprisingly, perhaps, fundamentalist and objectivist members of minority groups might also see this as a positive move, a step away from assimilation- ist attempts by dominant cultures, even if it meant coexistence with other cultures. Nevertheless, they might still wish to harbour their communities behind walls of thick trust; and the more that majority culture right-wing backlash occurred, and the more that they devel- oped a cultural self-confidence, the more they might feel inclined to build such walls. An 'anti-racist' argument would also develop which suggested that until majority cultures recognized that power struc- tures which disadvantaged minorities also needed to be dismantled, problems could not disappear. Nor should one forget that resistance from dominant social groups stemmed not only from an unwilling- ness to acknowledge previous discrimination, but also from holders of fundamentalist views within these dominant cultures. Neverthe- less, for a while movement towards some form of multiculturalism seemed inexorable, the high point probably being in 1999 in Canada, when Nanavut, a self-governing territory for the Inuit which occupies one-fifth of the entire geographical area of the country, was created.

But such changes have brought more problematic elements. 'Multi- culturalism', like 'excellence', 'quality' and 'standards' has become a 'hurrah' word – one which is criticized at your peril. Indeed, in the USA, other sources of affiliation – particularly national ones gener- ated in an earlier period by the dominant culture – have become increasingly less tolerable. Hollinger (2000: 157) suggests that anyone arguing that there exist viable and desirable affiliations beyond the level of the cultural group, is in serious danger of being branded as a right-wing reactionary monoculturalist: 'Closing down and exposing as reactionary those who try to address the question of the national culture has become a popular search-and-destroy sport.'

He and other critics argue that 'culture' as a symbol of a particular ethnic group has largely become uncriticizable, individual cultures being accorded a quasi-religious stature. There are a number of reasons for this. One is the influence of a woolly epistemological relativism, which declares that because cultures have different origins and different reasons for being, they are beyond criticism by other cultures, and particularly dominant cultures. Such relativism does not have to be invoked by sub-cultures: at the United Nations World Conference on Human Rights in 1993, China, Iraq and other Asian dictatorships invoked such cultural relativism when suggesting that western criticism of their human rights abuses was no more than western imperialism in another guise.

Another reason for rejecting intercultural criticism stems from the belief that cultures are organic unities, and that to pick at, or suggest the deletion of particular practices, will therefore and necessarily harm the entire 'body'. Rockefeller (in Clausen, 2000: 80), for instance, argues that:

> human cultures are themselves like life forms. They are the products of natural evolutionary processes of organic growth. Each, in its own distinct fashion, reveals the creative energy of the universe, working through human nature in interaction with a distinct environment, has come to a unique focus. Each has its own place in the larger scheme of things, and each possesses intrinsic value quite apart from whatever value its traditions may have for other cultures.

The result of such relativism and organicity, has led, suggests Wolfe (1998), to the creation of a new, Eleventh, Commandment – 'thou shalt not be judgemental', where cultures and their practices can then only be critiqued by members of those cultures themselves, though it becomes hard to see how minorities within those cultures could then do so against dominant power holders. Given such strong feeling, representatives of other cultures, and particularly dominant cultures, are driven towards either adopting an uncomfortable and dangerous relativism, where all and everything must be allowed if it is a product of a different culture; or they are driven to adopt a similarly entrenched but ideologically different fundamentalism, where the two communities build walls to keep the other out, just as much as to keep their members in. Communities then end up building strong trust between members, but then lack the means or desire to develop intercommunal values and understanding. The result may well be the creation of inter-communal uncertainty and tension as communication between communities diminishes.

Questions of absolutism

Movement towards fundamentalist or entrenched positions may be for epistemological reasons. But they are as likely to be derived from experience, personality and cultural attitudes. Where dominant cultures denigrate minority beliefs and practices, minority cultures are likely to retreat into more rigid positions, for denigration fuels resentment, and resentment fuels polarization, which eliminates the voice of the moderate, and which then allows those of extremist positions to come to the fore. Similarly, and as noted by Chua (2003), where economically dominant minorities exist, the same kind of reaction may also be seen in the disadvantaged majority. However, where concern, interest and respect for other views are shown, even for views which are very dissimilar from one's own, the chance of reaching a peaceful and enriching understanding is much more likely. They are even more likely to occur where social and economic changes occur at the same time. So leaders of dominant cultures, including educational leaders, precisely because of the power they hold, need to be first to attempt such measures.

Attempts at reconciliation are critical, as are wider social, economic and political changes. Nevertheless, any society attempting to establish principles of personal freedom, discussion of differences, and the use of reason and communication, must address absolutist viewpoints. In some cases, this leaves only one possibility. As Chesterton (1909: 58) argued over a century ago: 'there is a thought that stops thought. That is the only thought that ought to be stopped'.

This is an uncomfortable position, for it requires that a stand is taken which repudiates approaches denying personal liberty and individual autonomy. But absolutist problems are not just 'out there' – if educational leaders need to look outward to potential divisions within their society, they also need to look inward to the kind of organization they lead. If in the past intolerance came from 'professional absolutism, it is much more likely nowadays to come from the creation of the kind of 'performance training sects' discussed earlier. A training sect is potentially quite as fundamentalist and intolerant as anything outside of education, for both are arguments founded on authority and simple assertion rather than on debate and reason. They should be resisted as a matter of political, ethical and educational principle.

Questions of relativism

If the previous section suggested the need for a tolerance of different approaches, but that such tolerance can go too far, the same must be said with respect to the contrary position where all is tolerated, for a proper commitment to personal and social projects is thereby undermined. Relativism is corrosive: at the personal level it can lead to the belief that nothing is to be taken seriously – a contradiction which will be returned to. At the social level, it can undermine a commitment to notions of public good, to the creation of a better world, and thereby permit the continuance of an unjust status quo. In western societies, the ultimate beneficiaries of such a position would likely be those proposing the primacy of individual consumption, for this would result in individuals without social purpose, communities without commitment, but entrepreneurs with immense wealth, power and social control.

However, the answer is not for a reactionary swing to authoritarian and indoctrinatory positions, but for professionals to possess the arguments to reject relativism. For the educational leader this does not mean that we can know nothing, only that we cannot be *certain*. We can have good grounds for believing in and doing things, and we can work towards better ones. Karl Popper (1982: 111) writing on the provisionality of science, says this as well as any:

> the empirical base of objective science has ... nothing 'absolute' about it. Science does not rest upon solid bedrock. The bold structure of its theories rise, as it were, above a swamp. It is like a building erected on piles. The piles are driven down from above into the swamp, but not down to any natural or 'given' base; and if we stop driving the piles deeper, it is not because we have reached firm ground. We simply stop when we are satisfied that the piles are firm enough to carry the structure, at least for the time being.

Popper is pointing out that while we may never reach firm ground at the bottom of the swamp, our structure 'does the job' for the moment. Yet we have some stability, and the likelihood is that with continued effort, we can attain even more. While 'absolute' certainty may never be reached, our attempts can still provide a degree of confidence, which can strengthened with further effort. We do not need to believe that structures are not worth building, and attempts at improvement not worth attempting. Our attempts may not be perfect, but they can be adjudged as better or worse than previous efforts.

Relativism, then, can damage by suggesting that there can be no grounds for deciding between one stance and another. In so doing it can lead to a vacuous tolerance of all beliefs which corrodes attachment to communities, and can generate an egocentric individualism. Yet there is a profound weaknesses in the relativist viewpoint, for by its own logic, it cannot assert that its standpoint is more 'true' than any other. Yet to be put forward as a serious point of view, it has to make an exception for itself: it must assert that it is the one belief that can transcend cultures and be universally true: that all views are relative. This it cannot do. By its own logic, it cannot put itself forward.

All too frequently, however, such logical entailment is not seen, and from cultural relativism develops a relativism which suggests that not only should cultures be immune to outside criticism, but so should groups and individuals. When this happens, values and personal positions become no more than matters of choice, criticism of another becomes bad taste, and is counselled against as it leads to loss of self-esteem. This kind of individualism, fed by the flames of a rampant consumerism, is now seen as deeply problematic for western societies – a very different situation from 50 years ago, when books like Whyte's *The Organisation Man* (1957), and Riesman's *The Lonely Crowd* (1950) identified its antithesis, social conformity, as the major societal disease, while Milgram's *Obedience to Authority* (1974) portrayed the pathological consequences. Nowadays, the illness requiring treatment is seen as a corrosive individualism, and in order to bolster societies against this, the development of community spirit is seen as essential, the explicit teaching of 'good character' increasingly fashionable.

An important challenge for educational leaders, then, is the development of organizations which facilitate communication and critical dialogue between different 'cultural' groups, and which provide an overarching set of values to which all can commit themselves. While some communitarian suggestions, as well as allied character education approaches, seem to do little more than trade an unwelcome fragmentation of personal affiliation for an autocratic collective imposition, Ignatieff (in Hollinger, 2000: 134), rather unfashionably has called for a 'civic nationalism' which envizages the nation-state as a body beyond any group defined by race, colour, religious affiliation or ethnicity, in which individuals sees themselves as 'a community of equal, rights-bearing citizens, united in patriotic attachment to a shared set of political practices and values'.

While leaving until later major questions about the ability of the nation-state to take on such a role, this does at least suggest the need for a series of nested levels of affiliation, where meaning is not generated primarily by ties of history and ethnicity, but rather by overarching democratic political principles, underpinned by a tolerance and respect for others, located within a provisionalist epistemology. It is a theme which will be returned to in the next chapter.

Questions of identity

The kinds of fragmentation so corrosive of personal and social identity can then lead to demands for separatist communities and for excessive individual compliance to norms and rules, and indeed there is good evidence that some conservative proponents of community and character education would have us embrace such moves (Bottery, 2000). Certainly, communal affiliation is essential to individual psychological well-being, as well as in the quest for self-understanding, and as a base from which to explore people and groups beyond. Nevertheless, *enforced* identification and assimilation are neither necessary nor acceptable; and yet such positions occur when cultures are viewed as entities having lives in the same way as individuals do. When this happens, cultures cease to be vehicles for individual identity, betterment and purpose, and threaten individual liberties by assuming greater importance than their members.

This is understandable politically: members of dominant cultures tend to accommodate to organized minority groups rather to individual demands, and it therefore makes good political sense, in negotiating with others, to assert a cultural uniqueness and unity. Moreover, personal identification with a group may provide a sense of historical continuity and psychological security. However, cultural groups are not unchangeable entities, but a melange of previous culture and practice, borrowing from other groups, other quarters absorbing other practices and values all the time. Where cultural customs and practices are cocooned, guarded and rigidified, they become fossilized and may hinder individuals wishing to remain members, but who, through such things as inter-cultural marriage, may also wish to extend their conception of themselves and their possibilities by joining other groups as well. This is a natural consequence of intercultural exchange, yet it means that cultures are never complete and distinct entities, but amoeba-like, are influenced by, absorb, merge and in some cases are absorbed by other cultures. To protect them by building physical and psychological walls simply imposes on members what many minority cultures have accused majority cultures of – an enforced acceptance of values and practices, rather than the thoughtful, conscious and willing adoption by individuals.

Perhaps even more problematically, when cultural reification occurs, terms like 'culture', 'community', and 'ethnic group' become more than physical and psychological places for shared norms and values: they can become places where *truth* is decided and stipulated. A relativist epistemology provides no access for communicative critique by outsiders, and intercultural debates about the norms by which ideas are evaluated are discarded. Moreover, because the cultural group is ascribed primacy over the individuals within it, issues of power – who gets to decide which ideas are counted as true – may come to dominate internally. Educational leaders then must recognize that cultural groups provide valuable perspectives upon reality, which should be treated with respect, but which cannot all be equally valid 'takes' on reality. It suggests an epistemological provisionalism combining a respect for viewpoint, with a humility of appreciation, yet nevertheless with a rigour of investigative critique.

Conclusion

While this chapter began with an examination of the impact of global forces on questions of meaning, it has moved inexorably to questions of identity, and particularly the changing and increasingly multiple nature of individual identities within this complex world. Now the term 'identity' is a critical one, for it suggests a fixity and permanence when locating individuals within cultural or ethnic groups. In some societies, given the social and economic divisions, such fixity is probably inevitable. Yet for other societies, 'affiliation' may be a better term, for it suggests a more voluntary and conscious choice than a genetic or cultural imposition. It also suggests, rather better than 'identity' does, that in these societies, many individuals no longer live within the circle of one bounded community, but experience a shifting between several affiliations. One can then be English, black, of Barbadian/Irish parentage, living in Yorkshire, female, a geologist, married, a mother, a ten-pin bowler and a Christian. Some of these are of genetic or historical inheritance, some are self-chosen, many can be traded or discarded. This is a process which has occurred since time immemorial, only now the forces and changes which the individual confronts are more numerous, the fragmentation of structures both more facilitative and risky. The question for the educational leader then becomes: what should be *recognized*, what should be *accepted*, and what should be *supported*?

First is the need to recognize and support an epistemologically provisionalist view of the world. It is likely to be the most correct, and the most safe. It accepts that all visions may have some truth to them, and that a world where no one claims a monopoly on the truth is likely to be a safer, more tolerant, less violent one. In supports the vision of a pluralist society, with different values and views, for not only are these to be tolerated – as long as they tolerate others – but the exchange of viewpoints is seen as a valuable and worthwhile thing. The celebration of each 'take' on reality is the recognition that each most probably enriches our understanding of the world and of the challenges we face, and helps towards a better public good. A core professional ethic to be supported, then, would be one of a humility to other ideas and points of view, for there must always be some doubt that our view is superior to another, and far more certainty that it is not the complete picture.

Second, while such epistemological provisionalism suggests a celebration of different viewpoints, it also recognizes that views are grounded within particular cultural realities. It may be fine to embrace such provisionalism at one level; but when groups are economically and politically disadvantaged, such viewpoints need to be backed up by an understanding of political realities, and the need to work from such political realities towards this philosophical position.

Third, such provisionalism, endorsing a celebration of a variety of viewpoints, does not mean their uncritical endorsement. All attempts at the resolution of professional issues, or wider societal problems, must accept that insights, mores, practices and values of particular groups (including professional groups, and dominant cultures) are provisional and partial. The beliefs of any particular group should not be seen as permanent and inflexible entities, but as needing to be flexible and adaptive, leading always to the creation of new communities of meaning. There also needs to be recognition that there are tools by which the practices, beliefs and values of such communities can be critiqued. These may still provide no final answers, but they do support the view that educational leaders need not subscribe to an epistemological and value relativism.

Fourth, there is great political and psychological value in groups of affiliation, and such 'communities' need to be promoted either within or through educational systems, and because prescribed affiliations limit both individual freedom and commitment, communities need to be built upon the principle of voluntarism. Nevertheless, because such communities cannot exist without people contributing to them, educational leaders need to support notions of responsibility and duty as critical elements, as the other side of individual freedom in the promotion of healthy communities; it is unlikely that they will be realized without being pursued.

Fifth, given the dramatically expanded number of challenges and opportunities with which individuals are confronted, and the psychological need of these same individuals for affiliative groups, they will need the opportunity to move between different kinds of discourse.

Our English, black, Barbadian/Irish, Yorkshire, female, geologist, wife, mother, ten-pin bowling Christian, probably needs all of these to enjoy a fulfilling life, and educational organizations should support her attempts to access them. And when she can celebrate being both Barbadian *and* Irish, and this is not thought strange but an expression of her individuality, a vibrant 'post-ethnic' era will have been reached.

Finally, in a global world, with the challenges of epistemology and ethnicity, and with the need for individual psychological reaffirmation, different levels of discourse are needed, different levels for asserting identity, of cherishing our 'truths' while simultaneously critiquing them. The personal, familial, local, cultural, national, supra-national and global may all be sites for affiliation, and sites for nested identity, where individual freedoms and responsibilities are both exercised, which all may have legitimate claims to more equal support. Yet this has hardly been the case in the past. The key level for identity and obligation for the last few hundred years has been the nation-state. However, in a global age, where people look for, and are provided with, tangible symbols of legitimacy both below and beyond the level of the nation-state, confining allegiance to one level is increasingly problematic, and it is critical to the raison d'être and functioning of educational institutions, and for the students within them, to examine just what impact global forces are having upon such nation-state political identity. This is the subject of the next chapter.

8   *The impact on identity*

From personal to political questions of identity

In previous chapters, we have seen how global changes are creating issues of excessive control and standardization, how individualistic consumerism accelerates the atomization of communities, and how a relativistic epistemology facilitates a fragmentation of community and identity, and yet may also generate attempts at an authoritarian communal compliance. We have also seen how, in some societies, unmediated global ideas can lead to dangerous instability and violence.

We not only live in a changing world: we need to change to survive in it, and individuals need to be helped within educational institutions to deal with this complex of forces by a continued stress on criticality and autonomy, balanced by the cultivation of individual responsibility towards communities, for only by individuals recognizing communal needs can such communities provide the conditions within which freedoms can be enjoyed. Such communities, however, need to be as balanced as the individuals within them, by not only providing individual support and requiring a sense of individual responsibility, but also by not being so inclusive as to prevent individuals from moving and choosing between communities. This means recognizing that many lives are, and in some cases should be, increasingly founded upon sets of different allegiances, within different groups, different 'communities'. Individuals are, then, increasingly defined by a set of nested identities, rather than just by single hegemonic national ones.

So while much personal identity is not, and cannot be chosen, individuals need to be given the freedom to construct as much of themselves as they can. They cannot choose their genetic makeup, nor their early formative experience, and they cannot choose the 'community' into which they are born, just as they cannot choose their family. Yet individuality can be celebrated through the opportunity to select and join particular groups, interests and tastes. In a world of globalized opportunity and fragmentation, individuals are more likely to be healthy and stable, and communities vigorous and dynamic, if individuals, aware of the nature of this global world, are encouraged to use its opportunities rather than to suffer them, and if communities recognize the ever-changing needs of individuals and adjust to these as well. By charting and developing self-chosen identities, supported by and paying into a complex of communities and a nest of political options, individuals may well then make the most of the coming world.

This then is a conception of personal identity which asks for both greater freedom of choice and an acknowledgement of responsibility by individuals to their chosen affiliations. This is intimately linked to conceptions of political identity, for citizenship asks similar questions about personal freedom, commitment and community support, as it is a relationship between an individual and a larger body, this time political, in which that individual is provided with certain rights, while certain responsibilities are demanded in return. The conception of citizenship thus adopted largely determines the kind of political terrain within which the individual pursues his or her self-constructed identity. It is therefore vital to understand the kind of 'citizenships' – and the bodies who provide liberties and support in exchange for duties and responsibilities – with which individuals will be dealing in the future. This chapter will therefore examine why nation-state citizenship is increasingly seen as a construction rather than as a 'natural' level of allegiance. It will also describe and evaluate the kinds of responses which nation-states employ to meet such critiques, before it examines the effects of these changes upon conceptions of personal and political identity. Finally, it will ask what challenges this poses for educational leaders and their institutions.

The boundaries of citizenship

At the present time the nation-state is the political body which almost hegemonically defines the terms and boundaries of citizenship. Most people think they have a fair idea of what this means, yet 'nation' and 'state' are terms with quite different qualities, and combining the two can produce wide variations. 'Nation', suggests Anderson (1996) is a concept constituted by:

- Being *imagined* – for most members will never know the majority of their fellow members.

- Being *limited* – because all have finite (if sometimes elastic) boundaries.

- Being *sovereign* – for all are founded on notions of self-determination.

- Being a *community* – for despite vast differences of wealth and powers, all members share a sense of comradeship.

Conversely, the 'state', McCrone (1998) suggests:

- is partly defined by its *unity*;

- is partly defined by the fact that it is *artificial*: an institutional arrangement engineered for specific political purposes;

- is based on a *rational-legal legitimacy*, expressed above all in its complex of laws.

'Nation-states' can then occupy any position along a spectrum. At one end are (i) *'state-less nations'*, where groups see themselves as communities, yet which fail to have distinct territories over which they have sovereign command. These would include Basques, Catalans and Kurds, their treatment greatly depending upon the nation-states within which they are enclosed. At the other end of the spectrum, however, would be (ii) *'nation-less states'*, where multiple ethnic, linguistic and religious groups are incorporated and assimilated into deliberately engineered entities called states. Hobsbawm (1990: 88) thought this a good description of the USA, as, he argued, 'Americans are those who wish to be.' As we have seen, there is an increasing problem for such engineered entities constituted of more than one 'group' – a problem which increasingly confronts the USA.

However, nation-states don't just vary in shape and nature: there is actually very little about them – or the political hegemony they have enjoyed for the past 200 years – which is natural. The relationship between the individual and the larger political body has changed throughout recorded history, from the highly participative if parochial involvement of the citizen in the Ancient Greek city state, through the development of Roman notions of civic virtue, on to the variety of claims upon the medieval citizen, and then to the secular emphasis of the Renaissance. It is only relatively recently that citizen allegiance has been located with the claims of the nation-state. Yet even into the twentieth century its hegemony and people's allegiance to it was problematic. Fishman (1972: 6) tells the story of peasants in Western Galicia who, when asked if they were Poles or Germans, could only describe themselves as 'quiet', or 'decent', identifying as they did with the specific location they inhabited, not having travelled conceptually from such concrete geographic identity to a more abstract national one. Such 'voluntary' allegiance then has had to be constructed. As the Italian nationalist D'Azeglio declared after the Risorgimento, ' We have made Italy, now we have to make Italians' (Hobsbawm, 1990: 44). Part of this was achieved by the valuing of a national language as opposed to the local dialect. Part was by creating a national standing army (and its use against other 'national' foes), and part, as Green (1997) has shown, was by the creation of education systems with the explicit intention of inculcating a nation-state citizenship.

The nation-state, as a concept, then, is fluid, and historically and geographically contingent, and is not – as some would see it – a natural part of the political landscape. A growing awareness by individuals of this artificiality – and of its claims to citizen allegiance – is increasingly one of its problems, and a challenge which educational leaders running educational institutions, with the responsibility of inculcating a sense of citizenship, need to consider.

The nation-state citizenship bargain

Nation-state citizenship involves a form of exchange, even if such an exchange is in many cases never fully articulated. In return for a transfer of identification and loyalty by the individual from the local and regional to the national, most states have historically provided a greater liberty of the person, freedom of speech, rights to justice and the ownership of property – what Marshall (1950) called *civil citizenship*. As we have seen, Marshall argued that citizenship also needed to consist of *political citizenship* (the right to be involved in the exercise of political power) and finally *social citizenship* (the right to a degree of economic and health security, and educational provision), as essential to the exercise of the other forms. Moreover, by suggesting that these not only followed chronologically, but that they represented 'an evolution of citizenship which has been in continuous progress for some 250 years' (1950: 10) – he was suggesting a natural, almost inevitable progression from the earlier to the later, as nation-states perfected their citizenry arrangements.

Their success – and underpinning nationalist ideologies – is seen not only in terms of eruptions of radical 'hot' nationalism, but, as Billig (1995) suggests, in the way in which much nationalism is so obvious, so overt, and yet therefore so hidden, that we fail to recognize the 'flags' that constantly direct us to identify with it. On this account, even the weather forecast is about the weather of *this nation*. As Billig says: 'The metonymic image of banal nationalism is not a flag which is being consciously waved with fervent passion; it is the flag hanging unnoticed on the public building' (1995: 8).

Marshall's (1950) analysis probably accepts too easily the grounding of citizenship within a nation-state base; if this is the case, and the nation-state as an entity comes to be threatened, so also will be its role as primary guarantor of citizenship rights, and of people's instinctive identity with it. Citizenship of the nation-state, then, is a construction, which can be deconstructed, and an increasing awareness of the artificiality of the nation-state is therefore a developing threat to its perceived legitimacy.

In addition to this increased awareness, there are at least five other forces acting upon the nation-state which combine to undermine this legitimacy. These are:

1   The social citizenship critique.

2   Economic globalization and ensuing 'mean and lean' developments.

3   Political globalization and supranational developments.

4   Consequent Sub-national reactions.

5   The rise of 'citizen consumers'.

Threat 1: the social citizenship critique

While modern-day critiques of the individual's right to *civil* citizenship are still largely at the political periphery, there has been substantial debate regarding the need for an extensive *political* citizenship, particularly with respect to participation in the political process (see, for example, Schumpeter, 1942). Furthermore, with the resurgence of the political Right in the 1970s and 1980s, there has also been a sustained attack upon a *social* concept of citizenship, the provision of welfare goods in health, social security and education legislation – in essence, the provision of an extensive welfare state – in order to furnish individual citizens with essential prerequisites for political participation. Critiques have come essentially from three directions. The first has come from a philosophical and ethical aversion to a paternalistic, 'big brother' state; the second from a decline in the belief that the nation-state is capable of adequately providing such goods; the third from a belief that the market is a better provider of such 'goods'. All of these have affected the status and legitimacy of the nation-state, and therefore the citizenship bargain, for if the state is viewed as an essentially malevolent entity, needing to be kept as small as possible, having neither the capacity nor the capability of providing the goods it has claimed to provide, what right has it to demand allegiance, loyalty or duty from the individual? Why should individuals provide these when it does so little for them?

Together the arguments suggest that when governments embark on welfare legislation – and therefore on forms of social citizenship – they necessarily over-reach themselves, they encroach on individual liberties, and disrupt the efficiencies of normal market processes. These problems, it is argued, tend to lead to more government intervention, which in turn leads to a vicious circle of interventionism and the abrogation of personal liberties. Together, these arguments have helped forge a political consensus across the western world which remains very influential today. Even 'Third Way' approaches accept many of its tenets, for a limited and 'affordable' welfare state is still seen as the best that is possible or desirable, the public sector needing to emulate the practices and values of the private sector, as seen for instance, in the enthusiastic espousal by Clinton and Blair of the works of writers like Osborne and Gaebler (1992), and in the use of 'internal' and 'quasi' markets to increase the productivity and efficiency of the public sector. Such critiques argue that citizenship should not extend beyond Marshall's (1950) civil and political conceptions; yet such limitation would seriously weaken the bargain between the nation-state and citizens benefiting from an enhanced social citizenship. This is a process exacerbated by a second threat, the increased impact of global forces.

Threat 2: economic globalization and 'mean and lean' national developments

While present-day governments do not wish to return to the social democratic welfare policies of the mid-century, there is still evidence to suggest that states are *more* interested than previously in taking responsibility and central direction. The reasons for this lie in the rise of globalization forces. Two of them – the economic and the political – are directly implicated in threats to the legitimacy of the nation-state, and will be examined in this light as threats 2 and 3.

Economic globalization, as we have already seen, is that agenda aiming at the creation of unrestricted global free trade, and is increasingly influential in the functioning of nation-states, as more national policies are penetrated by global economic structures and demands. Such influence is spread by three main factors. A first is the ability of individuals and organizations to move finance easily and quickly around the world, thus preventing nation-states from creating 'fire-walls' to protect particular welfare or cultural agendas from the movement of finance out of a country. A second influence is the activities of supra-national organizations like the IMF, the World Trade Organization and the World Bank, which, while having different foci, lock nation-states into international free-market agreements which limit their room for individual manouevre. The third influence is the activities of trans-national companies (TNCs) who, because of their ability to relocate finance, plant and labour around the globe, are able to pressure and manipulate governments, not only into short-term acts of tax breaks and financial 'sweeteners', but also into longer-term policy changes.

Now it has already been mentioned that New Right responses to increased pressure upon welfare state expenditure have largely been predicated on attempts to reduce expenditures, primarily by emphasizing efficiency as a key value, the employment of a vigorous and assertive management ideology as opposed to a previously more facilitative administrative one, the re-education and employment of professionals as 'on tap' rather than 'on top', and the use of quasi-markets to heighten financial awareness and to stimulate entrepreneurialism. This financial austerity road continues to be travelled by many nation-states, despite changes in the colour of government. Hood (1995) in his analysis of such policies, argued that this may be for very different reasons, some nation-state governments, like that in the UK, believing that the hollowing out of state responsibilities, and reductions in welfare expenditure, will not only make the country leaner and fitter to compete on the global economic stage, but will also lead to a greater desired privatization. Others, like that in Sweden, he suggests, have adopted similar austerity policies precisely to *protect* the welfare state by making it more lean and efficient. In the USA, the advent of the Bush government increased this trend of state cutbacks and financial austerity. As already mentioned, Luttwak (1999) describes this approach as a 'turbocapitalist' one, where a widening of income differentials, a lower average wage, increased worker insecurity, and decreased welfare and labour protect, are seen as prices worth paying in generating greater economic growth, less bureaucracy and more entrepreneurship. Such policy approaches have, however, normally been correlated with increased wealth differentials, and with increasing crime rates and greater social dislocation, suggesting that their practice has led to a reduced citizenship allegiance, as individuals have felt less responsibility to a political body demonstrating increasingly less responsibility and care for them.

Threat 3: political globalization and supranational developments

If economic globalization is one form of threat to nation-state legitimacy, political globalization has added to this pressure. The drive to political organization above and beyond that of the nation-state has reduced many areas of traditional nation-state responsibility, and resulted in the formation of trans-national governmental organizations. Their increase has been dramatic: Held (1989: 196) estimates that in 1905 there were 176 international non-governmental organizations: by 1984 there were 4,615. Another critical aspect of political globalization has seen nation-states relocating themselves into larger trading blocks for greater political and economic leverage and protection, and to have access to enlarged markets. Yet such re-location moves the focus from the national to the transnational, and might involve jettisoning many (national) practices, and the acceptance of some new ones (honouring the EU flag?). In the process, it might well reduce allegiance to nation-states. A final aspect of this threat is seen in countries with economically dominant ethnic majorities. For when, as argued by Chua (2003), political globalization in the form of democracy is combined with the advocacy of global free markets, the result can be an even more dangerously unstable nation-state as groups fracture down cultural and ethnic lines, with impoverished majorities attempt to wrest economic and political power, and affluent minorities attempt to extinguish the democratic voice.

Finally, and as Billig (1995) argues, the impact of such personal relocation on political allegiances does not have to be positive. While it may help the individual choose a freer existence, it can also lead to a fragmentation and integration of purpose, for these global forces facilitate a postmodern stance of playing with ideas rather than being committed to them. By permitting personal exit from identification with the national, a postmodern psyche which 'is at home playing with the free market of identities' (1995: 134) is increasingly facilitated. In so doing, nation-state citizenship is undermined and degraded.

Threat 4: the sub-national development

Globalization and supra-national identities may have an air of inevitability about them, but this does not mean that people relish them. As already seen, the larger become those bodies and organiz-ations which control peoples' lives, the more individuals may feel distanced and alienated from the political process, the less loyalty they may feel, becoming global nomads, wandering between places which provide no sense of identity. As this happens, the more they are likely to relocate and define themselves at the local level, treasuring 'the traditions that spring from within' (Naisbett and Aburdene, 1988: 133). The increased political visibility of separatist movements in Quebec, Wales, Scotland, Macedonia, Catalonia, the Basque region, the Kurdish part of Turkey, Eritrea, and the general increase in intra-state rather than inter-state conflict, often defined around ethnic and religious identities, all suggest that current nation-states are failing to satisfy current needs for personal identity and allegiance. Such tensions may also be seen within a number of other nation-states in the future – China, for instance, has 56 regional groups within its boundaries. However, the interaction between economic and cultural factors is likely to be both extremely complex and difficult to predict. If nation-states becomes too small to deal with the big problems of life, and too big to deal with the small problems, complex, highly individual and problematic scenarios are likely to be created, and nation-state legitimacy will be threatened from below as well as from above.

Threat 5: the elite consumer development

A fifth threat, what Lasch (1995) called the 'revolt of the elite', is one in which the wealthy cease to identify themselves and their futures with any particular nation-state, and utilize the market option of 'exit' rather than the citizen option of 'voice' in order to achieve their personal aims. This 'elite consumerist' agenda stems from a combina-tion of political arguments and economic opportunities. A first may be found in a critique of Marshall's (1950) 'evolutionary' hypothesis of citizenship, for within it is embedded the notion that a necessary but insufficient condition for citizenship is the recognition and acceptance of equal rights between genetically *un*equal individuals, and that for this to happen, there has to be a measure of social and economic equality as well. However, once the wealthy can escape the demands of such citizenship, such allegiance is likely to founder

under the weight of the responsibility left to the rest. Furthermore, the argument that taxation is theft, and a violence to the person, in that the state arbitrarily extracts from its richer citizens' moneys to be redistributed to its poorer citizens, also lends support to those who would opt out of one national policy approach and locate themselves and their earnings within a more favourable regime. This, suggest Martin and Schumann (1997), is leading to a split between the 20 per cent elite of the world's population who are globally connected, and the 80 per cent who constitute the less privileged national majorities.

We have already seen how Davidson and Rees-Mogg (1999) have taken this analysis one stage further by extrapolating from the present to a situation, not too far-distant, where the cyber-economy will allow any individual, any organization, to relocate their financial holdings and themselves to the most profitable (i.e. least taxed) location around the world. The result could be, as Davidson and Rees-Mogg argue:

> you will no longer be obliged to live in a high-tax jurisdiction in order to earn high incomes. In the future, when most wealth can be earned anywhere, and even spent anywhere, governments that attempt to charge too much as the price of domicile will merely drive away their best customers. (1999: 21)

If this occurs on a large scale, the implications would be extremely serious, as 'the leading welfare states will lose their most talented citizens through desertion' (1999: 269), and through the widespread flight of capital and disappearance of major contributors, many nation-states would find it increasingly difficult to provide the basics of welfare. It would, however, be extremely risky for any nation-state to increase taxation, or even maintain it at present levels, for this would provide incentives to others to relocate their finances. The scenario is then for present fledgling competition between nation-states in terms of taxation policies to dramatically increase, and for citizens (at least the rich ones) to become consumers, 'shopping around' for the best 'deal' in low-cost citizenship. Davidson and Rees-Mogg's conclusion is that 'the massed power of the nation-state is destined to be privatised and commercialised' (1999: 259), and in the process citizenship in any recognizable form will disappear. While they believe that there will be 'transition difficulties' (1999: 224), prospects nevertheless are 'bullish' – even though the price seems likely to be walled enclosures for the rich, and the demand for new 'survival strategies' by the poor such as crime (1999: 256).

One must be careful to separate the prescriptive from the descriptive in this argument. While I personally find ethically grotesque their prescriptions for a world made up of competing tax havens, where the poor live either by serving the rich or by scraping a living in walled-off locations of alternating anarchy and tyranny, their arguments still require serious consideration and rebuttal, for the central argument is based upon a description of existing realities and extrapolations from these, and whether one likes the consequences or not, the possibility of individuals opting out of citizenship commitments and relocating to a more attractive state is an increasingly possible – even probable – one. Were this to happen on a sufficiently large scale, a nation-state's ability to demand responsibilities and duties from the remaining population would be severely threatened by the inability to deliver *its* side of any citizenship bargain. What then can be the responses of the nation-state to these threats to its existence, to current conceptions of citizenship?

Nation state responses to citizenship threats

If these developments threaten the existence of the nation-state, they also challenge current conceptions of citizenship. There exist at least six different responses by nation-state governments:

1 Responding to the rich.

2 Enhanced competitive skills.

3 The human capital option.

4 Intensifying citizenship.

5 The social capital option.

6 Enhancing participation.

Option 1: responding to the rich

If financial elites *are* increasingly 'shopping around' for the most competitive residence option (i.e. the state which provides them with the most security for their assets, and demands the least in return), one response might be premised on the assumption that while the rich can move, the poor cannot, so the emphasis should be upon meeting the needs of the rich. This is the option described critically by Luttwak (1999), and approvingly by Davidson and Rees-Mogg (1999), yet it seems to be a mixed blessing, whatever your income. It clearly rewards the rich and enterprising, but produces constant stress and insecurity for the less talented. It also seems to threaten the legitimacy of the nation-state. It would be an ugly place to live if you were not rich, ugly even if you were rich and used your money to ensure that this ugliness was kept out of sight. Moreover, Wilkinson's research (1996) suggests that societies with higher income differentials between rich and poor also have the lowest life expectancies, for both poor *and rich*. There is then some doubt whether such societies ultimately profit even the rich within them. It is also clear is that such states would not sponsor any form of citizenship worthy of the name.

Options 2 and 3: the enhanced competitive skills and human capital options

Considerably less odious, though still problematic, would be enhanced competitive skills and human capital options. These are placed together because they combine to form a particular approach to the development of workforce skills in a competitive economy. The *enhanced skills option* has formed the core of 'Third Way' approaches to education. It is predicated upon the belief that governments shouldn't provide the kind of extensive welfare safety net seen previously for individuals who fail, but rather should equip citizens with the requisite skills to make them employable in future job markets. And while Tony Blair may have declared 'education, education, education' as his policy priority at the 1997 UK general election, this is an education focusing tightly on employability, in the belief that an employed workforce is a more socially cohesive and prosperous citizenry. Social cohesion and prosperity, then, provide the props to support nation-state legitimacy. Yet there remain major problems with this approach. One is that a concentration upon skills for employability may fail to tackle issues of structural inequality, and thereby exacerbate an already unequal situation, for if governments fail to recognize that individuals do not begin from the same starting line, then they fail to provide equal entry into the competitive skills marketplace. While another strand of many government policies has been an emphasis upon inclusion agendas, some critics (for example, Clarke et al., 2000) argue that these two agendas are incompatible, and are being implemented with the managerialist approaches of administrations of a different political hue, and therefore are unlikely to be effective. A further problem is that an 'education for employability' agenda all too easily becomes rigid and dogmatic in what must be learned, leading as mentioned earlier to a 'trained incapacity' (Lauder et al., 1998) of individuals to adapt to rapidly changing scenarios. Governments may then have to place more emphasis upon freedom and creativity, as these facilitate the kinds of responsiveness which rapidly changing national and global economies demand.

The second part of this economic package, *the human capital option* has been a major way in which western governments have conceptualized education since World War II. Indeed, organizations like OECD seem, if anything, to be increasing this emphasis. This is in part due to the apparent success by Asian Tigers like Japan, Singapore, Taiwan and Korea, where governments have not only provided the training for workforces in competitive skills, but have been much more intrusive, attempting to mediate and fashion global forces to suit the particular talents and capabilities of the nation's workforce. Ashton and Sung (1997) provide a particularly good example of how the Singaporean government adjusted its education policies to match its economic objectives, prioritizing the raising of workers' skill levels to match the needs of 'preferred' multinationals, a policy which governments like that of the UK New Labour party have attempted to copy. Yet it is noteworthy that many of these Asian Tiger governments have changed tack in the last few years, recognizing the strength of the 'trained incapacity' argument mentioned above: their workforces have been compliant but unimaginative, hardworking but uncreative, and it is the nurturing of imagination and the fostering of creativity which, Tan et al. (1997) argue, are now seen as essential to successful competition in the future.

Options 4 and 5: the enhanced citizenship and social capital options

If the last two options concentrated upon the skills required by a workforce, the next two emphasize the attitudes and affective skills required. *The enhanced citizenship option* is concerned with sustaining the legitimacy of nation-states as definers of citizenship, by stressing the responsibilities and rights of citizenship, as well as by utilizing the flags of 'banal' nationalism. Formal education, and citizenship education in particular, are critical here. In England and Wales, for instance, citizenship education has become statutory in secondary schools, given the objective of helping students 'to become informed, thoughtful and responsible citizens who are aware of their duties and rights' (QCA, 1999: 12), and aided through the stipulation of critical study areas such as history, social studies and national literature which contribute to the contextual understanding of this particular form of citizenship. While some of the thrust of such educational legislation is more properly located within the 'Participation option' discussed below, nevertheless, part is much more directive, as exemplified in the widespread espousal in the USA, for example, of 'Character education' approaches, which stipulate the particular virtues which are societally desirable, and then attempt to inculcate these into populations (Bottery, 2000; Arthur, 2002). This helps to account for the paradox that in a culturally heterogeneous world, where the fragmentation of norms and values is a developing reality, teachers are experiencing an increasing control and direction of the content and practice of their work. Here then, education is being used by nation-states in attempts to bolster their legitimacy, and there exists the possibility that the more centralizing and directive that governments become, the more they will lose the support of at least part of their electorates.

The second option, *the social capital option,* is concerned with enhancing the social bonds between individuals to reduce fragmentation, and to increase cooperation and social cohesion within communities and workforces. While there is considerable debate in the literature as to the precise meaning of the term (see Baron et al., 2000), the present endorsement by a number of governments of Putnam's (2000) conception of benign social capital as a key force in generating trust and better relationships between individuals, and within fractured communities, is a strong pointer to its use as an aid in reducing a more general societal fragmentation.

Option 6: the active participatory option

Perhaps the most acceptable approach, from a liberal-democratic perspective, this is one which is less restrictive, less directive, more participatory. It sees the saving of the nation-state through its ability to motivate and engage all its citizens in societal projects to create not only a more equitable and harmonious society, but a more equitable and harmonious world as well. Current conceptions of citizenship education within the English National Curriculum, for instance, are fairly radical, arguing that citizens must 'shape the terms of such engagements by political understanding and action' (DfEE, 1998: 10), and that students must learn 'about and how to make themselves effective in public life' (1988: 64). Nevertheless, it is non-statutory in the early years; only 5 per cent of curriculum time is supposedly devoted to this area; it has a teaching force which is still largely ill-equipped to deal with it; and it is based around formal school education. This active participatory option is better seen in its wider expression in the Council of Europe project on Education for Democratic Citizenship (Council of Europe, 2002), which argues that the development of EC citizenship is a multistranded project, encompassing not just appropriate school curricula and organization, but life-long workplace and informal learning, which stresses inclusion and social cohesion. Crucially, it suggests that *'Education for Democratic Citizenship* is not mainly and essentially the inculcation of democratic norms, but more essentially the development of reflective and creative actors, the strengthening of the ability to participate actively and to question' (2002: 16).

Such aspirations address more directly concerns that nation-state citizenship is dying from within because of apathy, a fragmentation of values and the exclusion of minority groups, yet it remains to be seen whether a supra-national project can have genuine impact at the nation-state level, and whether sufficient individuals wish to commit to it as an at least part-replacement to nation-states in terms of citizen allegiance.

Whither citizenship? Whither personal identity?

Of the options considered, western nation-states seem to be converging around a conceptualization of their role as:

- The provision of an 'affordable' welfare state.
- An increase in the steerage of areas where they can exert effect, such as in education, and particularly in skills training, and in enhancing social cohesion.
- A re-assertion of notions of 'community' and 'duty'.
- A stress on the value of citizenship participation.
- The acceptance of the expanding influence of global markets and multinational forces.

However, this issue will not be resolved in purely planned, conscious, transactional terms, for citizenship is also determined by affective notions of identity, which run deep into the subconscious, underpinned by the hidden 'flags' of 'banal' nationalism, and aroused when ethnic and religious identities are threatened. In such circumstances, it is not enough to look at current governmental strategies, at the 'bargains' between state and citizen. One also needs to look at the ways in which citizenship is currently formed, and whether there is any evidence that individuals are beginning to conceptualize their relationship with the nation-state differently. Carrington and Short's (2000) study of citizenship conceptions by US and UK children is useful here, for it shows that while UK children are more likely to think of citizenship in terms of being born in the UK, and of being able to speak English, US children are more likely to identify citizenship in terms of its formal, juridical, components. This indicates that the USA, with an identity based historically upon a deliberate attempt to construct a nation through the prior assimilation of immigrant populations, but now facing a reaction by many groups against such policies of national assimilation, is increasingly producing individuals who see citizenship much more clearly as a construction. This is in contrast to the UK, where the evidence suggests that individuals still tend to see citizenship as a 'natural' and given identity, though the creation of Scottish and Welsh assemblies is increasingly developing perceptions of English, Scottish and Welsh nationalities, rather than a UK nationalism, which may lead to the same kind of constructivist perceptions.

Constructivist conceptions of citizenship were also (surprisingly) found by Parmenter (1999) when investigating children's attitudes to citizenship in Japan. This is a country wedded to a view of history as 'Kokkahattenshi' – as a description of national unity, whose official education policy has historically been, and continues to be, that of the inculcation of a conception of citizenship by ethnic-genealogical definitions of national identity. Yet Parmenter argues that: 'The majority of students . . . seem to believe that national identity is an identity that has to be constructed by the efforts of the individual through his/her acquisition of knowledge, development of abilities, maturity and way of living . . . the individual has a choice in whether to be "Japanese" or not' (1999: 6).

Furthermore, she found that many student teachers now believe that in a globalized world, national identity is becoming increasingly redundant. Such findings suggest that a global generation is growing up, more able than previously to see the ways in which nation-state citizenship is constructed. And once a construction is seen, it can then be asked whether it should be exchanged or broadened to include something else.

It must then be doubtful whether present strategies will enable nation-states to repel all the threats listed above, for their ability is compromised not only by some of the actions they take, and by an increased recognition by populations of the construction of nation-state citizenship, but also by an increased tendency for individuals to rationally calculate advantages. The result is likely to be a paradoxical combination of enhanced identity for some at the subnation-state level, and for others, an enhanced consumerist orientation towards nation-state citizenship. And as nation-states attempt to mediate the effects of global markets by relocating themselves within supranational bodies, *this* has the effect of spurring on identification at subnational levels, as people search for an identity which provides greater personal meaning.

However, perhaps the major conclusion is that because of the continued intrusion of the market into all walks of life, and the increased mobility of individuals and their capital, there is likely to be a new kind of citizen in the twenty-first century – the consumer citizen. In an increasingly mobile and knowledgeable world, there will probably be an increase in the number of individuals who actively choose their citizenship commitments. Nation-states will then have to compete for their custom. *Proprietor* and *customer* may be more frequently used terms in discussions on citizenship than *allegiance* and *duty*, and nation-states will have to be far more concerned with the views – or apathy – of their citizens than previously, because increasing numbers will be able to – and want to – vote with their feet if service is unsatisfactory. Exit rather than voice may, for many, become the preferred option. When bumper stickers appear in the USA which urge people not to vote, because 'it will only encourage them', then the leaders of national governments need to take note; and educational professionals will be asked to pick up some of the pieces.

Citizenship education and educational leadership

So what of citizenship education, and the responsibilities of educational leaders? What are the likely implications for political identity if trends follow the lines described above? If the political and economic threads are pulled together, citizenship education will probably be either an emphasis upon one, or a blend of the following four options.

One bleak scenario from a democratic point of view would be of nation-states, or those who control the reins of power, resorting to force, both mental and physical, in order to retain their power. They would then seek to increase control and direction of their educational institutions, not just in terms of the curriculum, by intensifying a skills/competency approach in those areas felt necessary to equip the nation's 'human resources' for successful competition on a global economic stage. But it would also be in terms of 'character education' and 'social capital' approaches, which would attempt to inculcate particular virtues and dispositions into a population, not only to further their attractiveness to trans-national companies as pliable and compliant workforces, but to also reduce the discontent consequent upon increasingly national economic 'mean and lean' policies. Such a prognosis would not only contradict the need for a flexible, creative and entrepreneurial workforce, but would also destroy the development of human potential and political freedoms, and educational leadership would be reduced to a limited implementational role. One could well envisage a depressing cycle of state domination, political protest and repressive state reaction, within which citizenship education and educational leadership became little more than mockeries of the true meaning of the terms. It is not a pleasant scenario to contemplate.

A second scenario, which might well be allied to the first, follows from the threats to identity, and is a citizenship education predicated upon a fear and exclusion of others, and an intense commitment to particular beliefs and practices, which would be indoctrinatory and intolerant of other beliefs. It would probably take all the elements of a 'hot' nationalism, based upon particular geographical, ethnic, religious, cultural or linguistic differences, and combine them with the elements of a 'banal' nationalism to inculcate an unthinking allegiance. It would be the domain of the fundamentalist or objectivist educational leader, and would prohibit the development of 'reflective and creative actors' who would wish 'to participate actively and to question' (Council of Europe, 2000). This is not only a scenario for distant underdeveloped countries, the 'Talibans' of the world: with an education sector constituted of performance training sects, there would be too many examples close to home to permit such complacency.

A third and more optimistic scenario would follow from the recognition by nation-states that nation-state citizenship is a concept which needs to be more participative, while nested within different levels of citizenship. Enhanced participation is an increasingly attractive notion to many developed nations, in part because of democratic ideals, in part because of the recognition of increased electoral apathy, and in part as an element of a larger agenda requiring citizens to take greater responsibility for things the state no longer feels capable of providing. There are then some hopeful signs here. 'Nested citizenship', an idea raised by Heater (1990), and recognized by the

Council of Europe (2002), nevertheless has yet to receive any real recognition by individual nation-states. However, were they to accept that some allegiance was better than none, and that they needed to work towards a global system within which some power was ceded both upwards and downwards, then national education systems would need to provide their citizens with an understanding of the different functions, rights, responsibilities and powers of these different levels, and with the skills to negotiate their way through such complexities.

A final scenario follows the trends of an increasingly consumerist world, where the market penetrates deeply into every form of societal activity, 'capturing' their discourses, and rendering their values second order to those of the market. In such circumstances, 'citizenship' becomes another consumer good, to be designed, displayed, marketed and sold like any other. Nation states would then not provide education, nor would they have ownership of plant, nor ownership of content and ideas. Educational opportunities for both child and adult would instead be the subject of intense competition between rival private organizations, who would sell not only different kinds of access, but different kinds of experience and different kinds of curriculum. We already live in an age where universities sell their products online around the world, and private companies see education as a huge market opportunity to be exploited like any other. On this scenario, nation-states would be no more entitled to a monopoly on educational provision than would any business. If citizenship became a market commodity, then the function of educational institutions and their leaders would likely be that of providing the discerning consumer with the knowledge and skills to make the right choice in selecting from the different 'brands' of citizenship on offer.

Conclusion

To draw some conclusions concerning the effects of citizenship developments upon individual identity, and of the challenges this poses for educational leaders, we need to retrace some steps to consider the future of the nation-state, and of citizenship within it, for on these rest the future of citizenship and political identity. An initial problem with talking about the 'death of the nation-state', as we have seen, is that it has no one Platonic form: it is possible to have forms which are driven primarily by the needs of the state, while equally possible to have forms driven by the needs of particular ethnic groups, linguistic minorities and religious communities. As a current nation-state splits, it is therefore possible to have smaller, but still viable, political entities which deserve the same name: the Czech Republic and Slovakia are as identifiable as 'nation-states' as was Czechoslovakia (and, some would argue, with even more justification than the previous entity). As current nation-state power is relocated below, there is reason to believe that such relocation of identity and allegiance may well result in the proliferation of new 'nation-states', rather than in the disappearance of this form and level of political organization. If this were the case, individuals may well continue to assign their primary political allegiance to the nation-state, and educational leaders will be asked to facilitate this.

However, as the forces of globalization drive nation-states to divest some of their powers to supra-national organizations, then at least three things happen to citizenship and personal identity. One is that people become more aware that nation-states, citizenship and its current location, are constructions, which can therefore be deconstructed. This might mean that citizenship does become a multilayered concept, that people locate their allegiance at different levels, and therefore begin to construct themselves differently. However, and secondly, given the fact that new 'nation-states' may be constructed out of amalgamations or dissolutions of existing arrangements, we may be faced with a complex of multilayered attachments which resist simplistic analysis – a conclusion arrived at by a different route at the end of the last chapter. It is highly likely, then, that people will come to more fully understand the constructed nature of citizenship, and by implication, their increasing freedom to choose in this construction, and thereby in what *they* would like to be.

So what does this suggest for educational leaders? It probably means that at a social and political level they will have more challenging careers, being perhaps more controlled and directed in the navigation of their institutions, yet forever open to the political winds of change. At the personal level, their students, their colleagues and they themselves, will face an increasingly less clear and fragmented political arena, where personal, political and educational ideals face implementation in much less certain scenarios. They will, as the Chinese curse says, live in interesting times.

PART 3
BEGINNING A RESPONSE

9 Learning communities in a world of control and fragmentation

This book has suggested that there is a paradoxical combination of control and fragmentation to be seen at global, national, institutional and individual levels. The control element is in large part a product of global movements towards standardization which are then seen at both governmental and organizational levels. Fragmentation, on the other hand, is in the main a consequence of new forms of knowledge capitalism, and of the effects of assaults upon the political certainties of the nation-state. As a consequence, both the state and the market are acting in ways which damage the public forms of discourse which allow citizenries to articulate, debate and determine ways of life not directed by state or market. If such forms of discourse are seen as valuable societal goods, then we need to ask how they can be supported, and what kinds of education system and schools would best serve in dealing with such pressures. This chapter then considers the responses of two contrasting kinds of schools, 'banking' and 'community' schools, while considering criteria by which their success or failure should be judged.

The existence of 'banking' schools

Educational systems and professionals are constantly urged to meet the challenges of a rapidly changing age, and to provide individuals with new skills, new competencies, and new attitudes, to help them succeed in a competitive economy. This is often seen as the key ability of 'learning how to learn', and 'learning', rather than 'teaching' is therefore increasingly given the pivotal role within education systems. Some of this constitutes exciting, even

165

liberating exhortation, yet much of this thinking derives from a business sector (particularly a US sector) obsessed since the 1980s with global economic competition. This obsession has translated into similar calls within educational systems, without it being fully appreciated that education is concerned with more than economic productivity, and that while unceasing change *may* be the economic answer, it is not always so for education, and particularly for social, moral and political aspects of its work. When the difference of these agendas is not acknowledged, excitement and liberation can quickly turn into confusion and both personal and societal fragmentation are then produced. And when this happens, calls are made for a reassertion of the 'community' to prevent such fragmentation, and to halt perceptions of social and moral slide. While it is unsurprising to find that 'learning' and 'community' are joined together to become flagship terms in an advocacy of 'Learning Communities', a careful eye needs to be kept on the ultimate purposes of such communities.

The adoption of this idea needs careful consideration, for it is neither simple, nor an unalloyed good. Perhaps the best way to illustrate this is to begin in the negative and describe schools which are *not* learning communities. Strike (1999, 2000) suggested that many such schools – which he termed 'banking schools' – have large and diverse student populations. They also have stakeholders with differing views on the goods education supplies, and thus may differ considerably on the meaning of 'human flourishing'. These schools, having to respect such diversity, do so, Strike suggests, not by adopting any one view of human flourishing, but instead by attempting to provide a broad and instrumental menu, in the hope that such provision is valued by all even if no ultimate ends are vocalized. Schools on this account are like banks, providing students with credentials to be cashed in for other goods, like income, status, jobs, powers. Strike here extends Freire's (1972) 'banking' concept of education, in which knowledge 'deposits' are placed in the individual learner's head, to be 'withdrawn' on suitably profitable occasions. Knowledge is then a commodity, and education is instrumentalized, for schools are created to provide educational services for individual purposes.

Now there are a number of reasons for the continued existence and support of such schools. One is as a consequence of a commitment, widely held in politically liberal societies, and particularly in the USA, to provide public institutions celebrating a diversity of views. Society is then constituted by different visions of the good, the state ensuring that all are permitted such liberty, as long as particular visions of the good do not prevent others from celebrating their versions. The state itself, then, cannot be a community, and should not aspire to be one: it is consituted primarily to secure and implement a shared view of justice. And state schools, as representatives of such a state, also should not be community schools, for they must be no more than educational representatives of that liberal view. Schools then should do no more than help individuals to extract from the education system what they need to build and celebrate their personal visions.

Such liberal inclinations, many would argue, are essential to societies trying to promote respect and tolerance for different values and lifestyles. However, there is clearly a sting in the tail of this position, for the logical endpoint of such a view must be that schools cannot, as public institutions privilege one vision of the good over another, and therefore cannot be communities. This, for some at least, links liberal views uncomfortably closely to the kinds of relativist postmodern perspectives outlined earlier, which lead to an inability to recommend or condemn any other view. They also seem to support the kinds of consumerist perspectives where the only thing that matters is the satisfaction of individual consumer need. And both of these perspectives undermine larger, shared conceptions of any society, liberal or otherwise.

The result, critics would argue, is a liberal expression of schooling which in reality has no vision of the good life, for by attempting to cater for all, none are celebrated – the vision is simply too 'thin'. Questions of epistemology are now being reframed in organizational terms, for if 'liberal' schools admit of too much, they embrace a relativist standpoint; while if they attempt to shore themselves up by embracing particular communally oriented viewpoints, it becomes difficult to maintain a liberally-oriented set of public values. The two can sit very uneasily together.

A second reason for the support for such non-communal schools may be creation by default – legislative frameworks and social and political thinking may have prevented the construction of much else. Thus, across the western world, as initiatives by both right- and left-wing governments over the last 15 years have tended to homogenize school output, individual communal visions have also been curtailed. Centralizing national curricula, literacy and numeracy initiatives, and external accountability mechanisms, have all contributed to the creation of standardized cultures of teaching. And while the paradoxical and simultaneous espousal of market-led policies was in part to generate greater school variety, it has also steered schools into consumer-led policies, rather than vision-led ones. Finally, while governmental adoption of 'Third Way' approaches has largely consisted of state-led attempts to provide the skills required for competition in the job market (Bottery, 2000), it has seldom developed into the specification of greater societal goods.

Such legislative initiatives provide a final reason for the existence of such schools – a lack of commitment, or an inability, by school leaders to interpret their role through a particular set of values. Writers like Ball (1999) and Wright (2001), for instance, argue that headteachers are now so deluged with legislative implementation that they actually have little time or room for manoeuvre to vocalize and implement a set of core values, while my own research (Bottery, 1998) has suggested that the professional is drawn into a process of self- and role definition determined principally by the implementation of external directives, rather than by definitions of the meaning and purpose of the job. To be fair, there is other research (see, for example, Day et al. (2000); Gold et al. (2003), suggesting that the best school leaders are capable of framing events and responding to policy through clearly articulated personal visions. This is a debate which will be revisited in the final chapter.

Are banking schools the answer?

Whatever the reasons for 'banking schools', they tend to exacerbate the paradoxical trends towards both fragmentation and control/standardization. Thus, by being susceptible to both relativist and consumerist agendas, they accelerate societal fragmentation; and to the extent that they reproduce central dictates, they standardize educational ends. And as these agendas develop, notions of public good and common goals either cease to be important, for these schools are primarily about servicing private consumer wants, or these notions are defined by central agencies determining much of what is to be taught and how it is to be taught. Second, such schools instrumentalize and commodify knowledge, because such knowledge is increasingly valued for its use in other purposes, rather than for any intrinsic value. Less and less is the need seen for a deep understanding of the nature of knowledge, normally through the study of a particular subject discipline, which not only provides an understanding of this world, and a sense of awe and wonder, but also tells us something about our limitations. Indeed, it is telling that anyone who now talks of 'learning for its own sake' is probably seen as slightly quaint and outdated.

A third result is that because of the instrumentalization of knowledge, such schools – and the education they provide – enhance the view and project of education as a competitive exercise, for now knowledge is a positional good, to be used by students as a way of gaining (limited) admission to colleges or jobs, or providing access to (limited) positions of power. As not all can have these things, so schools become places where individuals compete for them, rather than as places where some greater good is defined and worked towards, and to which each has the responsibility of making some contribution. And finally, on this model, equality is no more than equal opportunity, which comes to mean fair competition, because educational knowledge being a positional good, selects some, and bars others. Banking schools then lead down a path to standardized, instrumentalized, commodified and competitive education. In so many ways, then, 'banking' schools fail to provide the qualities needed to critique restrictive economic agendas of change, and to encourage participation in wider and more inclusive agendas.

The rise of 'community' schooling

Perhaps, then, while 'banking schools' may have initially been conceived as one response to a philosophic dilemma at the heart of the liberal democratic agenda, their development has produced as many problems as solutions, and it should then be no surprise if policy makers have increasingly turned from them to the notion of 'community' schooling. The benefits claimed for these are impressive:

- Unlike banking schools, which of their nature tend to produce alienated learning, such schools are said to provide more emotionally secure learning environments.

- Unlike the individualistic competitive ethos of banking schools, such community schools are predicated upon a concern for the welfare of all in the organization.

- While banking schools emphasize individual choice and personal rights, communal schools tend to place as much emphasis upon individual responsibility to others within the organization.

- While banking schools generate a view of educational knowledge as a positional good, communal schools celebrate a shared and public view of knowledge, from which all can benefit.

- While banking schools are essentially instrumental organizations, communal schools claim to provide intrinsic non-educational goods like belonging, identity, trust, friendship, loyalty and care.

However, 'community' as a concept is not a neatly defined notion, and there is considerable debate as to its meaning. Beck (1999), for instance, suggests at least six different metaphors for educational communities:

1   *Ontological* metaphors – those based around the notion of the caring family, or rustic support ('it takes a whole village to raise a child'), or music (the orchestra as producing more than the sum of the parts).

2   *Psychological* metaphors – those referring to long-term relationships of intimacy and commitment, which suggest strong ties, psychological safety, a sense of agency and individual and corporate identity.

3   *Behavioural* metaphors – those which talk of relationships characterized by caring, modelling, dialogue, confirmation, cooperation, cohesion and purpose.

4   *Structural* metaphors – ones which suggest structures of openness and inclusivity, which are natural and organic, and are opposed to fragmentation, bureaucracy, compartmentalization, external imposition, or artificiality.

5   *Political* metaphors – ones which talk of inclusivity, participation, and care, and which stress the equitable distribution of power in decision making, and the enhanced choice of stakeholders.

6   *Ethical* metaphors – ones which emphasize the values of critique, justice, care, empowerment, values expressed in day-to-day actions and structures.

The sheer number of such metaphors might suggest an over-rich concept, but a number of key themes constantly occur:

●   These organizations are united by a set of shared beliefs and values; they develop agreed projects based upon such beliefs and values;

●   Such beliefs, values and projects create a sense of membership, ownership, and loyalty.

●   Such organizations are familial and nurturing, and create a sense of interdependence, as opposed to independence.

●   They are concerned with both individual and minority viewpoints.

- Relationships within them are informal, meaningful and non-bureaucratic.

- They involve relationships of considerable interaction and participation.

- Such relationships occur in multiple contexts which are mutually reinforcing.

Nevertheless, and despite such claims, community schooling is not an unqualified good: there are a number of problems which need to be recognized and addressed.

Questions for community schooling

A first issue is that arguments for community schools come from different sources, and may have different objectives. Many proposals come from social theories of the community, not only intended to counter feelings of anomie and alienation, but also to reassert the need for a greater sense of individual responsibility, in reaction to an over-long fixation on rights. However, interest by policy makers is as much because some research (see, for example, Bryk et al., 1996; Bryk and Schneider, 2002) suggests that their communal nature is a key feature of academically successful schools. So while social community rhetoric may see community development as an intrinsic good, school improvement literature tends to see it in more instrumental terms. When this happens, it is easy to slip into the kind of 'hard' instrumental thesis of Fukuyama (1996) – where community, trust, and 'social capital' simply become ends to the attainment of the twin gods of economic competitiveness and national prosperity.

A second issue is that people may take the notion of 'community' too seriously for policy makers' liking, the adoption of the term having ramifications far beyond policy makers' original endorsement. Thus, Sergiovanni (1994), echoing Tonnies' (1957) basic distinction between *gemeinshaft and gesellshaft,* and Macmurray's (1950) distinction between the personal and the functional, argues that changing the metaphor changes the nature of educational activity, and that we should move from talking of schools as 'organizations', to talking of them as communities. Innocent as this may sound, such adoption suggests dispensing with a whole load of conceptual baggage, for relinquishing 'organization' as a metaphor would mean rejecting many organization theory assumptions, and its parent, economics; it would mean rejecting the view of human nature as motivated by individual self-interest, where extrinsic rewards and punishments are seen as essential to performance (such as through the use of PRP); it would mean ceasing to view schools as needing to be based upon bureaucratic codification, where activities are grouped into a logical, linear order, whose purposes are decided externally, where control is hierarchical and executed by rules and regulations, monitoring and supervision. Instead, adopting a 'community' metaphor would suggest that human nature is as much constituted by ties of affection and empathy as self-interest; that much performance is motivated by intrinsic interest and enjoyment in the nature of the work and in the relationships developed through that work. Schools would be seen as principally concerned with developing relationships and nurturing interdependence, and their purposes would be constructed through shared values and commitments, and activities determined by projects forged through such communal value commitments. As Sergiovanni argues: 'Instead of relying upon control, communities rely more on norms, purposes, values, professional socialization, collegiality, and natural interdependence. Once established, the ties of community become substitute for formal systems of supervision, evaluation and staff development' (1994: 216).

The full implications of this for policy makers wedded to a rational, bureaucratic, *gesellschaft* view of organizations are so revolutionary as to make one doubt that sufficient consideration has been given to the implications of the full-blooded adoption of such communal values.

A third issue is that 'community' is not an unequivocal good. Communities have their darker sides, and the values which members embrace may not always be ones which a wider society would want to support. At its most extreme, the Mafia is a community of sorts, as it has a code of values and accepted practices. Many street gangs are also centred on loyalty to the group, but on ongoing hostility and acts of violence to outsiders. One does not have to provide such extreme examples, however: the same issue applies to fundamentalist communities which eschew wider societal values in the belief that they alone possess the 'truth', who attempt to isolate themselves and their members from other communities, other societies. This points to a wider philosophic and ethical problem raised earlier: that the creation of communities and community schools within a larger society does not remove the necessity of providing some extra-communal examination of communal values. Indeed, before a society permits the existence of such, there has to be some articulation of the principles upon which they can be accepted within the larger society. A standard response, as we have seen, is the liberal one, but we have also seen the difficulties that this leads to.

A fourth issue is that the espousal of community schools is likely to clash with another highly valued policy – that of inclusivity. The reason for this is simple: the very essence of being a community implies the selection or self-selection of a body of people, defined in terms of their adherence to a particular set of values and practices. In so doing, they define themselves within the community, but necessarily exclude others who do not share their core values and practices. A policy of 'community' might then clash directly with a policy of inclusivity. Even if it does not, at the very least, an articulation of the principles upon which the exclusivity of communities is reconciled with the policies of societal inclusivity needs to be clearly spelt out.

A fifth problem is that such exclusion may lead to an intolerance of other beliefs, and a failure by communities to provide members with an appreciation and respect of other communities and their value systems. Such exclusivity seems closely related to the strength with which values are held – whether communities are 'thick' or 'thin'. Strike (2000) argues that different kinds of communities will provide different possibilities, and suggests the following four:

1 Communities as tribes, where there is not only a shared consciousness, but shared beliefs and practices, and an agreed way of life. This is the true *Gemeinshaft* community.

2 Communities as congregations, where there are common values and a shared view of human flourishing, which leads to common projects, though such communities are not predicated upon shared forms of life.

3 Communities as orchestras, where there are common aims and shared practice.

4 Communities as families, where the basis is that of extended natural sentiments, principally that of the requirement to care for others.

Now it may be that these are best thought of as on a continuum. At one end, the thin end, would be communities as families. Yet communities as 'families' may be too 'thin' a conception of community, for while 'care' is a valuable attribute of any person or organization, it may not be sufficiently distinctive to define an organization as a community. Communities may need 'constitutive' values, like specific religious or democratic values, which would frame the direction and nature of specific projects. Other constitutive values in educational communities would be ones which specifically embraced particular views of learning, such as child-centred approaches, or ones where schools specialized in sporting or artistic curricula. While one would expect all such schools to 'care' for those within their community, one would also expect the exclusion of those not wanting to adopt specific values or organizational aspirations.

So this would raise real difficulties with the sufficiency of the 'family' community. Yet at the other end of the spectrum, communities as tribes may be so 'thick' as to be too exclusive, thereby creating problems of intolerance and misunderstanding. To specify not only a shared consciousness, but also to share beliefs, practices and an agreed way of life, may well be so embracing, and so exclusive, as to prevent the embrace of wider societal values. For an educational community, then, such a 'thick' description might actually be anti-educational, excluding as it did consideration of other points of view and ways of life.

On this basis then, a community school would need to be one somewhere between the two ends of the continuum, having different weaknesses, different strengths, depending upon where on this continuum they were situated.

Learning communities and the rise of the learning organization

If one side of the learning community is that of 'community', the other side is clearly that of 'learning', and there seems little doubt that much of the inspiration for this side of the equation comes from currently popular notions of 'learning organization'. Now, once again, this is a term which began its existence in the business literature and was then transferred to educational concerns. Its major impetus came when the western business world felt that global changes and competition necessitated a paradigm shift in business thinking, along with new conceptions of business leaders and workers. What was required, instead of hierarchical organizations peopled in typically Fordist manner, were flatter organizations with more multi-skilled workforces, in which, as Casey (1995: 43) suggests, 'the worker's ability to learn and adapt becomes more important than his past training'. Part of this change would be achieved by espousing transformational theories of leadership, as such leaders would lead the new workers through this new paradigm; but all within the organization would need to play their part in such change. From such beginnings a widespread, almost universal, enthusiasm in the business world developed for organizations which adopted the following kinds of principles:

- Ones that created continuous learning opportunities for all their members.

- Ones that promoted continuous dialogue and inquiry between members, even when (perhaps particularly when) this exposed deeply held and unexamined assumptions.

- Ones which created climates within which people felt encouraged to share ideas and collaborate on developing new ones.

- Ones which could establish systems which would 'capture' and further distribute such learning.

- Ones which empowered people towards the articulation and embrace of collective visions.

- Ones which recognized the need to understand, interact and adapt to a constantly changing environment.

Some writers were very upbeat about such change. Zuboff (1988: 6), for instance, suggested that, 'the new technologies will provide workers with opportunities in which they can exercise new forms of skills and knowledge . . . As work becomes more abstract . . . workers [will] experience new challenges and new forms of mastery.'

The new organization then needed to be a one of constant learning, a place where, according to Senge (1990: 3) 'people continually expand their capacity to create the results they truly desire, where new and expansive patterns of thinking are nurtured, where collective aspiration is set free, and where people are continually learning how to act together'.

Senge went on to suggest that these kinds of organization needed to develop and interweave five particular forces or 'disciplines' if they were to become learning organizations:

1 Personal mastery: the need to make clear personal capacities and dreams.

2 Mental models: the need to make public, critique and, where necessary, overturn deeply held personal beliefs, and instantiate new ways of thinking.

3 Team learning: the need for those within organizations to collaborate in developing and sharing knowledge in small groups.

4 Shared vision: the need to build collective dreams which can then be used to guide future actions.

5   Systems thinking: the need for employees to develop the ability to
    place and understand their own views or actions within a larger,
    organizational perspective, and to accept that there is a fundamen-
    tal inter-connectivity between their actions and all others within
    the organization.

Central to such learning organizations is the acceptance of the need
for critical reflection and open dialogue, with individuals being
willing to talk about, share and have critiqued their own belief
systems, and to apply the same processes to their colleagues. Such
challenge was acknowledged as threatening for many, but was seen
as essential if organizations and their employees were to break free
of outdated, unhelpful, or dysfunctional thinking patterns in the
quest for innovative ways of dealing with a rapidly changing
environment. Through such openness, sharing and systems thinking,
learning then becomes organizational rather than individual in
nature, as knowledge comes to be seen principally as that which can
be spoken and shared between individuals.

Now there seems good reason to believe that Senge's views were
developed from the best of motives. Fielding (2001: 19) for instance,
is convinced that his is a 'deeply humanistic' view, driven by a desire
to help individuals 'express themselves creatively through the process
of work'. Yet, as Fielding and others point out, accounts like that of
Senge's account are seriously flawed, and, particularly with respect
to their translation into education, need to be carefully examined.

To begin with, it is important to note that, initially being a business
model, it encourages critique of organizational procedures, thought
processes and actions, but not of the purposes to which organizations
are put. It is a view of knowledge which is almost completely
instrumental in nature, for the model emphasizes only two kinds of
knowledge: that used for innovative problem solving, and that used
for detecting error. While employees are then encouraged to reflect
critically upon the operational procedures of organizations, they are
not encouraged to reflect critically upon power structures, nor upon
ultimate purposes. The 'learning organization', then, is yet one more
example of an idea which has been taken from a business literature,
which non-critically accepts current economic paradigms, and which,
if uncritically transferred to education, can result in a non-critical
acceptance of current market- and state-led aspirations for educational institutions. In its sphere of origin, as well in education, it then
reduces thought and learning to the instrumental, discouraging
exploration and criticism of currently existing economic paradigms,
and of education's role in these.

Such concerns link strongly with the influence of economic and commercial forces upon the public sector, and on education in particular; and there does seem good reason to believe that educators are being encouraged to create learning organizations which critique practices and processes *within* these paradigms, but are not being encouraged to develop learning organizations which are critical *of* such paradigms. There are a number of different paradigms which might drive learning purposes. One paradigm is that which sees education as a principal tool in the production of an economically more competitive workforce – what might be called the *economic productivity* function. However, another paradigm would be that which provided students with a kind of 'intellectual capital', allowing them to 'bank' qualifications and records of attainment for 'spending' later on, either in gaining places at university, or in having the qualifications to apply for a job. These would then be part of a *banking* function, concerned with learning for individual advancement. A third paradigm would be the transmission of a culture's norms, values, heritage, intellectual, scientific and artistic achievements – the *cultural transmission* function, while a fourth paradigm would be that of responding to and building from the learner's interests and abilities – a *person-centred* function. Finally, there is the paradigm of providing future citizens with the skills and self-belief to effect change, and with the ability to critically discuss current practices, values and norms – what might be called a *social reconstruction* function. There may well be other functions, but the point is that these approaches to education, and the purposes to which learning can be put, can all be critiqued. Yet dominant 'learning organization' models largely do not explore them, as their concerns are restricted and the learner is drawn away to other concerns.

Not only do current learning organization paradigms raise issues of the direction and control of educators, they also increase the sense of fragmentation. Fenwick (2001: 85) for instance, argues that 'the warm rhetoric in the literature of connectedness, trust and opportunity is unfurled in a climate darkened by the ethos of anxiety' for, as organizational members find themselves having to survive and prosper within a volatile, unpredictable global economy, they are asked to 'learn continuously and embrace instability as the normal order of things' (2001: 83). In such circumstances, expertise is an ever-changing, transient commodity, and the likelihood is that workers will then be reduced to a situation of 'eternal, slippery deficiency'. Echoing Sennet's (1998) concerns regarding the corrosive effects of such processes upon an individual's character, this suggests that when continual innovation is the order of the day, the individual can never be content in having reached a degree of expertise which provides satisfaction and stability, for, as Fenwick suggests this is an ideology of constant improvement which creates a competitive racing track 'where the racing dogs never reach the mechanical rabbit' (2001: 79).

Now such personal anxiety is one aspect of a much bigger picture of personal pressure, which combines elements of both fragmentation and control. Comment has already been made upon the effects of targets and performativity, and Casey (1995) extends this picture when she argues that the organizational focus is not just upon the individual's learning *per se*, but rather upon the mind and the heart, the commitment of the worker, as well. It has already been noted how we live in age of increasingly 'greedy organizations', which want and expect commitment beyond normal working hours. Casey argues that part of this is accomplished through the emphasis within 'learning organizations' upon both the socialization of the individual into desired learning habits, and induction into wider corporate values and procedures, largely through the creation of 'pseudo-family values'. The individual, impelled to participate in such cultural rituals and to personally identify with the corporate culture, is thus seduced into the 'corporate family.' For Casey, this leads to either willing collusion by some, active defence against such personal invasion by others, or an ultimate and unhappy capitulation. This has all the hallmarks of the dilemmas Lispky (1980) described in his classic work of street-level bureaucrats.

This corporate demand for personal loyalty increasingly limits an individual's psychic space, and through learning organizational rhetoric, businesses then increasingly assert their power and right to submit the individual to a public scrutiny of personal beliefs and assumptions. For Fenwick (2001: 83), this is tantamount to surrendering 'the last private space of personal meaning to the public space of workplace control'. However, it also constitutes the ultimate in personal surveillance, for now there is no private space left to the individual: all must be made public in the name of organizational improvement. The result, as the personal is increasingly utilized for the functional, is, as previously suggested, that the functional and the personal collapse into each other. This bears an uncomfortable similarity to the kinds of 'contrived collegiality' which Hargreaves (1994) described as the experience of teachers pressured to work in teams, whether this made sense either personally or creatively.

This discussion suggests a fourth and wider issue with much learning organization literature: there is a real danger with it of political naïvety, for much of it ignores not only the realities of the asymmetrical distribution of power within organizations, but also the economic and commercial imperatives of the business environment. To uncritically assume the transference of such a theory, from a highly politicized, value- and power-laden private sector, to a public sector requiring a different set of values, but which is already heavily influenced and steered by the private sector, simply fails to recognize the political and economic realties within which educational organizations find themselves. This is not a value-neutral theory, and it does not result in value-neutral practice. It cannot and should not be treated as such.

A final but important point is that by failing to locate the dynamics of learning organizations within particular political and economic contexts, the theory's central tenets may fail to blossom because of the conditions that those supposedly working to implement them actually encounter. Thus, while learning organization theorists in the business sector may have called for workers to engage in critical debate, knowledge exploration, and innovative practice, the reality has been very different. Argyris (1998), for instance, argues that private sector worker empowerment is still mostly an illusion. Part of the reason for this is the collision with systems which, as Fenwick (2001: 85) argues, demand very different 'organisational norms of productivity, accountability and results-based measurement using predictable outcomes'. This is a very good description of what currently seems to exist in many educational systems. If 'learning organization' theory doesn't work well in its private sector home of origin, there must be real doubt that an uncritical transference will work outside of it.

Combining 'learning' and 'community' for educational purposes

The danger then is that those espousing the creation of 'learning communities' fail to see the hidden assumptions of a functional organization, fail to see the values which come with the uncritical importation of a term from the private sector, and fail to see the political and economic imperatives of currently contextualized learning organizations. When this happens, as Fielding (2001: 27) points out, community then becomes no more than an 'ideological cosmetic: to clothe the functional in the language of the communal'.

Furthermore, while it is easy to understand why 'learning community' is a phrase of the moment, it, like so many other concepts, can be easily fitted into the agendas of different pressure groups, to be 'filled up' with different meanings. The concept then can appeal to policy makers and politicians, who might wish to see 'learning communities' as a convenient shorthand for institutions engineered to meet the demands of a 'knowledge economy' and the need for 'intellectual capital', and to facilitate the production of flexible workforces which know how to learn how to learn. But it can also appeal to those concerned with a perceived decline in social consensus, ethical values or communal cohesion, and who wish to stress the values and morals of the 'community' side of 'learning communities'. Finally, it can appeal to educationalists wanting the term used as a vehicle for moving educational policies away from a punitive 'results' and 'accountability ' orientation, towards one more concerned with the processes of learning, and even with the notion of learning as a good in itself. And the concept of 'leadership' would also be given an appropriate emphasis or twist to bring it into line with the desired conception of the learning community. It is therefore very important to know what the term is being filled up with – and by whom.

So, a composite version of current views probably incorporates the following qualities for a learning community:

- that members continually expand their capacity;
- that they develop new and expansive patterns of thinking;
- that they have collective aspirations;
- that they learn together;
- that they invest in their own learning.

However, this does not exhaust the possibilities. One might also wish, when specifically considering educational institutions as learning communities, to add other qualities. These might include:

- that they prioritize the personal and social above the purely functional;
- they are not exclusive for reasons of finance, race or religion;
- that they act as a bulwark for thinking determined neither by state nor by market;
- that they are not only reflective and reflexive about learning but about the cultural and political conditions surrounding that learning;
- that such reflexivity of learning lead to a criticality of existing frames of reference, of organizational structures, and of economic and political contexts.

Some will agree with these, some will disagree, while others will want to add more items and take others out. But the point is clear: conceptions of 'learning communities' are built upon different social, educational and political values, and we need to be clear of an advocate's views on these matters before any particular definition is accepted. Indeed, as communities can be located at thick and thin ends of a spectrum, and as there are at least five different functions of learning, it is perfectly possible to combine these in different ways and produce, as in Table 9.1, at least 20 different kinds of learning communities.

If this is true, then this is no transparently clear term: for meanings will be filled up with different values, functions and ends, and its leaders will also have different values, functions and ends. It also means that some kinds of learning communities – perhaps our most preferred versions – may not be realized because of the forces that surround them, whether these be local, national or global.

Table 9.1 *Possible varieties of 'learning communities'*

Learning for	Economic productivity	Individual banking	Cultural transmission	Person centredness	Social reconstruction
Communities as Tribes					
Communities as Congregations					
Communities as Orchestras					
Communities as families					

Conceptions of the learning community

From the foregoing analysis, it would seem that the creation of genuinely extensive learning communities need to prioritize the following agendas.

First, the provision for future citizens of an educational overview of such changes, so that they better understand the world in which they are living. This will mean, minimally:

- the provision of a global perspective on the changes that are occurring;

- the provision of an 'ecological' perspective – one which shows how the parts interconnect and produce the effects experienced.

Second, the provision of an educational system which ameliorates excessive elements of control. To do this, it would need to:

- provide an educational perspective which is neither simply representative of state or market, but provides a 'public' space for their debate;

- provide students with a critical perspective;

- provide them with an empowered perspective;

- provide an approach which demands that both political authority and professional practice be based upon the production of research-based information.

Third, the provision of an educational system which ameliorates excessive elements of fragmentation. To do this, it would need to:

- provide a greater sense of cohesion to learning and social life;

- provide a greater sense of the cooperative nature of learning;

- provide a greater continuity of values;

- provide for a greater continuity of the project of the self;

- provide for a public rather than a private celebration of the educational project.

These changes could then lead to the fourth, a view of learning which neither fragmented nor controlled, but which provided the ability to rise above the two. It would be one:

- where learning was less about delivery, and the solving of technical-rational problems, but was recognized in many instances as being non-linear in nature;

- where learning was at least in part concerned with an experimentation of thinking which did not have all end-points already defined;

- where a proper conception of the subject matter of learning was not restricted to the politically pragmatic and the economically essential, but transcended such concerns and embraced the broad, rich and varied;

- where learning was seen as a cooperative activity; as much a contribution by, and a responsibility of the individual, to society, as an instrument of individual, competitive advantage;

- where a proper conception of learning was one which not only adapted central directives to local situations, but which accepted the location and ultimate meaning of much learning and development as being within and for the personal and local;

- where it was accepted that a sign of societal health was one where a reflexivity of learning could lead to a criticality of existing frames of reference, of organizational structures, and of economic and political contexts.

At the present time, the jury must still be out on whether current conceptions of learning communities meet such agendas and the challenges which underpin them.

Conclusion

The project of creating learning communities is for many the result of deeply-felt imperatives about the ultimate purpose of formal education as a contribution to human flourishing. But it is also a project borne out of pragmatic considerations for the tailoring of educational policies to fit the demands of a new knowledge economy and of concerns for dealing with a perceived fragmentation of societal values and practices. Given this, the actual shape and functioning of such learning communities is likely to be a mixture of such imperatives, and the results are likely to be unpredictable. It is certainly unlikely that policy makers fully appreciate where a too-enthusiastic adoption of community rhetoric could take them. Yet it is also the case that those of a more 'educational' orientation do not fully appreciate the degree to which instrumentalist, economic and social forces steer this agenda; and the creation of such learning communities will fail if the concerns over 'community' and 'learning' discussed in this chapter are not fully appreciated. It is then vital that the different strengths and weaknesses of 'thick' and 'thin' conceptions of community are fully realized and addressed. Thin communities may provide defence for those who would see schools as a support and exemplification of liberal democratic principles, and as a bulwark against those (including the state) who would prosecute a single vision of human flourishing, which would ultimately contribute to the internal collapse of a liberal-democratic state, founded as it is upon the celebration of different lifestyles, different visions of life's ultimate purposes. Yet at the same time, thin communities will ultimately fail if they cannot provide a sense of purpose and meaning to the educational project. In such circumstances, they may well lead to no more than an anomic concentration upon individual self-gratification, where learning is seen as no more than a personal means to instrumental gain. Ultimately, then, thin communities may lead to the collapse of both tolerance and support, for they may fail to provide the kind of sufficiently structuring and supportive vision which individuals seek and need. Yet the opposite end of the continuum presents the mirror image of such problems: too 'thick' a community may provide such a structure and supportive vision, yet exclude consideration of other visions. Learning would then become a different kind of tool, one employed in the promotion of a particular kind of vision, and outputs might well become myopic and intolerant. In such circumstances, communities which were too thick are as likely as thin ones to produce a weakening of any overarching political vision which attempted to provide a larger framework within which such communities could flourish.

The same kind of considerations need to be applied to 'learning', for learning has functions beyond the needs of particular communities. Clearly it has instrumental functions, and it would be foolish and unwise to dismiss such needs, as part of the foundations of national economic wealth is based upon its use in this way. Yet learning also needs to be seen as concerned with a respect for logic, for evidence and rationality as means of settling disagreements, and for a necessary objective criticality of opinions regardless of the status of the person holding those opinions. It needs to be seen as concerned with the affective, the social and the moral. It also needs to be utilized for wider issues, so that the learner understands not just *how* to do things but also appreciates *why* such things are important. To realize these aims, educational systems and learning communities within them need to have the 'space' to develop such a capacity. If education system are seen as no more than handmaidens to the economic, social and political objectives of states, learning communities will not have that room. They are also unlikely to realize that role if they are designed to do no more than serve the whims of the market. The success or failure of community schools should be judged, then, on the willingness of governments to relinquish some control, on a clarity of vision which circumscribes the influence of the market and its tendencies to fragmentation, and on the understanding of those within the system of the need to embrace and practice such public and civic principles.

10 Professionals at the crossroads

Late in 2003, two editions of the *Times Educational Supplement*, the premier UK teacher's journal, led with very different stories about the condition of England's state schools. One, a report entitled 'Schools without Teachers' (5 December 2003), was concerned with an official government paper, *Workforce Reform – Blue Skies*, which claimed that there was need for only one qualified teacher in each school. The other story, entitled 'Call me Mr Forgettable' (19 December 2003), reported that over half of the teachers in a *TES* survey had no idea who the current Secretary of State for Education was. Both of these stories are highly significant for this book, the first because it suggests that official thoughts on the deprofessionalization of education may be further advanced than many have thought; the other, because many of those directly affected by such changes don't seem to have the faintest idea of what is going on. Both of these issues are extremely worrying and need to be examined in more detail.

Blue Skies thinking

The first document, *Blue Skies*, had been written by a senior government official and circulated to external signatories of an earlier workload agreement. The document talked of the 'essential but presentationally uncomfortable' need to make the case to cut teacher numbers to pay for more support staff. The paper stated that:

> the legal position . . . is that a maintained school must have a head with qualified teacher status (QTS), but beyond that the position is very much deregulated. The school need not employ anyone else – other staff need not have QTS and staff could be bought in from agencies or come in on secondment. . . . Gone are the days of every school having

to have a full complement of directly employed QTS teachers.

The document accepted that current regulations required support staff to be supervised by qualified teachers when they were used for teaching purposes. *'But'* , the document went on, '[the] *teacher might of course be the head.'* It also suggested that recruitment targets for teachers should be abandoned in favour of targets for higher-level assistants. When qualified teachers were used, their time would be *'ruthlessly focused on expert teaching, planning and pupil assessment'.* Other work with pupils could be taken by *'a range of other adults'*, support staff then playing *'increasingly important roles in direct teaching'.* It also envisaged that management posts in schools would be transferred to non-teachers to *'embrace modern management practices'.* The model for schools was one of a single professional educator supervising the work of non-qualified staff, while non-educational managers took over the headteacher's responsibilities. The one qualified person in the school would then oversee the work of technicians who would do most of the teaching, with lesson plans provided for them, most probably by government web sites.

Now while the DfES hastily insisted that the paper had been produced without the authority and knowledge of ministers, it was sent out as an official DfES document, and it was clearly believed that it would be viewed sufficiently sympathetically by these other signatories to be sent to them. It does not seem unfair, therefore, to suggest that it did reflect an official governmental train of thinking. It was also clear that it was largely driven by two factors. The first was concern over spending, for the paper warned that the government's next spending review, 2005–2008 would be *'very tight'*, and that the proposed changes would help to keep spending at current levels. This was a theme revisited repeatedly throughout the document. The second factor was the concern raised in 2001 when the then Secretary of State warned that there would be a shortfall of 30,000 teachers by 2006 (Morris, 2001).

It might be tempting to assume that these two factors – problems with finance and recruitment – are peculiarly English problems, but this book has shown how these are much wider problems, and are generated by global issues such as ageing populations and reductions in the number of tax-payers, limits on governmental spending through neo-liberal global market requirements, and by low-trust and standardizing regimes reducing the commitment and morale of public sector workers. So by taking a long view of education and educational leadership, this book has argued that such commonalities between economically developed nations are not matters of coincidence, but are located within larger fragmenting and controlling/standardizing agendas, which may be mediated at national level, but which largely originate elsewhere.

Call me Mr Forgettable

This example is but the tip of a much larger iceberg. While global forces impact upon national funding of education and the recruitment of teacher workforces, they also impact upon wider relationships. They do so through limiting the abilities of individuals and groups to trust one another; they impact upon wider questions of meaning by affecting people's perceptions of what is true and worth knowing; and they impact upon people's sense of identity by fracturing communities and creating consumerist self-images. In so doing, these forces generate challenges for educational leadership not just through issues of funding and recruitment, but through reducing a wider population's commitment to a common good, and to the good of future generations. They also generate wider challenges by standardizing work, and reducing the judgements of professionals to the extent where they may be incapable of responding to such challenges. A Chinese epigram, used at the beginning of a previous book (Bottery, 1992), suggested that those who lowered their heads to pull their carts were less likely and capable of raising their heads to look at the road they were travelling down. It is a caution of which educators need to be constantly aware, for if they are not, one has to worry down which roads they may be encouraged to travel, and at which destinations they and their societies will arrive. Indeed, given the second *TES* article, that less than half of the teachers questioned knew the identity of the man directing the government's education policies, there is probably real cause for worry. Yet perhaps this finding should be not that surprising. Previous research (Bottery, 1998) had found that not only many teachers, but nurses and doctors as well, significantly failed, either through lack of interest or simple overwork, to be aware of the social and political context within which their work was located. Moreover, research following this (Bottery and Wright, 2000), suggested that most teacher INSET in England was short-term, technical-rational and implementational in nature. Such INSET is located within an educational system where the teaching profession has been deluged over the last two decades with initiative after initiative, and where the consequences of non-compliance have been both public and punitive. Such a system damages teachers by reducing their practice to external requirement, rather than encouraging a flexible response to context, and prevents the use of subject and pedagogical expertise and local knowledge not only to more helpfully implement policy, but to critique and amend policy by feeding back the negative effects. It damages students by preventing teachers from adjusting to individual problems, and by limiting expertise to the exercise of the competent rather than the excellent. It prevents consideration of the kind of flexible skills required in new economies, as well as failing to highlight the dangers of excessive fragmentation and control which can be consequent upon them. It damages education by capturing a discourse which should be concerned with exploring a range of possibilities, rather than being reduced to a cipher of economic policy; and in so doing it damages society by closing down possible visions of the good society, including critical explorations of future demands and possibilities. Finally, it damages global society by preventing a sustained gaze upon the effects of such policies, and by suggesting that present economic arrangements are natural and inevitable, when in fact they are conscious choices engineered by powerful individuals and groupings. Indeed, if the situation is one where governments seem even more intent on reducing the scope of education and professional input, while at the same time there exists a profession which does not seem to have much of an idea about what is going on, it does not seem too apocalyptic to suggest that the teaching profession – and indeed society itself – is at a crossroads, and its leaders need to think very carefully about the profession's future direction.

'Call me Mr Forgettable' doesn't mean, as the article suggested, that the principal problem was that the current Secretary of State for Education had so little impact that few teachers could remember him. It meant instead that few teachers knew the identity of the man who headed the government department which had dramatically and was continuing to change their work, their practice and their values. It is a stunningly worrying condemnation of the political awareness of the English teaching profession. At the same time, *Workforce Reform – Blue Skies*, while extreme, does follow the trend of the kinds of predictions made so far in this book, suggesting a model for a future teaching force which effectively leaches anything professional out of such practice. It suggests a model of teaching which lacks both subject knowledge and pedagogical expertise, for teachers would not require expertise in a subject area, nor how to teach it; the objective would be to have classroom technicians delivering downloadable lesson plans by teams of government-sponsored writers in manners even more carefully prescribed than the UK National Numeracy and

Literacy Strategies, or the US *Success for All*. It would be an educational world light-years from one where a profession, through a deep knowledge of the structure of a subject area, and an expertise in pedagogy, was aware of and capable of communicating that deep structure to students, who would then come to understand the ways in which knowledge is constructed, the ways in which personal meaning affects such knowledge, and the ways in which individuals, values and cultures necessarily place their own interpretation on understandings of the external world. Under a regime such as that proposed, none of this would be possible. It would be a desperately impoverished society. It is genuinely alarming that members of a government could think such things, never mind feel that it was a sufficiently 'safe' proposition to be sent to external parties for discussion.

Six professional requirements

So the question is: given the kind of alternate model of professional educator which this book has argued for, what do educational leaders need to promote as a model to realize this role? Building on earlier work (Bottery, 1998), this chapter suggests six professional require-ments needed for such achievement, which need to guide educational leaders as they frame their understanding and actions, not only within the organization, but in managing its boundaries, and in responding to and participating in future proposals for professional formation.

A first requirement, clearly, is an *ecological and political awareness,* the necessity for all educators to be aware of the factors beyond their institutions which constrain, steer or facilitate their practice. This requirement, underpinning the whole thrust of this book, suggests a need for awareness beyond the local and the national right through to the global. But it also requires a professional self-consciousness, an understanding of how professionalism has changed, and how the role of professional educators needs to change in the future as well. Table 10.1 illustrates how societal views of professionals have changed during the last 50 years, from ones of high trust, peer-based accountability, and mystique, where considerable autonomy and discretion were exercised, to a kind nowadays which is predominant-ly low-trust, based on extensive external quantitative accountability, and limited professional discretion.

Part of this has been due, as Marquand (1997: 141) suggested, to neo-liberal views which have seen professionals as little more than

Table 10.1   *Changing views of public sector educators*

	Welfare state	*Neo-liberal/New modernisers*	*Preferred future?*
Internal/external accountability	peer	external	mixed
Accountability based on	values and peer judgement	process and output	values, process and output
High/low trust	high	low	high
Trust based on	values and mystique	external audit	values and 'open' practice
Technical/Critical knowledge base	technical	technical	mixed
Prof. discretion/ External direction	high discretion	external direction	earned discretion

'market distorting cabals of rent seekers, engaged in a collaborative conspiracy to force the price of their service above their true market value'. Yet despite the fact that Reagan and Thatcher shuffled off the political stage, the professional position did not improve significantly under the New Modernist, 'Third Way' regimes of Blair and Clinton. Indeed, as Fergusson (2000: 208) argues, New Labour is actually 'much more interventionist and considerably more managerialist'. Moreover, by moving from a former norm-referenced emphasis on comparing performance between institutions, to a criterion-referenced emphasis on performance to externally defined targets and benchmarks, the impact on teachers has been even more marked, more stressful. Nevertheless, while the style may have changed, the substance has remained much the same, and the impact, if anything, has intensified. Such 'third-way' regimes then continue at least in part to accommodate a continuing dominance of neo-liberal premises, derived from wider global economic notions.

This continuing low-trust culture led to what Power (1994: 38) called 'an audit explosion', which not only stresses the measurement of professional work by external quantitative measures, but emphasizes a shift to administrative control, where professionals are there, as Pollitt (1993) suggests, not to be 'on top' in autonomously deciding how their practice is best used, but instead to be 'on tap' to managerial strategic decisions. In the process they service a mindset which asks not 'is it true?' but 'is it useful?', and where educators committed to the pursuit of truth become, in Parker's (2001: 139) terms, no more than 'court jesters' who live out their professional lives being 'noisy, but largely ineffectual'.

Despite this situation, it is pointless and unhelpful to hark back to some fondly remembered 'good old days'. Such days may have been good for professionals, but they were much less good for others who depended on their service, as the mystique and protection afforded by professional peers all too often left clients powerless, ignorant and dependent. To suggest then, that trust can be regenerated by a return to the past is both quixotic and unhelpful. If trust is to return it will be by recognizing those factors which placed professionals in the situation they currently find themselves and by addressing them. And that, I suggest, means in part a very urgent need for a professional transparency, openness and accessibility to the public, and to a wider educational role than has formerly been conceived. This then points to two more professional requirements.

A second requirement, if such professionalism is to be grounded in a service to the public and the local community, is for educators to be much clearer and vociferous in espousing a *notion of the public good*. As argued in previous chapters, this requires that education be seen as more than a private consumable item, and what Hirsch terms a 'positional good', but instead needs to be seen, as Grace (1994: 214) argues, as ' a public good' which develops 'a moral sense, a sense of social and fraternal responsibility for others'. This is closely linked to the need to develop notions of social citizenship, and to the argument that a publicly provided education is one of the foundation stones for a welfare state which provides people with the abilities by which to engage on an equal footing with others, not just in the competitive race of life (which is essentially the 'Third Way' vision), but which is also part of a cooperative project, aiding all in contributing to the building of a better society, and which actively redresses societal inequities. This means that not only should educational leaders recognize the political context within which their work is encompassed, but that they should more actively engage with it. Not only do professionals need to situate their work within an ecological and political awareness; they need to critique changes in this context in the light of the kind of educational vision they are trying to achieve.

This leads directly into a third requirement, for perhaps the most influential 'ecological' force directly impacting upon professionals at the present time is the form of accountability which is exercised over their practice. This, as already described, is one which is normally an external, quantitative and low-trust form of audit, which attempts to replace public trust built upon mystique with one based on quantitative transparency. Yet we have already seen how such approaches, linked to systems of targets and performativity, not only generate poor morale in those made so accountable, but also fail to be fully transparent because they fail to understand, appreciate, value or encourage other aspects of professional practice which make this practice successful. A third professional requirement, therefore, is the development of *an extended, proactive and reflexive accountability*. This recognizes that forms of accountability are a product of, and contribute to, the ecology within which professionals practice. Professionals must recognize that because global and national contexts, as well as perceptions of their own practice, affect the kinds of accountability they face, they must not accept that accountability is something simply 'done' to them. Instead, they need to proactively work towards new forms which display how current officially neglected aspects of professional practice are essential to a rich conception of education.

Current forms of accountability are predicated upon two models. One model is driven by the market and the search for financial efficiencies, and is underpinned by what Broadbent and Loughlin (1997: 37) call two assumptions of 'accounting logic': (i) that any activity needs to be evaluated in terms of some measurable outputs achieved and the value added in the course of any activity; and (ii) that it is possible to undertake this evaluation in and through the financial resources actually received.

The other form of accountability is driven by standardizing and controlling agendas, and this book has shown that current accountability is not only steered by governments wishing to satisfy the demands of the market, but by other state-sponsored imperatives – such as its need to bolster its own legitimacy – which also require control of professionals' work.

The overall result is what Power (1994: 8–9) describes as Style A of audit. This, as shown in Table 10.2, is a quantitative, low-trust single-measure approach using external agencies. It asks for distilled judgements within simple reassuring categories, which allow governments to claim effective functioning, both for themselves and for the institutions being audited. It also enables them to identify where 'blame' can be located. Power believes that the best approach may be one marrying Style A with Style B, rather than simply seeing them as in opposition. 'As in all things,' he suggests (1994: 9), 'the key is to achieve a balance and compromise.'

Yet, given the different kinds of drivers mentioned above, there are many pessimistic of such internal/external compromise. Jary (2001:

Table 10.2 *Two different styles of audit*

Style A	Style B
Quantitative	Qualitative
Single measure	Multiple measure
External agencies	Internal agencies
Long-distance methods	Local methods
Low trust	High trust
Discipline	Autonomy
Ex-post control	Real-time control
Private experts	Public dialogue

51) for instance, concludes that 'the general exigencies that are driving audit will continue to sustain Style A audit and preclude any widespread move to Style B'.

Nevertheless, there is some reason to believe that richer forms of audit, more extended versions of accountability, might be achievable. Misztal (2001), for instance, points to management theorists who argue that if organizations are to be successful in the knowledge economy, they need to generate greater creativity, teamwork and problem-solving, and that this entails a more extensive sharing of information within a flatter organizational form. As she says 'the organisation of the future is interested in fostering trust among its members and partners because it is recognised that centralised bureaucratic control is too weak, too costly and incapable of performing in a new competitive environment where cooperative relationships are the main sources of productivity gains' (2001: 26).

There is also evidence that governments, even those reluctant to relinquish control, are influenced by such dominant private sector ideas, and therefore may be encouraged to adopt a mixture of types A and B accountability. Nevertheless, it is important to recognize, as Power (1997: 145–6) argues, that governments work within political climates, and therefore 'such institutionalised capability for evaluating audit which avoids reproducing the very problems it is intended to solve could only be created by a confident society. This would be *a society capable of knowing when to trust*, and when to demand an audited account' [emphasis added].

How, then, does one go about creating a society 'knowing when to trust'? Part undoubtedly comes from a private sector eager to encourage such practices; part also comes from an official sponsorship. But part must also come from those who wish to be trusted. So a fourth requirement of professionals is for a deliberate move towards *constituency building.* This is in part a need for public sector professionals to build support for their practice by involving and educating those stakeholders around them in the nature, purpose and constraints of their job. This clearly aligns with a focus on a transparency, openness and accessibility of accountability. But it is also a move towards three larger political objectives.

- One is the encouragement within the profession and beyond for support for a public sector vision and a healthy welfare state.

- A second is the belief that such a constituency has to be one dedicated to more than just the support of educational practice; this constituency must consist of *all* those with a shared vision of a public sector.

- A final objective is the building out from a vision of such a role for education, and this vision for a public sector, to a vision for society as a whole, one in which members understand the ecology of forces surrounding, steering and constraining their own existences and that of their society.

Such sharing, joint support, and consciousness-raising makes the fifth requirement for educational leaders an essential for any society. Discarding the belief in the justifiability of a profession built on mystique, and moved towards the acceptance of a profession based upon transparency, this entails epistemological change as well. If professional educators previously thought that they alone possessed the 'truth' of their practice, as they alone were the experts, so now, with the recognition of the need to listen to others, they need *to embrace an epistemological provisionality* – a requirement to be suitably humble about their own capacity to 'know' any final answers, and to recognize that others have significant input here, and not least those normally described as 'clients'. Yet this transcends professional knowledge, and the needs of education. As argued in previous chapters, such embrace of epistemological provisionality helps to counter both corrosive relativism, and dogmatic and uncritical fundamentalism. Professional educators then need to embrace such provisionality not only in pursuit of a better understanding of their own practice; they need to be at the front of a movement which recognizes and counters contrary but mutually dangerous tendencies of relativism and absolutism in society. Ultimately, this position needs to be one not only for educators and other professionals, but for society as a whole.

A sixth and final requirement follows from all that has been discussed previously. More than ever before, professional educators need *a much greater professional self-reflection*. They need to appreciate the contexts within which they find themselves, debate the purposes of their profession, and the balance between those purposes, and then interrogate these in the light of the requirements above. This calls for a degree of professional self-knowledge and self-reflection which, under the current strain of work intensification, is all too absent. Yet upon it depends in large part the ability to make a difference to education, and indeed in the long term to society at large. If professional education means anything, it means an awareness of these issues and the ability to debate them. Such education should begin in the induction stages, and continue as an integral part of educators' continuing professional development. It should be a critical part of any leadership education, for such leaders frame and steer the context within which their fellow professionals work. If *they* fail to keep this as a constant mirror by which to interrogate the long-term validity and use of their practice, what hope has the rest of the profession? Yet, if one looks at the materials of any of the national initiatives for school leadership, such awareness is sadly lacking. One could be polite and believe that this is simply an oversight, that the press of day-to-day work, and of the medium-term management of institutions, attract so much attention that this longer-term issue is simply neglected. If this is the reason, then it says little for the overall understanding or commitment of educators – and policy makers – to debate ultimate purposes. If, on the other hand, it is simply because educational leaders think this unimportant, and policy makers remain happy to reassure them in their lack of commitment, for *they* can perform the simple matter of deciding such ultimate purposes, then we already have a situation where educational leaders are shorn of any proper leadership. They will be hardly worthy of the name, for if they are incapable or fail to articulate what education is *for*, they fail to be leaders, and become no more than servants of the powerful.

Conclusion

Educational professionals are at an important crossroads. Given the kinds of global pressures, national government aspirations and professional compliance, many retreat into the antithesis of globalization – the retreat to the parochial and insular, in the hope that at this level, true meaning, personal identity, enriching relationships can be found. There is some sense in such movement, in that much of the essence of the human is to be found in the personal, and it is at this intimate level that such relationships are likely to be realized. Yet ignoring the powerful doesn't make them go away; it just provides them with even more room and power to exert their effects. Whatever level individuals retreat to in search of ultimate spiritual support, larger national and global forces are ignored at their peril. And for educators, having accepted the responsibility of helping others in facing the demands of today and tomorrow, there can be no greater abnegation of such responsibility than to do others' bidding without questioning whether this constitutes what they believe to be good education.

As argued above, this does not mean returning to a previous period where professionals believed that it was their right alone to define such issues: the professionals' responsibility is to *add their voice* in a larger dialogic project. Professionals do have their understandings and expertise to share, and they should not be shy in declaring these; but they need to recognize other understandings, others' expertise, in a societal-wide debate on what is needed to improve what exists.

The professional requirements outlined in this chapter are a first step towards this realization. An *ecological and political awareness* allows professionals to understand the context in which they find themselves and their society; espousing a *notion of a public good* allows them to raise their sights, and that of fellow societal members, above the level of the self-gratifying consumer to this larger project. The call for *an extended, proactive and reflexive accountability* requires that they see accountability as more than something external 'done' to them, but as something they can and must feed into, not only to make their own lives more tolerable, but in order to provide non-educators with a better appreciation of what they, the professional educators, should be aiming to achieve, and what they need to do in order to achieve this. To realize this objective, however, they need to be involved in *constituency building*, which is more than simply cultivating allies in the pursuit of a more fulfilling occupation, but is instead the building of a community which recognizes the global and national context within which all work, and upon which all need to cooperate if they are to have significant input. Such cooperation, such acceptance of the need to listen to others, requires, but also produces an *embrace of epistemological provisionality*, which also reduces the tendency for some to claim relativist or absolutist positions. Finally, *professional self-reflection* does not mean an appeal to introversion, but precisely the opposite, for greater self-knowledge is only possible where the person is situated within contexts and when the impact of such contexts is appreciated. By specifying this last, then, we return to the first requirement to be aware of and understand the ecological and political context of professional practice.

Given these conditions, what kind of educational leader is required? This book began by stating that it did not wish to become involved in disputes over definitions of leadership, but, nevertheless argued that some definitions actually constrained and steered the actual practice and, in so doing, intensified the pressure on leaders. So there are occasions when awareness of officially sponsored models is not only useful but perhaps even vital, for such models also form part of the ecological context within which leaders work. And similarly, the final call to professional self-reflection demands that leaders contribute to their own ecology by arguing for particular practices, particular models of leadership. This book, then, concludes by examining a number of educational leadership models and asks: given the situation that education finds itself in, what model should be the one that educational leaders adopt and recommend to others?

11 Models of educational leadership

The last chapter argued that due to current pressures on educational practice, educational leaders needed to embrace the following requirements as integral to their role:

- An ecological and political awareness extending beyond the institutional and local, to the national and global.

- The espousal of a notion of public good, drawing people beyond the personal and consumerist.

- A proactive and reflexive approach to a rich and extended version of accountability.

- The building of constituencies with others, professionals and non-profesionals, to develop extended partnerships not only to improve professional practice, but society in general.

- An embrace of epistemological provisionality, not only as a reflection of humility in such partnerships, but also as a counterweight to moves towards absolutist and relavist views.

- A continued need for professional self-reflection as the interrogation and understanding of practice within larger contexts.

It was further argued that not enough attention was being paid to the policy and economic context within which educational leadership is practised, and that the nature and gravity of the challenges which this book has discussed might not be fully appreciated. Wright (2001) provides support for this position in the UK in arguing that the economic and political climate has effectively reduced the ability of school principals and other educational leaders to transcend matters of government policy, their own values and preferred practice being submerged beneath a deluge of managerialist rhetoric, paperwork and legislated practice. Ball (1999) has adopted a similar position in arguing that much school autonomy is little more than rhetoric, where greater local management of finance is effectively negated by what it can be spent upon. Contrary to such a position has been research by writers like Day et al. (2000), Moore et al. (2002), and Gold et al. (2003) which suggests that while external forces continue to impinge upon educational leaders' values and practice, the best practitioners nevertheless still find it possible to retain and practice their deeper personal values – as Moore et al. (2000: 178) argue, a 'conscious eclecticism at its core'. Indeed, and as one principal said (Bottery, 1998: 24), his attitude to legislation was one which ran 'from *defy* through *subvert* to *ignore*, on to *ridicule*, then to *wait and see*, and in some exceptional cases to *embrace*'.

Yet it is still likely that an incremental assimilation of thought and practice to current managerialist norms is likely to occur – particularly by those principals whose schools, for one reason or another are the subject of constant inspection, who are not so mentally agile or ethically driven, or who are inclined to pragmatism or entrepreneurialism. Fergusson (1994: 213) suggests that an acculturation then takes place, where educationalists 'come gradually to live and be imbued by the logic of the new roles, new tasks, new functions . . . in the end [they] absorb partial re-definitions of their professional lives, first inhabiting them, eventually becoming them'.

It may well be then that there is a spectrum of accommodation, from those who do become largely cyphers for current government thought and suggested practice, to those who are able to stand back and continue to deliver their own view of what good education is for. Yet it is likely that the ends of such a spectrum are unrepresentative of the profession as a whole. Common sense suggests (and much research agrees) that much practice is a pragmatic compromise between personally held views and external pressures. Nevertheless, the evidence which began this book indicates that even this pragmatic compromise may be failing as increasing numbers of leaders come to view the job as simply too onerous.

In the light of this evidence, and in the light of the leadership requirements detailed above, it is important to interrogate a number of different leadership models and ask how likely they are of being capable of responding to such pressures, and how well equipped they are to take on the requirements listed above. This final chapter will interrogate five such models:

1 The opportunist.
2 The corporate implementer.

3   The instructional leader.

4   The moral community leader.

5   The ethical dialectician.

The opportunist

Of all the leadership types, the opportunist is the most free-floating, the most de-contextualized. This is in part because such leadership does not exist as an objective phenomenon: it is in large part a construction by individual leaders themselves. Such leaders have drive, ambition and 'actively shape our interpretation of the environment, the challenges, the goals, the competition, the strategy and the tactics' (Grint, 2000: 4). They are very contextually and politically aware, even if they do not identify with this context, for they try instead to persuade others that their interpretation of the context, and of the manner of dealing with it, is the correct one. Opportunist leadership, then, is a personal, interpretive affair, a leadership built on a leader's *artistry* in the creation of a leadership persona, and the function of an organization under such a leader would be a similarly individualistic creation, founded upon the leader's strategic vision, created as a painting rather than a photograph. Of course, while vision is a critical skill of such a leader, it is a personal vision, and is not necessarily one which furthers the good of others.

However, opportunist leaders, as Grint argues, do have other interesting qualities, for to achieve such personal visions, opportunist leaders must be master tacticians, individuals better envisaged as martial arts experts than as mathematicians, because there is an inherent indeterminacy of outcome which such leaders must surmount, an indeterminacy they might actually encourage, confident as they are in using a fluidity of situation to establish the primacy of their version of reality. And others may well follow this leader because of another of their arts – that of persuasive communication, the ability to induce belief in a world painted by words and props.

Such leaders, then, are highly individual, very idiosyncratic, their success resting not only upon what ends they are trying to achieve, but on how they achieve them. Ethical considerations do not necessarily intrude too far in their contemplation of either means or ends, so if education is seen as an activity which needs to be underpinned by ethical considerations and different value perspectives, then an opportunist whose major motivation was one of self-advancement would hardly be educationally desirable, even if there must be some educational leaders who fit this bill very well. Furthermore, if the opportunist leader's vision is so personal, it might well be asked how such a person could be trusted to deliver a vision of a public good, or build a wider constituency towards such a vision. Finally, present educational policy contexts leave limited room for such a highly individualistic, non-bureaucratic model. Given strong direction from the centre, and the degree of surveillance currently in evidence, the permissiveness needed to allow such individual artistic creations to succeed seems unlikely. Having said all of this, their contextual awareness, their ability to paint a compelling vision, and their mastery of strategy, make these formidable individuals, and there are no doubt some who do manage to reinvent themselves in officially favoured garb in order to survive and prosper. The conclusion must probably be that while ethically unpalatable, they may have qualities of which the more ethical might need to take note. They are likely to be survivors, and that seems no bad thing to be.

The corporate implementer

For some, the corporate implementer is that species of leader who is hardly worthy of the name. This is the individual who, unlike the opportunist, has no final goals, no picture to be painted, except in the most limited sense, for the subject of this leader's picture has been painted elsewhere, and it is his/her job to realize this vision. Their epitaph might well be: I did what I was told, and I did it extremely well. In England, much of the literature would describe them as managers rather than leaders, in the USA as administrators. In both countries they would be seen as having transactional skills, but lacking the vision to transform a situation. Others would say that this underestimates what the corporate implementer does. After all, was not the subject matter of some of the greatest paintings dictated by others to the artist? And if the task is to implement a vision, might not this involve many of the tasks of the opportunist or the community leader? Is it not likely that the corporate implementer will have to inspire others to believe in this (external) vision in order to motivate them? Will not this individual need the strategic skills of the martial artist? May they not need to be master persuaders, especially if this external vision is not to the liking of the teaching force? And if they have to implement external agendas – curriculum requirements, performance targets, personal appraisals – do not these skills all apply? It will help, of course, if those who are to be the follower/implementers are clear in their role – as lower-grade members of a hierarchy whose job is to follow a vision and then implement an external agenda. They need to be empowered, but such empowerment is carefully circumscribed in its scope. As Murgatroyd and Morgan (1992: 121) argue:

> What a team or an individual is empowered to do is to turn the vision and strategy into reality through achieving those challenging goals set for them by the leadership of the school. *Individuals are being empowered in terms of how they can achieve the goals set, not in terms of what the goals might be.* [emphasis added]

Corporate implementers and their followers, then, are people whose professional parameters are very carefully specified. A variety of critical literatures suggests that this has been the position for quite some time – and the DfES document which began Chapter 10 suggests that it remains the key model for many in government. Glatter (1999: 263) also suggests that currently 'institutional leaders are seen as conduits of government policy'; Wright (2001: 280) similarly suggests that 'Leadership . . . is now very substantially located at the political level where it is not available for contestation, modification or adjustment to local variations.' And work by Hargreaves (2003) and Gronn (2003b) suggest that this is not just a problem for the English.

So why would such followers accept such leadership? They may on occasion be seduced by the corporate implementer who can 'sell' them this vision, by a calculated persuasion and rhetoric similar to that of the transformational opportunist; but essentially they will be persuaded not by educational or moral visions, but by a managerial system built around systems of legislative dictation, target setting, external and internal surveillance, and by a professional development system built around the reward of the individual through compliance with such dictation and the achievement of such targets. Its moral basis lies in the claim that because governments are elected on democratic mandates, they deserve the right to direct and dictate, and it is the duty of teacher-implementers to comply. This kind of approach has little time for the literature on the need for bottom-up mediation and interpretation of policy (for example, Parsons (1996), Fullan (1992)), or for the need to address the concerns of lower levels in this system. Bluntly, it sees lower level employees as implementers of wider policy aims, and because this approach is hierarchical in nature, it has great potential to frustrate the development of a distributed leadership beyond those officially appointed. Furthermore, it can be a soul-less, mechanical version of education for both leader and followers, and is probably a strong contributory factor to the widespread crises in teacher recruitment in a number of countries. The message from such statistics seems clear: the model of leader as corporate implementer fails to motivate, and those practising it or those on the receiving end are likely to be victims of value conflict, stress, overwork and burnout. Crucially, as Day et al. (2000) point out, this is what those advocating hierarchical, control-oriented, transactional forms of leadership for schools seem not to understand, for as they argue:

> There can never be enough rules to ensure that those we do not trust do the right thing. And as rules are added to prevent more and more anticipated future diversions from the right thing, we inadvertently constrain people from using their problem-solving capacities on behalf of the organisation's purposes. (2000: xv)

Its greatest danger, however, is that on so many of the leadership requirements listed above, it would have no voice. It need have little ecological awareness, for the wider social and political context is taken as a given, one which must be worked within rather than critiqued; it would only espouse notions of public good, and build constituencies towards this if these were officially prescribed, and it would see no need to build towards a proactive accountability, for the form of accountability would be unquestioningly accepted as that which was 'given' by those in authority. And finally, given its acceptance of hierarchy and authoritarian commands, it is predisposed to absolutist rather than provisionalist views of knowledge. It is a model which might satisfy the short-term aims of some policy makers, but continues to be disastrous in the achievement of a rich and diverse educational system.

The instructional leader

Change is slow in coming. Most centres for developing leaders have concentrated, not unsurprisingly, on the pragmatics of leadership – the setting of directions, the development of people and organizations, and all within fairly predictable and functionalist frameworks. In the UK, for example, the initial prospectus for the National College for School Leadership (DFEE, 1999) was written very much in corporate implementer mode. The opening paragraph made it clear that the intention was to provide 'a coherent national training framework for headship so that all heads have access to high quality, practical and professional training at every stage of their careers'.

This, and the following pages, emphasized that this framework was about *training, about practical* issues, and about the enhancement of *skills.* There was little here to suggest that leadership need be concerned with moral compasses to interrogate questions from the community, the society, nor from global pressures. There was little focus upon the developing *education* of the leader.

Nevertheless, there have been a few indications of change. The UK publication, *Schools Achieving Success* (DES, 2001) acknowledged the possibility of teacher overwork, of unnecessary bureaucracy, of insufficient flexibility in curricular provision, and of the need for leaders to provide a personal perspective on the development of their schools. It was now believed that 'the evidence shows that schools with a distinct identity perform best, with the ethos acting to motivate staff and students across a wide range of subjects and activities, improving teaching and learning' (2001: 38, para. S.3).

The UK National College for School Leadership (2001: 3) also seemed to be adjusting its ground when it argued that 'leaders who are capable of transforming their schools are driven by a passionate commitment to a set of educational and moral values; they need time and opportunity to explore and test their values so that they can act consistently and with confidence in the school workplace'.

Moreover, it initiated a series of think-tanks to establish the kind of educational leader that was required, the kind of issues that needed to be addressed, the kind of research needed to be covered. A key document here was the 'Think Tank Report to Governing Council' (NCSL, 2001) which came out strongly in favour of what was described as an 'Instructional Leader'. Such an instructional leader was committed to the idea of the school as centrally concerned with learning and instruction for all, and with an ability to flexibly implement in the light of the particular context. Such a leader, it was claimed, needed to be 'infused with a moral purpose', the reason for this being 'the vital importance of closing the gap between the highest and lowest achieving students and to raise standards of learning and achievement for all' (2001: 8).

This, we were informed, was 'the contemporary moral purpose of school leadership'. It undoubtedly was a development beyond the corporate implementer, and now followers were permitted – even required – to have a moral purpose to their work, one of providing students with core learning abilities, a focus combined the mission to ensure that this was *every* student's entitlement.

Yet while this *was* a development, it still left a number of questions. For a start, this seems a circumscribed and second-order moral purpose: essentially, it does no more than ensure that more students achieve standards set elsewhere. There is little here about plurality, diversity, discussion of varieties of the good society, of the good life, or of different ways of achieving this – nor of the leadership of such schools as being major players in participating in such wider moral and educational aims, nor of their developing such a vision with their colleagues. While it is encouraging to hear talk of moral purpose at last infusing educational leadership, it remains a very limited purpose.

Moreover, such limitations to its vision were also to be seen in the belief that such an organization was there, above all, to prepare its learners (and this includes not only students, but staff, and possibly the wider community as well) for a future in a knowledge society where the flexibility of learning how to learn was *the* critical skill. Such instructional leadership, then, is based within the wider paradigm of the learning organization and 'the learning society'. Substantial comment has already been made on the possible limitations of a learning organization, and on the increasingly fashionable learning 'community', and in terms of a learning society, the rhetoric is also very familiar. Ransom (1998: 86), for instance, suggests that such a society is one transformed by economic, social, cultural and political changes, where the production of knowledge and information increasingly supplant manufacturing and industry, and where society must therefore be viewed as having learning as its organizing principle, where the instructional leader is a 'natural' educational figurehead. Some of this is fair enough: we do live in an age of rapid change, where flexibility, adaptability and the ability to learn how to learn, are essential survival skills, and where the ability to provide them to students of all ages is going to be a critical leadership quality. Nevertheless, there must be the worry that 'learning' once more becomes a non-problematized term, where the job is to learn 'how' rather than 'why' or 'for what', and where the critical question is not 'is it true' but 'is it useful?' This suspicion is strengthened when writers like Hopkins et al. (1994) argue that 'school improvement, like the human condition, is largely about problem-solving'. Really? Is the human condition – and school improvement – to be predominantly concerned with and resolved by an ability to solve problems, rather than with a wider and richer appreciation of social, cultural, religious and ethical issues, with a concern for debating what is a good society, and what place education might play in these? As Masschelein (2001) argues, going down such a problem-solving/learning route has the potential to make education no more than a technical-rational exercise, where ideological superstructures (such as that the human condition is largely about problem solving, or that the primary function of schools is to provide its students with the problem-solving skills to work within a capitalist knowledge economy) are kept off the agenda. Would this not impoverish the mission and value of a school and of educational purpose?

It is reasonable to believe, then, given the description of the policy context above, that this model is still largely driven by the political and economic discourse of global capitalist agendas, and where the role of government is to adopt strategies ensuring that all students are provided with the problem-solving skills to become members of a national workforce competing on a global stage. We do not seem to have come very far from the views of David Blunkett (1988), who when Secretary of State for Education, asserted in the Foreword to 'The Learning Age' that

> Learning is the key to prosperity . . . investment in human capital will be the foundation of success in the knowledge based global economy of the 21st century . . . Learning throughout life will build human capital by encouraging the acquisition of knowledge and skills and emphasising creativity and imagination . . . The fostering of an enquiring mind and the love of learning are essential for our future success.

This is no selective quotation: it formed virtually the entire introduction to a key political document. There must then be concern that such driving forces continue to have their effects upon the conception and creation of this leadership model, and that the result is a narrow, rather rigid instructional leader, whose function – defined largely from above – is the paradoxical one of constructing an inclusive, flexible, adaptable workforce, within tight economic/skill parameters. Yet a genuinely extensive definition of an 'instructional leader' would embrace the following viewpoints:

- that learning is not so much about delivery, or even about the solving of technical-rational problems, as an acceptance of the non-linear nature of much thinking;

- that learning must at least in part be concerned with an experimentation of thinking which does not have pre-defined end-points;

- that a proper conception of the subject matter of learning is not restricted to the politically pragmatic and the economically essential, but must transcend such concerns and embrace the broad, rich and varied;

- that a proper conception of learning is one which not only adapts central directives to local situations, but which accepts the location and ultimate meaning of much learning and development as being within and for personal and local situations;

- where it is accepted that a sign of societal health is one where learning is viewed as potentially subversive of existing views, for a reflexivity of learning may well lead to a criticality of existing frames of reference, of organizational structures, and of economic and political contexts.

There was some movement in 2003 with the recognition in the NCSL's *Annual Review of Research* of the need to appreciate the context of leadership and of developing innovative and leading edge thinking, signalling perhaps policy makers' recognition that 'instructional leadership' needed to entail less central direction, more tolerance of new strategies that did not produce immediate results, and were evaluated in other than purely instrumental terms. Yet, at the end of the day this does not actually develop leadership beyond instructional preoccupations, and it remains a long way from sponsorship of the kinds of leadership requirements which began this chapter.

The moral community leader

A more appealing model, perhaps, is the moral community leader of the sort depicted by writers like Serglovanni (1996), or the servant leader variation suggested by Greenleaf (1977), both of whom believe, as Greenleaf says, that 'if we are to have a more moral society, then moral man [sic] must also care for institutions' (1977: 53). Such a person is in most ways the antithesis of the opportunist, for this leader, rather than inventing an image, and constructing a persona calculated to appeal to followers, instead sees the school as a community, and embraces and reflects back the core educational and moral values of that community. School life, then, is defined at its core as the public celebration of certain values, and it is the leader's role to articulate and provide leadership in the attempted resolution by the school community of those problems that are defined by such educational and moral values. As Sergiovanni says (1996: 15), 'For schools to work well, we need theories of leadership that recognise the capacity of parents, teachers, administrators, and students to sacrifice their own needs for causes they believe in.'

For those who hold similar educational and moral values, then, this will be a good place to work, for they will have leaders who articulate what they *know* to be good education. Members of such communities are likely to be empowered and committed, as they will feel that they are backed by someone who thinks and feels the same way they do. Such school communities, as Bryk et al. (1996) and Bryk and Schneider (2002) have found, are likely to be tightly focussed, have high self-esteem, and may also produce strong academic results. In a number of ways, this model of leadership might also fit current policy demands rather well. There is, for instance, a clearly perceived concern at policy level for measures to counteract what is perceived as a general community decline, and writers like Etzioni (1993, 1997) and Putnam (2000) have been taken extremely seriously by politicians on both sides of the Atlantic, as they have advocated a greater emphasis on individuals' responsibility to their community, and of the need for the generation of 'social capital', the 'relationship glue' that binds individuals in communities together, as well as many of the elements of trust covered earlier. They also fit some of the leadership requirements listed above. They clearly rise above the personal in the search for the building of a constituency which builds values and support between people. Moreover given the strong commitment to a particular set of values, they have a moral grounding which enables them to critique external policy and which leads them to an awareness of the political and social context which impinges on their values. Given such awareness, they are likely to want to argue for a form of accountability which recognizes and celebrates the values, knowledge and practices which they as a community value. These are all very hopeful signs for the development of a viable leadership.

Yet such conceptions have potential downsides. A leader's ability to rise above the personal to embrace the communal cannot remain at the local, and the prosecution of such local 'community' values then needs to be tempered by a recognition of such larger purposes, and there might then be real tensions between such community-focussed schools and nationally stated polices, which such community leaders might fail or be unwilling to mediate. Further, given the extremely strong hold over policy direction that many governments currently practise, considerable community variation may be difficult to tolerate, particularly if such attention displaces a concern for academic results. A final concern is that, as already pointed out, a community that espouses certain values excludes as well as includes, and by creating versions of 'thick' trust, and by insulating the next generation from understanding others of different background, such communities might then actually work against the development of 'thin' trust, and a national or even global sense of community. Ultimately, 'public good' has to transcend the parochial, and there is real potential here for the pursuit of the larger public to be lost in the pursuit of the smaller communal.

Greenleaf's (1977) *Servant Leader* is also likely to encounter problems. This is the kind of leader whose first question is 'what can I do for my students, my teachers, my community?' and then makes their betterment and their development his/her driving passion. The danger here is that such a leader may then see the function of the organization as the realization of whatever it is that its community wants to achieve. This will be an attractive model to those who similarly want to serve the needs of the school community, articulating as the servant leader does, their moral principles. Yet, once again, a number of questions must be asked. What happens, for example, when what a community wants is not what it needs? What happens when what it wants is not ethical? Does the servant give them what they want, even when he/she knows it is not what they need, nor indeed what they should have? Further, what happens when such local wants/needs conflict with centrally-defined national requirements? Greenleaf's best test (1977: 13–14) of leadership is to ask the questions: 'Do those served grow as persons? Do they, *while being served,* become healthier, wiser, freer, more autonomous, more likely themselves to become servants?' [original emphasis].

Yet these do not provide resolution, for if the judgement is that their growth depends on giving them what they need rather than what they want, it is difficult to see how this person is a *servant* leader any longer. It is also difficult to see how such a model can fit very well with strong central direction. It is likely, then, that currently this model has limited opportunity for realization: while some of its 'moral' aspirations would be welcomed by policy makers, many of its more local concerns and parochial values would not fit with a policy direction which saw primary attention to local concerns and values as an impediment to central direction. Perhaps more importantly, it is likely that it would fail to meet the leadership requirements listed above, for it is not clear that such reflection of communal needs would automatically include greater social and political awareness, an enlarged vision of the public good, of the need to build a constituency beyond this local community, or that it needs to be proactive in terms of mechanisms of accountability. Finally, there are likely to be communities committed to forms of absolutist knowledge which, by followership criteria at least, the leader would have great difficult in disputing. Perhaps the time has come for an ethical dialectician.

The ethical dialectician

Ethical dialecticians are individuals with an internal moral compass. They know who they are, they are centred, they don't arrive at a situation trying to work out what other people think they should do, but arrive with a particular moral stance. In part this is why people trust such leaders, for they may well share the same values, and others will certainly have a good idea of how and why such individuals will deal with particular situations. Yet such ethical dialecticians don't drive through their vision with no regard to other views. While being individuals with moral compasses, they are sufficiently aware of the ecological complexity of the external world, and of their own personal and epistemological limitations, to know that they need to listen to others, and to adopt a 'provisionalist' attitude to the world. They need to move from thesis to antithesis to synthesis. However, as conditions change, or as a wider picture is understood, their synthesis may be challenged, and they must engage in a process of dialectic once more. This then entails much more work than simply driving through their own or a government's vision; it entails a willingness to put in the time to forge joint visions, and from there to develop these into working realities. As Day et al., argue (2000: xv) 'When we judge people to be principled, committed to a vision we also value, to respect our contributions, and to be willing to work tirelessly on behalf of our organization, we trust them to do the right thing.' Moreover, such a leader is capable of producing a creative synergy with others because 'when a school gets to the point where trust is mutual . . . then rules become largely unnecessary, and the full capacity of the school's members can be unleashed on behalf of its mission'.

Such leaders work from within a strong ethical and educational vision, yet they also possess considerable political and pragmatic astuteness, for they need this to work outwards from a personal vision of the school as community, towards one which is jointly owned and increasingly articulated and transformed into a shared public statement. Such leaders then acknowledge that communal visions have to be worked towards rather than being thought of as neatly packaged personal creations. As this is done, so a shared purpose and a shared sense of trust are developed.

However, this combination of ethical vision and political and pragmatic astuteness means that they also recognize the legitimacy of demands beyond their community. Government have claims both legislative and moral, and such leaders need to engage in a further dialectic between their own shared understanding of what they believe should be done and what the government of the day asks of them, in the light of the facilitators or constraints which policy parameters provide. There is, then, in the ethical dialectian, the same recognition as with Grint's (2000) opportunist leader, of the necessity to recognize the social and political context, as well as the practicabilities and the achievability of particular projects at any moment in time. However, with them, the ends are very different, as are the beneficiaries, for the ethical dialectian, unlike the opportunist, has a moral compass.

Yet such dialectic does not stop there. Such leaders are ecologically aware to the extent that they recognize that governments are not necessarily the final source of understanding: they too are driven by demands, imperatives and claims beyond the national level, and may well be in a position of mediation and interpretation, just as much as the ethical dialectician is at the local level. This adds a further level of dialectic to their task, for now they must engage in a debate which asks of them to think through the effects, not only of local and national but of global pressures as well. Theirs is a role of increasing complexity and it would be all too easy to think it impossible, but given an acceptance of personal limitations, but of an ethical compass nevertheless, it does allow the ethical dialectician to accept that they can only do the best that they can.

Leaders in some ways very similar to these were seen in the survey carried out by Day et al. (2000) when surveying the characteristics of successful principals. They too began from such internal compasses, they too recognized the need to dialogue, they too recognized the complexity and the need for the time to make best sense of a situation. Yet there are reasons for doubting their full official espousal. One reason for such doubt returns us once more to the question of trust. Day et al.'s conception of 'trust' is generated by others' recognition of leaders who are principled, who are committed to a valued vision, who respect contributions, and who work tirelessly to that end. In contrast, the governmental vision of trust as articulated by Morris (2001: 26) is a colder, more limited beast: 'It is important to trust our professionals to get on with the job. That does not mean leaving professionals to go their own way, without scrutiny – we shall always need the constant focus on effective teaching and learning, and the accountability measures described above'. The message here seems clear. Trust is limited in scope, and any flexibility in getting on with the immediate job will be determined by a continuing battery of external accountability measures.

A second reason for doubt lies in the lack of partnership in this statement: there is nothing within it to suggest that professionals or their leaders might actually be consulted on the schools of the future, or on the likely impact of national and global pressures on contextualized learning communities, or on the best ways of mediating such pressures. There is, sadly, a great deal from previous experience to suggest that the professionals' job is to be merely one of putting into practice decisions once more made elsewhere. To use an ugly but fashionable term, current policies suggest a 'responsibilization' of the profession, but only to accept the jobs allocated to them, and to get on with implementing them. So, finally, trust means only limited permission in the deliverance of targets set elsewhere: it does not mean trust to participate in developing or modifying policy based on the dialectically developed moral understandings of a school community interrogating legislation in the light of local, national and global circumstances.

In the circumstances, there must be real concern that many will fail the tricky balancing act between the ethical and the pragmatic. Lipsky's (1980) discussion of the tensions facing the street-level bureaucrat, and of the kinds of strategies adopted in order to maintain their idealism while dealing with the practicalities of their work, seems very relevant here. Some, he suggested, will be seduced by the practical, and may find themselves on a slippery ethical slope down to the cynical land of the opportunist. Others, in order to maintain some vestiges of moral idealism, will sideline the greater vision, and restrict their ethical practice to particular instances and problems; and others, tragically, will give too much of themselves and end up either 'downshifting' to more acceptable levels of pressure, or need time off on extended sick leave, and from there to retirement. The problems of principal recruitment, stress and early retirements which began this book, support such an interpretation. A principled moral vision is essential to the educational leader, and a process of moral dialectic is also vital, but current policies of control – as well as stresses from societal fragmentation – probably create such intense pressures as to prevent the full development currently of an ethical dialectic model of leadership. A policy orientation from the centre which acknowledged the need for leaders to begin from an ethical centredness in the moderation of central policy in order to meet the particular contexts of educational problems, may need to be more centrally strongly endorsed before the ethical dialectician is a genuine system-wide possibility.

Conclusion

If the leadership of educational organizations, and particularly that of schools, is embedded within networks of regional, national and global policy making, then acceptable and practical forms of leadership need to interrogate such policy making. Leadership of a value-driven and essentially moral organization *needs* to ask awkward questions about the policy networks that facilitate, constrain or direct the work of education. This chapter has argued that such questions have probably not been asked enough.

This chapter has also suggested five possible models of leadership, while the book has discussed a number of policy contexts within which to evaluate them. Clearly, any list of leadership models described is not exhaustive, and there are also many different policy contexts. Nevertheless, there is little doubt of genuine similarities between policies in many countries. In particular, in the western world at the present time, many governments are struggling to energize populations to be more flexible and creative, and there is some small evidence that a few recognize the need for contextualization, trust and a moral purpose to educational activity. However, most continue to be wedded to a vision of education and educational leadership which constrains, even prohibits, such realizations. This may be a case of a lack of 'joined-up' thinking, but the consequences for the achievement of such aims are likely to be extremely damaging. While there may be some movement from the adoption of a 'corporate implementer' model of leadership to an 'instructional leader' model, mixed with a little of the 'moral community' model, this chapter has argued that the realization of an education system which not only provides adaptability and economic competitiveness, but which also provides a personally enriching and rewarding education, lies with the espousal of the practice of 'ethical dialecticians'. At their best, such leaders incorporate many of the 'instructional' and the 'moral community' leader traits, while transcending both these and the corporate implementer through recognizing that ultimately the process of education, and the institutions which deliver it, have to be concerned with governmental agendas and their delivery, but must also incorporate other communal and societal concerns.

At their best, these ethical dialecticians take due cognisance of the need for educational organizations to engage in national endeavours delineated and organized by the government of the day, but recognize that they have a responsibility to do much more than this. Educational leaders also need to help individuals look into themselves, to stand back from the demands of everyday life, and reflect upon how current circumstances and problems provide new insights into who they are, into the nature of their mortality, and into how values fashion and shape such reality to provide personal meaning to their lives. As individuals recognize that their being is fashioned by, dependent upon and responsible to others, so they move back up through levels of concern: they transcend the personal and reflect upon their relationships with others, upon their rights, and of their responsibilities to other individuals, communities and the global society. A leader who fails to have such a moral compass is very likely to fail to recognize and make central these other educational requirements. It remains to be seen whether official conceptions can encompass and develop policies which deliver on these concerns.

Bibliography

Anderson, B. (1996) *Imagined Communities: Reflections on the Origin and Spread of Nationalism*. London: Verso.

Argyris, C. (1998) 'Empowerment: the new Emperor's new clothes', *Harvard Business Review*, May–June: 98–105.

Arthur, J. (2002) *Education with Character*. London: RoutledgeFalmer.

Ashton, D. and Sung, J. (1997) 'Education, skill formation and economic development: the Singaporean approach', in A.H. Halsey, H. Lauder, P. Brown and A.S. Wells (eds), *Education, Economy, Society*. Oxford: Oxford University Press. pp. 207–18.

Axelrod, R. (1986) *The Evolution of Cooperation*. New York: Basic Books.

Ball, S. (1999) 'Global trends in educational reform and the struggle for the soul of the teacher'. Paper presented at the British Educational Research Association Annual Conference, University of Sussex.

Ball, S. (2001) 'Performativities and fabrications in the education economy', in D. Gleeson and C. Husbands, *The Performing School*. London: RoutledgeFalmer. pp. 210–26.

Banks, J. and Banks, C. (eds) (1996) *Multicultural Education: Issues and Perspectives*. New York, Chichester: Wiley.

Barber, B. (1996) *Jihad V. McWorld*. New York: Ballantine Books.

Barber, M. (2000) 'High expectations and standards for all – no matter what'. Edited version of a speech delivered to the Smith Richardson Foundation in Washington <www.tes.co.uk>.

Barber, M. (2002) 'From good to great: large-scale reform in England'. Paper presented for the School Development Conference, Tartu University, Estonia.

Baron, S., Field, J. and Schuller, T. (2000) *Social Capital*. Oxford: Oxford University Press.

Bass, B. (1985) *Leadership and Performance Beyond Expectations*. Cambridge, MA: Harvard University Press.

Bates, R. (2003) 'Can we live together? The ethics of leadership and the learning community'. A paper presented at the BELMAS annual conference, Milton Keynes, October.

Bauman, Z. (1996) 'From pilgrim to tourist – or a short history of identity', in S. Hall and P. Du Gay (eds), *Questions of Cultural Identity*. London: Sage. pp. 18–36.

Beck, L. (1999) 'Metaphors of educational community: an analysis of the images that reflect and influence scholarship and practice' *Educational Administration Quarterly*, 35 (1).

Beck, U. (2001) 'Living your own life in a runaway world: individualization, globalisation and politics', in W. Hutton and A. Giddens (eds), *On the Edge: Living with Global Capitalism*. London: Vintage. pp. 164–74.

Billig, M. (1995) *Banal Nationalism*. London: Sage.

Blackmore, J. (1995) 'Breaking out from a masculinist politics of education', in B. Limerick and B. Linguard (eds), *Gender and Changing Educational Management*. Hodder: Sydney.

Blunket, D. (1998) Preface to *The Learning Age*. London: DFEE.

Bottery, M. (1992) *The Ethics of Educational Management*. London: Cassell.

Bottery, M. (1998) *Professionals and Policy*. London: Cassell.

Bottery, M. (2000) *Education, Policy, and Ethics*. London: Continuum.

Bottery, M. and Wright, N. (2000) *Teachers and the State*. London: Routledge.

Boulding, J. (1968) 'The economics of the coming spaceship earth', in M. Allenby (ed.) (1989) *Thinking Green: An Anthology of Essential Ecological Writing*. London: Barrie and Jenkins. pp. 133–8.

Broadbent, J. and Laughlin, R. (1997) ' "Accounting logic" and controlling professionals', in J. Broadbent, M. Dietrich and J. Roberts (eds), *The End of the Professions?* London: Routledge. pp. 34–50.

Brown, P. and Lauder, H. (2001) *Capitalism and Social Progress*. Basingstoke: Palgrave.

Brundrett, M. (2002) 'The development of school leadership preparation programmes in England and the USA: a comparative analysis', *Educational Management and Administration*, 29 (2): 229–45.

Bryk, A., Lee, V. and Holland, P.(1996) *Catholic Schools and the Common Good*. Cambridge, MA: Harvard University Press.

Bryk, A. and Schneider, B. (2002) *Trust in Schools*. New York: Russell Sage Foundation.

Bryman, A. (1992) *Charisma and Leadership in Organisations*. London: Sage.

Burns, J.M. (1978) *Leadership*. New York: Harper and Row.

Bush, T. and Jackson, D. (2002) 'A preparation for school leadership: international perspectives', *Educational Management and Administration*, 30 (4): 417–29.

Campbell, C. (1982) 'Romanticism and the consumer ethic: intimations of a Weber-style thesis', *Sociological Analysis*, 44 (4): 279–96.

Carrington, B. and Short, G. (2000) 'Citizenship and nationhood: the constructions of British and American children', in M. Leicester, C. Modgil and F. Modgil (eds), *Education, Culture and Values Vol. VI: Politics, Education and Citizenship*. London: Falmer.

Casey, C. (1995) *Work, Self and Society*. London: Routledge.

Casey, C. (2001) ' "New Age" religion and identity at work', in M. Dent and S. Whitehead (eds), *Managing Professional Identities*. London: Routledge. pp. 201–15.

Castells, M. (1998) *End of Millennium*. Oxford: Basil Blackwell.

Castells, M. (2001) 'Information technology and global capitalism', in W. Hutton and A. Giddens (eds), *On the Edge: Living with Global Capitalism.* London: Vintage. pp. 52–74.

Chesterton, G.K. (1909) *Orthodoxy.* London: John Lane Company.

Chua, N. (2003) *World on Fire.* London: William Heinemann.

Clarke, J., Gewirtz, S. and McLaughlin, E. (eds) (2000) *New Managerialism, New Welfare?.* London: Sage.

Clausen, C. (2000) *Faded Mosaic.* Chicago: Ivan R. Dee.

Collins, R. (1990) 'Market closure and the conflict theory of the professions', in M. Burrage and R. Torstendahl (eds), *Professions in Theory and History.* London: Sage. pp. 24–43.

Council of Europe (2002) *What is Education for! Democratic Citizenship – Concepts and Practice.* <http://www.coe.int/T/e/Cultural_Co-operation/ Education/E.D.C/What>.

Couzens, J. (1921) 'What I learned about business from Ford', *System* Vol. 40.

Crowther, F., Hann, L., McMaster, J. and Ferguson, M. (2000) 'Leadership for successful school revitalisation: Lessons from recent Australian research'. Paper presented at the annual meeting of the American Educational Research Association, New Orleans, LA.

Dasgupta, P. (1988) 'Trust as a Commodity', in D. Gambetta (ed.), *Trust: Making and Breaking Cooperative Relations.* Oxford: Basil Blackwell. pp. 49–73.

Davidson, J.D. and Rees-Mogg, W. (1999) *The Sovereign Individual.* New York: Touchstone.

Day, C., Harris, A., Hadfield, M., Tolley, H. and Beresford, J. (2000) *Leading Schools in Times of Change.* Buckingham: Open University Press.

Delors, J. (1996) *Learning: The Treasure Within.* UNESCO.

DES (2001) *Schools Achieving Success.* London: DES.

DfES (2003) *Final Report of the External Evaluation of England's National Literacy and Numeracy Strategies.* Nottingham: DfES.

DfEE (1998) *Education for Citizenship and the Teaching of Democracy in Schools* (The Crick Report). London: Falmer.

DfEE (1999) *National College for School Leadership: A Prospectus.* London: DfEE.

Drucker, P. (1993) *Post-Capitalist Society.* New York: HarperCollins.

Dychtwald, K. (1999) *Age Power.* New York: Tarcher Putnam.

Elliot, J. (2001) 'Characteristics of performative cultures' in D. Gleeson and C. Husbands *The Performing School.* London: RoutledgeFalmer. pp. 192–209.

Elliot, L. and Atkinson, D. (1999) *The Age of Insecurity.* London: Verso.

Etzioni, A. (1993) *The Spirit of Community.* London: Fontana.

Etzioni, A. (1997) *The New Golden Rule.* London: Profile Books.

Evans, R. (1995) 'Getting real about leadership', *EducationWeek* 16 April.

Evans, R. (1996) *The Human Side of School Change.* San Francisco: Jossey Bass.

Faux, J. and Mishel, L. (2000) 'Inequality and the global economy', in W. Hutton and A. Giddens (eds) *On the Edge: Living with Global Capitalism.* London: Vintage. pp. 93–111.

Fenwick, T. (2001) 'Questioning the concept of the learning organisation', in C. Paechter, M. Preedy, D. Scott and J. Soler (eds), *Knowledge, Power and Learning*. Milton Keynes: Open University Press. pp. 73–83.

Fergusson, R. (2000) ' "Modernising managerialism" in education', in J. Clarke, S. Gewirtz, and E. McLaughlin (eds.), *New Managerialism: New Welfare?* London: Sage. pp. 202–21.

Fielding, M. (2001) 'Learning organisation or learning community? A critique of Senge', *Reason in Practice* 1 (2); 17–29.

Fielding, M. (2003) 'Working the soul: the earnest betrayal of high performance schooling'. A paper given at the ESRC seminar series, University of Sussex, October 2003.

Fineman, S. (2000) 'Commodifying the emotionally intelligent', in S. Fineman (ed.) *Emotion in Organisations* (2nd edn). London: Sage. pp. 101–14.

Fink, D. (2001) 'The two solitudes: policy makers and policy implementers', in M. Fielding (ed.) *Taking Education Really Seriously: Four Years Hard Labour*. London: RoutledgeFalmer.

Firat, F. and Dholakia, N. (1998) *Consuming People: From Political Economy to Theaters of Consumption*. London: Routledge.

Fishman, J. (1972) *Language and Nationalism*. Rowley, MA: Newbury House.

Fitzgibbon, C. (2000) 'School effectiveness and education indicators', in D. Reynolds and C. Teddle (eds), *International Handbook of School Effectiveness*. London: Falmer.

Frank, T. (2002) *One Market Under God*. London:Vintage.

Freire, P. (1972) *Pedagogy of the Oppressed*. Harmondsworth: Penguin.

Friedman, M. (1962) *Capitalism and Freedom*. Chicago: University of Chicago Press.

Fromm, E. (1942) *The Fear of Freedom*. London: RKP

Fukuyama, F. (1996) *Trust: the Social Virtues and the Creation of Prosperity*. London: Penguin.

Fukuyama, F. (1999) *The Great Disruption*. London: Profile Books.

Fullan, M. (1992) *The New Meaning of Educational Change*. London: Cassell.

Fullan, M. (1997) *What's Worth Fighting for in the Principalship?* (2nd edn). New York: Teacher's College Press.

Fullan, M. (2001) *Leading in a Culture of Change*. San Francisco: Jossey Bass/Wiley.

Fullan, M. (2003) *The Moral Imperative of School Leadership*. Thousand Oaks, CA: Corwin Press.

Gambetta, D. (1988) 'Can we trust Trust?', in Gambetta D. (ed.), *Trust: Making and Breaking Cooperative Relations*. Oxford: Basil Blackwell. pp. 213–19.

Giddens, A. (1990) *The Consequences of Modernity*. Stanford: Stanford University Press.

Gilliat, S., Fenwick, J. and Alford, D. (2000) 'Public Services and the Consumer: Empowerment or Control? *Social Policy and Administration* vol. 34, no. 3, pp. 333–49.

Glatter, R. (1999) 'From struggling to juggling: towards a redefinition of the field of educational leadership and management', *Educational Management and Administration*, 27 (3): 253–66.

Gleeson, D. and Gunter, H. (2000) 'The performing school and the modern-ization of teachers', in D. Gleeson and C. Husbands, *The Performing School*. London: RoutledgeFalmer. pp. 139–58.

Gold, A., Evans, J., Earley, P., Halpin, D. and Collarbone, P. (2003) 'Principled principals? Values-driven leadership: evidence from ten case studies of "outstanding" school leadership', *Educational Management and Administration*, 31 (2): 127–38.

Grace, G. (1994) 'Education is a public good: on the need to resist the domination of economic science', in D. Bridges and T. McClaughlin (eds), *Education and the Marketplace*. London: Falmer. pp. 126–38.

Gray, J. (1998) *False Dawn*. London: Granta.

Green, A. (1997) *Education, Globalization and the Nation State*. London: Macmillan.

Greenleaf, R.K. (1977) *Servant Leadership*. New York: Paulist Press.

Grey, C. and Garsten, C. (2001) 'Trust, control and post-bureaucracy', *Organization Studies* 22 (2): 1–15.

Grint, D. (2000) *The Arts of Leadership*. Oxford: Oxford University Press.

Gronn, P. (2003a) *The New Work of Educational Leaders*. London: Paul Chapman Publishing.

Gronn, P. (2003b) 'Leadership: who needs it?', *School Leadership and Management*, 23 (3): 267–91.

Gunter, H. (2001) *Leaders and Leadership in Education*. London: Paul Chapman.

Hallinger, P. and Heck, R. (1996) 'Reassessing the principal's role in school effectiveness: a critical review of empirical research 1980–1995', *Educational Administration Quarterly*, 32 (1): 5–14.

Handy, C. (1989) *The Age of Unreason*. London: Business Books.

Handy, C. (1994) *The Empty Raincoat*. London: Hutchinson.

Handy, C. (1997) *The Hungry Spirit*. London: Hutchinson.

Hargreaves, A. (1994) *Changing Teachers, Changing Times*. London: Cassell.

Hargreaves, A. (2003) *Teaching in the Knowledge Society*. Milton Keynes: Open University Press.

Harris, A. (2002) *School Improvement. What's in it for Schools?* London: Falmer Press.

Harris, A. (2003) 'Teacher leadership as distributed leadership: heresy, fantasy or possibility', *School Leadership and Management*, 23 (3): 313–24.

Harris, A. and Lambert, L. (2003) *Building Leadership Capacity for School/Improvement*. Maidenhead: Open University Press.

Hayek F. (1944) *The Road to Serfdom*. London: Routledge and Kegan Paul.

Heater, D. (1990) *Citizenship*. London: Longman.

Held, D. (1989) 'The decline of the nation state, in S. Hall and M. Jacques (eds) *New Times*. London: Lawrence and Wishart.

Hersh, R., Paolitto, D. and Reimer, J. (1980) *Promoting Moral Growth*. New York: Longman.

Hertz, N. (2001) *The Silent Takeover*. London: William Heinemann.

Herzberg, F., Mausner, B. and Snyderman, B. (1959) *The Motivation to Work*. New York: Wiley.

Hobsbawm, E. (1990) *Nations and Nationalism Since 1780*. Cambridge: Cambridge University Press.

Hofstede, G. (2003) *Culture's Consequences* (2nd edn). New York: Corwin Press.

Hoggett, P. (1996) 'New modes of control in the public service', *Public Administration*, 74 (Spring): 9–32.

Hollinger, D. (2000) *Postethnic America*. New York: Basic Books.

Hood, C. (1995) 'The new public management in the 1980s: variations on a theme', *Accounting, Organisations and Society*, 20 (2/3): 93–109.

Hopkins, D., Ainscow, M. and West, M. (1994) *School Improvement in an Era of Change*. London: Cassell.

Hopkins, D. (2001) *School Improvement for Real*. London: Falmer Press.

Huntington, S. (1998) *The Clash of Civilizations and the Remaking of the World Order*. London: Touchstone.

Hutton, W. (2001) 'Anthony Giddens and Will Hutton in conversation', in W. Hutton and A. Giddens (ed.), *On the Edge*. London: Vintage. pp. 1–52.

Janis, I. (1972) *Victims of Groupthink*. Boston: Houghton and Mifflin.

Jary, D. (2001) 'Aspects of the "audit society" ', in M. Dent and S. Whitehead (eds), *Managing Professional Identities*. London: Routledge. pp. 38–60.

Jeffrey, B. and Woods, P. (1998) *Testing Teachers: The Effect of School Inspections on Primary Teachers*. London: Falmer Press.

Kipnis, D. (1996) 'Trust and technology', in R. Kramer and T. Tyler (eds), *Trust in Organisation*. London: Sage. pp. 39–50.

Kohlberg, L. (1981) *The Philosophy of Moral Development*. San Francisco: Harper and Row.

Korten, D. (1996) *When Corporations Rule the World*. London: Earthscan.

Kramer, R. and Tyler, T. (eds) (1996) *Trust in Organisation*. London: Sage. pp. 39–50.

Laabs, J. (1996) 'Downshifters: workers are scaling back', *Personnel Journal*, 75 (3): 62–76.

Lasch, C. (1995) *The Revolt of the Elites*. New York: W.W. Norton.

Lauder, H., Jamieson, I. and Wikeley, F. (1998) 'Models of effective schools: limits and capabilities' in R. Slee, G. Weiner and S. Tomlinson (eds), *School Effectiveness for Whom?* London: Falmer. pp. 51–69.

Leadbeater, C. (1998) 'Who will own the knowledge economy?', *Political Quarterly*, 375–85.

LeGraine, P. (2002) *Open World: The Truth About Globalization*. London: Abacus.

Leithwood, K., Jantzi, D. and Steinbach, R. (1999) *Changing Leadership for Changing Times*. Buckingham: Open University Press.

Levin, B. (2001) *Reforming Education*. London: RoutledgeFalmer.

Lewicki, R. and Bunker, B. (1996) 'Developing and maintaining trust in work relationships', in R. Kramer and T. Tyler (eds), *Trust in Organisations*. London: Sage. pp. 114–40.

Lindblom, C.E. (1959) 'The science of muddling through', *Public Adminstration Review*, 19: 78–88.

Lingard, R., Hayes, D., Mills, M. and Christie, P. (2003) *Leading Learning*. Maidenhead: Open University Press.

Lipsky, M. (1980) *Street-level Bureaucrats*. New York: Russell Sage Foundation.

Louis, K.S. (2003) 'Trust and improvement in schools'. Paper presented at BELMAS annual conference, Milton Keynes, October.

Luhmann, N. (1988) 'Familiarity, confidence, trust: problems and alternatives', in D. Gambetta (ed.), *Trust: Making and Breaking Cooperative Relations*. Oxford: Basil Blackwell. pp. 94–109.

Luttwak, E. (1999) *TurboCapitalism*. London: Orion

MacMurray, J. (1950) *Conditions of Freedom*. London: Faber.

Marquand, D. (1997) 'Professionalism and politics', in J. Broadbent, M. Dietrich and J. Roberts (eds), *The End of the Professions?* London: Routledge. pp. 140–147.

Marshall, T.H. (1950) *Citizenship and Social Class and Other Essays*. Cambridge: Cambridge University Press.

Martin, H-P. and Schumann, H.(1997) *The Global Trap: Globalisation and the Assault on Prosperity and Democracy*. London: Pluto Press.

Maslow, A.H. (1954) *Motivation and Personality*. New York: HarperCollins.

Masschelein, J. (2001) 'A discourse of the learning society and the loss of childhood', *Journal of Philosophy of Education*, 35: 1–20.

McCrone, D. (1998) *The Sociology of Nationalism*. London: Routledge.

McLagan, P. (1998) *Management and Morality*. London: Sage.

Meier, D. (2002) *In Schools We Trust*. Boston: Beacon Press.

Merton, R. (1952) 'Bureaucratic structure and personality', in R. Merton, A. Gray, B. Hockey and H. Selvin (eds), *Reader in Bureaucracy*. Glencoe: The Free Press. pp. 361–72.

Meyerson, B., Weik, K. and Kramer, R. (1996) 'Swift trust and temporary groups', in R. Kramer and T. Tyler (eds), *Trust in Organisations*. London: Sage. pp. 166–96.

Micklethwait, J. and Wooldridge, A. (1996) *The Witch Doctors*. London: Heinemann.

Middlehurst, R. and Kennie, T.(1997) 'Leading Professionals' in J. Broadbent, M. Dietrich and J. Roberts (eds), *The End of the Professions?* London: Routledge. pp. 50–69.

Misztal, B.A. (2001) 'Trusting the professional', in M. Dent and S. Whitehead (eds), *Managing Professional Identities*. London: Routledge. pp. 19–37.

Moore, A., George, R. and Halpin, D. (2002) 'The developing role of the headteacher in English schools: management, leadership and pragmatism', *Educational Management and Administration*, 30 (2) 175–88.

Morris, E. (2001) *Professionalism and Trust – The Future of Teachers and Teaching*. A speech given to the Social Market Foundation. London: DES.

Murgatroyd, S. and Morgan, C. (1992) *Total Quality Management and the School*. Milton Keynes: Open University Press.

Naisbett, J. and Aburdene, P. (1988) *Megatrends 2000*. London: Sidgwick and Jackson.

NCSL (2001) *Think Tank Report to Governing Council*. Nottingham: NCSL.

NCSL (2001a*) Leadership Development Framework*. Nottingham: NCSL.

NCSL (2003) *Annual Review of Research 2002–3*. Nottingham: NCSL.

Neef, D. (ed.) (1998) *The Knowledge Economy*. Oxford: Butterworth-Heinemann.

Northouse, P. (2003) *Leadership: Theory and Practice*. London: Sage.

Nye, J. (2002) *The Paradox of American Power*. Oxford: Oxford University Press.

Ohmae, K. (1995) *The End of the Nation State*. New York: Free Press.

Osborne, D. and Gaebler, T. (1992) *Reinventing Government*. New York: Plume.

Ozga, J. and Lawn, M. (1981) *Teachers, Professionalism and Class*. London: Falmer.

Palan, R., Abbott, J. and Deans, P. (1999) *State Strategies in the Global Political Economy*. London: Pinter.

Parker, M. (2001) 'The romance of lonely dissent', in M. Dent and S. Whitehead (eds), *Managing Professional Identities*. London: Routledge. pp. 138–56.

Parmenter, L. (1999) 'Constructing national identity in a changing world: perspectives in Japanese education', *British Journal of Sociology of Education*, 20 (4): 6.

Peters, T. and Waterman, R. (1982) *In Search of Excellence*. London: Harper and Row.

Peterson, P. (2000) *Gray Dawn*. New York: Three Rivers Press.

Piaget, J. (1932) *The Moral Judgement of the Child*. London: RKP

Pollard, A. and Trigg, P. (2001) *What Pupils say: Changing Policy and Practice in Primary Education*. London: Continuum.

Pollitt, C. (1993) *Managerialism and the Public Services* (2nd edn). Oxford: Basil Blockwell.

Popper, K. (1982) *The Logic of Scientific Discovery*. London: Hutchinson.

Power, M. (1994) *The Audit Explosion*. London: Demos.

Power, M. (1997) *The Audit Society: Rituals of Verification*. Oxford: Oxford University Press.

Putnam, R. (2000) *Bowling Alone*. New York: Simon Schuster.

Qualifications and Curriculum Authority (1999) *Citizenship*. London: DfEE.

Ransom, S. (ed) (1998) *Inside the Learning Society*. London: Cassell.

Reich, R. (1991) *The Work of Nations*. New York: Vintage.

Ribbins, P. (1993) 'Conversations with a *condottiere* of administrative value', *Journal of Educational Administration and Foundations*, 8 (1).

Rifkin, J. (2000) *The Age of Access*. London: Penguin.

Ritzer, G. (1993) *The McDonaldization of Society*. London: Sage.

Ritzer, G. (2004) *The Globalization of Nothing*. Thousand Oaks, California: Pine Forge Press.

Rorty, R. (1989) *Contingency, Irony, Solidarity*. Cambridge: Cambridge University Press.

Schorr, J. (1992) *The Overworked American*. New York: Basic Books.

Schumpeter, J. (1942) *Capitalism, Socialism and Democracy*. London: Allen and Unwin.

Scruton, R. (1997) *Modern Philosophy*. London: Arrow.

Senge, P. (1990) *The Fifth Discipline*. London: Century Business.

Sennet, R. (1998) *The Corrosion of Character*. New York: W.W.Norton & Co.

Sergiovanni, T. (1994) 'Organizations or communities? Changing the metaphor changes the theory, *Educational Administration Quarterly*, 30: 214–26.

Sergiovanni, T. (1996) *Leadership for the Schoolhouse*. San Francisco: Jossey Bass.

Sergiovanni, T. (2001) *Leadership: What's in it for Schools?* London: RoutlegeFalmer.

Sitkin, S. and Stickel, D. (1996) 'The road to Hell: the dynamics of distrust in an era of quality', in R. Kramer and T. T'yler (eds), *Trust in Organisations*. London: Sage. pp. 196–216.

Smart, B. (ed) (1999) *Resisting MacDonaldisation*. London: Sage.

Spillane, J., Halverson, R. and Diamond, J. (2000) 'Investigating school leadership practice: a distributed perspective', *Educational Researcher*, 30 (3): 23–8.

Stewart, T. (1998) *Intellectual Capital*. London: Nicholas Brealey.

Strike, K. (1999) 'Can schools be communities' the tension between shared values and inclusion', *Education Administrator*, 35 (1).

Strike, K. (2000) 'Community, coherence and inclusiveness' A paper given at the 5th Annual Values and Educational Leadership Conference, 28–30 September, Barbados.

Tan, J., Gopinathan, S. and Kam, H.W. (1997) *Education in Singapore*. Singapore: Prentice Hall.

Tonnies, F. (1957) *Community and Society*. East Lansing, MI: Michigan State University Press.

Troman, G. and Woods, P. (2000) 'Careers under stress: teacher adaptations at a time of intensive reform', *Journal of Educational Change*, 1: 253–75.

Troya, B. and Williams, J. (1986) *Racism, Education and the State*. London: Croom Helm. p. 12.

Urwick, L. (1943) *Elements of Administration*. London: Pitman.

Uslaner, E. (2002) *The Moral Foundations of Trust*. Cambridge: Cambridge University Press.

Wallace, M. (2002) 'Modelling distributed leadership and management effectiveness: primary school senior management teams in England and Wales, *School Effectiveness and School Improvement*, 13 (2): 163–86.

Weber, M. (1948) *From Max Weber*. London: Routledge and Kegan Paul.

Webster, D. (2002) Personal correspondence.

Wilkinson, R. (1996) *Unhealthy Societies: The Afflictions of Inequality*. London: Routledge.

Williams, R. (2001) 'Unrecognised exodus, unaccepted accountability: the looming shortage of principals and vice principals in Ontario public school boards', *Queens University School of Policy Studies*, Working paper no. 24.

Wolfe, A.C. (1998) One Nation After All. New York: Viking Press. p. 54.

Woods, P. (2003) 'Democratic leadership: drawing distinctions with distributed leadership', in *International Journal of Leadership in Education* (in press).

Wright, N. (2001) 'Leadership, "bastard leadership" and managerialism: confronting two paradoxes in the Blair education project', *Educational Management and Administration*, 29 (3): 275–90.

Wurzburg, G. (1998) 'Markets and the knowledge economy: is anything broken? Can government fix it?', *Journal of Knowledge Management*, 2 (1): 32–46.

Yukl, G. (1999) 'An evaluation of conceptual weaknesses in transformational and charismatic leadership theories', *Leadership Quarterly*, 10 (2): 285–305.

Zuboff, S. (1988) *In the Age of the Smart Machine*. New York: McGraw Hill.

Zuboff, S. and Maxmin, J. (2003) *The Support Economy*. London: Allen Lane.

Index